"This exploration into the mind of evangelical Christianity is one of the most courageous books of our time. In language that is thoroughly erudite but compassionate, theological but practical, and scriptural but entirely relevant to today, the author presents the deeper significance of Paul's plea to the Christians at Phillipi: 'Let this mind be in you, which was also in Christ Jesus.'"

—The late D. JAMES KENNEDY, who for many years served as senior minister, Coral Ridge Presbyterian Church, Fort Lauderdale, Florida

"J. P. Moreland exemplifies the Christian mind as it ought to be: tough and analytical but also generous and caring. Christians who want to develop their minds in the service of Christ couldn't find a better teacher or book for the task."

—PHILLIP E. JOHNSON, author of *Darwin On Trial*

"Perhaps as never before, the church needs to grapple with the issue that J. P. Moreland has so eloquently presented. In a day when experience has become the driving force in our thinking, we must recapture the biblical importance of the mind. Dr. Moreland spells out the issues in a profound yet understandable way so that this book is essential reading for anyone who takes his or her faith seriously."

—CLYDE COOK, president, Biola University

"In today's climate of increasing secularism, Christians must stop retreating from the arena of ideas and heed the call of this book to retake the ground the church has ceded to the university. More than a call for action, this book provides the historical, biblical, and philosophical groundwork for Christians to actually begin reclaiming their secular world. For many, this will be a whole new paradigm of how to be a Christian in our world. If only 10 percent of today's evangelical Christian leaders study this book and take it to heart, the church will once again transform the world!"

—EDWARD KANG, JD, MDiv, pastor, Berkland Baptist Church, Berkeley, California; campus minister, U.C. Berkeley with A.B.S.K.

# LOVE YOUR GOD WITH ALL YOUR MIND

THE ROLE OF REASON IN
THE LIFE OF THE SOUL

*J . P . Moreland*

NAVPRESS
Discipleship Inside Out®

Discipleship Inside Out®

NavPress is the publishing ministry of The Navigators, an international Christian organization and leader in personal spiritual development. NavPress is committed to helping people grow spiritually and enjoy lives of meaning and hope through personal and group resources that are biblically rooted, culturally relevant, and highly practical.

**For a free catalog go to www.NavPress.com**
**or call 1.800.366.7788 in the United States or 1.800.839.4769 in Canada.**

NavPress titles may be purchased in bulk for ministry, educational, business, fund-raising, or sales promotional use. For information, please call NavPress Special Markets at 1.800.504.2924.

ISBN: 978-1-61747-900-7

Some of the anecdotal illustrations in this book are true to life and are included with the permission of the persons involved. All other illustrations are composites of real situations, and any resemblance to people living or dead is coincidental.

Unless otherwise identified, all Scripture quotations in this publication are taken from the *Holy Bible, New International Version*® (NIV®). Copyright © 1973, 1978, 1984 by Biblica, used by permission of Zondervan. All rights reserved. Other versions used include: the New American Standard Bible® (NASB), Copyright © 1960, 1962, 1963, 1968, 1971, 1972, 1973, 1975, 1977, 1995 by The Lockman Foundation. Used by permission; and the King James Version (KJV).

Moreland, James Porter, 1948-
  Love your God with all your mind : the role of reason in the life of the soul / J.P. Moreland. —2nd ed.
    p. cm.
  Includes bibliographical references (p.   ).
  ISBN 978-1-61747-900-7
  1. Faith and reason—Christianity. I. Title.
  BT50.M62 2012
  230.01—dc23
                                      2011053526

Printed in the United States of America

2 3 4 5 6 / 16 15 14 13

# CONTENTS

# ACKNOWLEDGMENTS

There are several people who played an important role in helping this book see the light of day. First, I wish to thank my friend and research assistant, Glenn Cudzilo, to whom this book is dedicated. Glenn gave me helpful feedback on a very rough draft of the manuscript.

Second, the president of Biola University, Clyde Cook; the provost, Sherwood Lingenfelter; and dean of Talbot School of Theology, Dennis Dirks have helped create a stimulating place to teach and study, and they gave me a sabbatical to work on the project. I am grateful to them for their confidence in me and in this book.

Third, my faculty colleagues at Talbot — including Alan Gomes, Mike Wilkins, Clint Arnold, Klaus Issler, Scott Rae, and John Mark Reynolds at the Torrey Institute, Biola University — are a team of which I feel honored to be a part. They live what this book is all about. Also, my graduate students in the Talbot MA in philosophy and ethics are partly responsible for my own life of study. Their questions in class are so sophisticated that I am frequently sent back to my study to find answers that satisfy them. God bless them for pushing me as they do.

I cannot adequately express my indebtedness to my mentor and friend Dallas Willard. For some time now, he has been my most important role model for combining a rigorous intellectual life with a vital spiritual devotion to Jesus and His kingdom. I also want to thank my friend and editor Steve Webb. His encouragement and excellent editorial suggestions made this book much better than it would have been without his help. Thanks as well to the whole NavPress team, who've worked so hard at excellence in the publishing experience.

Finally, my precious wife, Hope, and my lovely daughters, Ashley and Allison, are simply what make my life possible. I have never met anyone with as gracious and tender a spirit as my wife's, and I love her for who she is. My prayer is that this book will contribute to restoration of the church's intellectual life because it is the church that is the pillar and support of the truth.

J. P. Moreland, 1997

# PREFACE TO THE REVISED EDITION

Since its publication in 1997, *Love Your God with All Your Mind* has had an impact for the cause of Christ that goes considerably beyond anything I could have imagined. It would be a significant understatement to say that I am grateful to God for this fact. The majority of the first edition's content is as relevant today as when it first appeared in print. But some updating was needed and, in my view, the reader could be better served by changing a few of the chapters.

So you hold in your hands a revised and updated version of the book. In chapter 1, I added a brief section about the current three-way worldview struggle in Western culture, and in chapter 2, I have included a new section on the nature of knowledge and its importance to Christianity. No author likes to remove material from his or her writing, and I am no exception to this rule. But, in my opinion, chapters 7–9 of the original edition, though useful, were not as helpful as the rest of the book. Moreover, I had additional content I wanted in the book. So chapters 7–9 of the original have been removed and replaced with three new chapters providing an outline of how to present a case for God's existence and the historicity of the life, teachings, deeds, death, and resurrection of Jesus of Nazareth.

Further, the appendices, which provide further resources for cultivating an integrated Christian mind, have been thoroughly updated and expanded. I am deeply indebted to Joseph Gorra for his work on the appendices. So it is with gratitude and expectation that I offer to you, the reader, this improved and significantly altered edition of *Love Your God with All Your Mind*. May God be pleased to use it as He sees fit.

J. P. Moreland, 2012
www.jpmoreland.com

# PART ONE

# WHY THE MIND MATTERS IN CHRISTIANITY

# CHAPTER ONE

# HOW WE LOST THE CHRISTIAN MIND AND WHY WE MUST RECOVER IT

I had just returned from the mailbox and opened a letter from a woman who had attended a series of lectures I had recently given at her church. One never knows what a letter from a parishioner will say, so it was with a certain ambivalence that I opened the envelope. Here is what I read:

> My life has changed drastically during the past few weeks since you have been teaching and encouraging us to think. I used to be deathly afraid of witnessing and terribly fearful that someone might ask me something about my faith. Whenever I got into any kind of discussion, I was rather defensive and nervous. Well, I have been reading, rather, plowing, through some of your lecture notes at church. As I absorb the information and logically understand the foundations for my faith, a calm is resting in my soul. I have been a believer for a long time and the Lord has done marvelous, specific things in my life. But now I understand why I believe, and this has brought me both peace and a non-defensive boldness to witness to others. Please don't stop encouraging people to risk thinking objectively and arriving at conclusions based on logic and fact. My life will never be the same because of this encouragement.

My heart was at once deeply grateful and profoundly saddened. I was grateful to think that God could use someone like me to help one of His children. I was saddened to be reminded of how unusual it is for Christian people to be taught how to think carefully and deeply about what they believe and why they believe it. Not long ago, the newspaper featured a leading politician's statement about the Christian political right in which he charged that the Christian right was populated by dumb, uninformed people who are easily led by rhetoric. While I would dispute the complete accuracy of this charge, nevertheless, we Christians must ask ourselves why, if there is not a grain of truth in it, someone would think to make this accusation of us in the first place. Judged by the Scriptures, church history, and common sense, it is clear that something has gone desperately wrong with our modern understanding of the value of reason and intellectual development for individual discipleship and corporate church life.

It doesn't take a rocket scientist to recognize that our entire culture is in trouble. We are staring down the barrel of a loaded gun, and we can no longer afford to act like it's loaded with blanks. The guidance counselor at a public high school near my home confessed to a parents' group that the teenagers who have attended the school during the last ten years are the most dysfunctional, illiterate group he has witnessed in close to forty years at the same school. Our society has replaced heroes with celebrities, the quest for a well-informed character with the search for flat abs, substance and depth with image and personality. In the political process, the makeup man is more important than the speech writer, and we approach the voting booth, not on the basis of a well-developed philosophy of what the state should be, but with a heart full of images, emotions, and slogans all packed into thirty-second sound bites. The mind-numbing, irrational tripe that fills TV talk shows is digested by millions of bored, lonely Americans hungry for that sort of stuff. What is going on here? What has happened to us?

There are no simple answers to these questions, and I don't pretend to offer a full analysis as a solution to this quandary. But I do think the place to start looking for an answer is to remind ourselves of something Jesus Christ said long ago. In His inaugural address, He spelled out how

His community of followers were to understand themselves. With characteristic insight, He asserted that "You are the salt of the earth. But if the salt loses its saltiness, how can it be made salty again?" (Matthew 5:13).

One job of the church is to be salty to the world in which it finds itself, so if that world grows saltless, we should look first to the church herself to glean what we can about her contribution to the situation. In the rest of this chapter, I will demonstrate that a major cause of our current cultural crisis consists of a worldview shift from a Judeo-Christian understanding of reality to a post-Christian one. Moreover, this shift itself expresses a growing anti-intellectualism in the church, resulting in the marginalization of Christianity in society—its lack of saltiness, if you will—and the emergence of the most secular culture the world has ever seen. That secular culture is now simply playing out the implications of ideas that have come to be widely accepted in a social context in which the church is no longer a major participant in the war of ideas.[1] In the rest of this book, then, I'll try to demonstrate how the church must overcome the neglect of this critical area of the development of the Christian mind, perhaps the most integral component of the believers' sanctification. The role of intellectual development is primary in evangelical Christianity, but you might not know that from a cursory look at the church today. In spite of this, if we are to have Christ formed in us (Galatians 4:19), we must realize the work of God in our minds and pay attention to what a Christlike mind might look like. As our Savior has said, "Love the Lord your God with all your heart and with all your soul and with all your mind" (Matthew 22:37). To do this, we cannot neglect the soulful development of a Christian mind.

## THE LOSS OF THE CHRISTIAN MIND IN AMERICAN CHRISTIANITY

Two major developments emerged in the late nineteenth century that contributed to the loss of the Christian mind in America. The legacy of the Pilgrims and Puritans waned, and two new movements emerged from which the evangelical church has never fully recovered. Let's take a brief look at these two movements, and then we'll examine the deeper problems that have resulted.

## Historical Overview

**1. The emergence of anti-intellectualism.** While generalizations can be misleading, it is safe to say that from the arrival of the Pilgrims to the middle of the nineteenth century, American believers prized the intellectual life for its contribution to the Christian journey. The Puritans were highly educated people (the literacy rate for men in early Massachusetts and Connecticut was between 89 and 95 percent)[2] who founded colleges, taught their children to read and write before the age of six, and studied art, science, philosophy, and other fields as a way of loving God with the mind. Scholars like Jonathan Edwards were activists who sought to be scholarly and well informed in a variety of disciplines. The minister was an intellectual, as well as spiritual, authority in the community.[3] As Puritan Cotton Mather proclaimed, "Ignorance is the Mother not of Devotion but of HERESY."[4]

In the middle 1800s, however, things began to change dramatically, though the seeds for the change had already been planted in the popularized, rhetorically powerful, and emotionally directed preaching of George Whitefield in the First Great Awakening in the United States from the 1730s to the 1750s. During the middle 1800s, three awakenings broke out in the United States: the Second Great Awakening (1800–1820), the revivals of Charles Finney (1824–1837), and the Layman's Prayer Revival (1856–1858). Much good came from these movements. But their overall effect was to overemphasize immediate personal conversion to Christ instead of a studied period of reflection and conviction; emotional, simple, popular preaching instead of intellectually careful and doctrinally precise sermons; and personal feelings and relationship to Christ instead of a deep grasp of the nature of Christian teaching and ideas. Sadly, as historian George Marsden notes, "anti-intellectualism was a feature of American revivalism."[5]

Obviously, there is nothing wrong with the emphasis of these movements on personal conversion. What was a problem, however, was the intellectually shallow, theologically illiterate form of Christianity that came to be part of the populist Christian religion that emerged. One tragic result of this was what happened in the so-called Burned Over District in the state of New York. Thousands of people were "converted" to Christ by revivalist preaching, but they had no real intellectual grasp of Christian teaching. As a result, two of the three major American cults began in the Burned Over District among the unstable, untaught "converts": Mormonism (1830) and the Jehovah's Witnesses (1884). Christian Science arose in 1866 but was not connected with this area.

**2. Evangelical withdrawal began.** Sadly, the emerging anti-intellectualism in the church created a lack of readiness for the widespread intellectual assault on Christianity that reached full force in the late 1800s. This attack was part of the war of ideas raging at that time and was launched from three major areas. First, certain *philosophical ideas* from Europe, especially the views of David Hume (1711–1776) and Immanuel Kant (1724–1804), altered people's understanding of religion. Hume claimed that the traditional arguments for God's existence (for example, the world is an effect that needs a personal cause) were quite weak. He also said that since we cannot experience God with the five senses, the claim that God exists cannot be taken as an item of knowledge. In a different way, Kant asserted that human knowledge is limited to what can be experienced with the five senses, and since God cannot be so experienced, we cannot know He exists. The ideas of Hume and Kant had a major impact on culture as they spread across Europe and into America.[6]

For one thing, confidence was shaken in arguments for the existence of God and the rationality of the Christian faith. Additionally, fewer and fewer people regarded the Bible as a body of divinely revealed, true propositions about various topics that requires a devoted intellect to grasp and study systematically. Instead, the Bible increasingly was sought solely as a practical guide for ethical guidance and spiritual growth.

Second, *German higher criticism* of the Bible called its historical reliability into question. The Mosaic authorship of the Pentateuch was challenged and the search for the historical Jesus was launched. Believers grew suspicious of the importance of historical study in understanding the Bible and in defending its truthfulness. An increased emphasis was placed on the Holy Spirit in understanding the Bible as opposed to serious historical and grammatical study. Third, *Darwinian evolution* emerged and "made the world safe for atheists," as one contemporary Darwinian atheist has put it. Evolution challenged the early chapters of Genesis for some and the very existence of God for others.[7]

Instead of responding to these attacks with a vigorous intellectual counterpunch, many believers grew suspicious of intellectual issues altogether. To be sure, Christians must rely on the Holy Spirit in their intellectual pursuits, but this does not mean they should expend no mental sweat of their own in defending the faith.

Around the turn of the nineteenth century, fundamentalists withdrew from the broader intellectual culture and from the war with liberals that emerged in most mainline denominations at the time. Fundamentalists started their own Bible institutes and concentrated their efforts on lay-oriented Bible and prophecy conferences. This withdrawal from the broader intellectual culture and public discourse contributed to the isolation of the church, the marginalization of Christian ideas from the public arena, and the shallowness and trivialization of Christian living, thought, and activism. In short, the culture became saltless.[8]

More specifically, we now live in an evangelical community so deeply committed to a certain way of seeing the Christian faith that this perspective is now imbedded within us at a subconscious level.

This conceptualization of the Christian life is seldom brought to conscious awareness for debate and discussion. And our modern understanding of Christian practice underlies everything else we do, from the way we select a minister to the types of books we sell in our bookstores.

It informs the way we raise our children to think about Christianity; it determines how we give money to the cause of Christ; and it shapes our vision, priorities, and goals for both local and parachurch ministry. If our lives and ministries are expressions of what we actually believe, and if what we believe is off center and yet so pervasive that it is seldom even brought to conscious discussion, much less debated, then this explains why our impact on the world is so paltry compared to our numbers. I cannot overemphasize the fact that this modern understanding of Christianity is neither biblical nor consistent with the bulk of church history.

What, exactly, is this modern understanding of Christianity?

### Anti-Intellectualism's Impact on the Church

I believe it is critical that the evangelical church overcome these characteristics and move toward a clearer, more biblical understanding of the Christian mind and how Christ Himself wants to shape our thinking. The rest of this book will attempt to provide countermeasures to these unbiblical problems so that our spirituality is informed by an appropriate biblical view of the mind and how Jesus Himself wishes to transform the mind by renewing it (in fact, we'll look at Romans 12:1-2 in some depth later). Five characteristics capture the essence of the impact of anti-intellectualism on today's evangelicalism. Read carefully and see how these may have impacted your own ideas.

*1. A misunderstanding of faith's relationship to reason.* First, while few would actually put it in these terms, faith is now understood as a blind act of will, a decision to believe something that is either independent of reason or that is a simple choice to believe while ignoring the paltry lack of evidence for what is believed. By contrast with this modern misunderstanding, biblically, *faith is a power or skill to act in accordance with the nature of the kingdom of God, a trust in what we have reason to believe is true.* Understood in this way, we see that faith is built on reason. We should have good reasons for thinking that Christianity is true before we dedicate ourselves completely to it. We should have solid evidence that our understanding of a biblical passage is correct before we go on to apply it. And so on.

If this is correct, then sermons should target people's thinking as much as their wills and feelings. Sunday school should be more effective in training believers how to think carefully about their faith. Training in apologetics should be a regular part of discipleship. Apologetics is a New Testament ministry of helping people overcome intellectual obstacles that block them from coming to or growing in the faith by giving reasons for why one should believe Christianity is true and by responding to objections raised against it. Local church after local church should be raising up and training a group of people who serve as apologists for the entire congregation.

Unfortunately, our contemporary understanding of these important concepts treats faith and reason as polar opposites. Let me give you two illustrations from my own ministry.

Years ago I conducted a series of evangelistic messages for a church in New York. The series was in a high school gym, and both believers and unbelievers attended each night. The first evening I gave arguments for the existence of God from science and philosophy. Before closing in prayer, I entertained several questions from the audience. One woman (who was a Christian) complained about my talk, charging that if I "proved" the existence of God, I would leave no room for faith. I responded by saying that if she were right, then we should pray that currently available evidence for God would evaporate or be refuted so there would be even more room for faith! Obviously, her view of faith utterly detached itself from reason.

The second illustration comes from repeatedly hearing small group Bible studies go straight to the question, What does this passage mean to me? while bypassing the prior question, What does the passage say and why do I think my interpretation is correct? We allow one another to get away with applying an understanding of a passage that is based on vague feelings or first impressions and not on the hard work of reading commentaries and using study tools such as concordances, Bible dictionaries, and the like. Why? Because a careful exercise of reason is not important in understanding what the Bible says for many of us. Besides, it takes work!

For many, religion is identified with subjective feelings, sincere motives, personal piety, and blind faith. As the song puts it, "You ask me how I know He lives, He lives within my heart." In other words, we test the truth of our religion not by a careful application of our God-given faculties of thought, or even by biblical mandates (see, for example, 2 Corinthians 10:5), but rather by our private experiences. For the most part, theoretical reason is just not part of our local church life any longer. We often hear it said in church that we don't want a discussion to get too theological, we want to keep it practical, as though good practice did not require careful thought to direct it. We sing, "In my *heart*, Lord, be glorified," but when was the last time you heard someone sing, "In my *intellectual life*, Lord, be glorified"? Unfortunately, this misunderstanding of the relationship between faith and reason has led to an even more sinister trend among modern evangelicals.

**2. The separation of the secular and the sacred.** There has emerged a secular/sacred separation in our understanding of the Christian life with the result that Christian teaching and practice are privatized and placed in a separate compartment from the public or so-called secular activities of life. The withdrawal of the corporate body of Christ from the public sphere of ideas is mirrored by our understanding of what is required to produce an individual disciple. Religion has become personal, private, and too often, simply a matter of "how I feel about things." By contrast, the culture encourages me to invoke my intellect in my secular, public life. By way of example, I'm always encouraged to use my intellect in how I approach my vocation, select a house, or learn to use a computer. But within the sphere of my private, spiritual life of faith, it is my heart, and my heart alone, that operates. The life of the mind is thus separated, broken off, and compartmentalized as a function of the "secular" life instead of more naturally being integrated with the spiritual. As a result, Sunday school classes, discipleship materials, and sermons too often address the heart and not the head, or focus on personal growth and piety and not on cultivating an intellectual love for God in my vocation.

When was the last time your church had Sunday school classes that were divided up by vocations—classes for thinking Christianly as a lawyer, businessman, health care professional, educator, and so forth? Parachurch ministries have produced excellent tools for training the private, "spiritual" lives of converts. But where are the tools that take ten or fifteen different university majors and spell out issues and resources for integrating ideas in those majors with Christian theology? We have organizations for businessmen that emphasize personal testimonies, devotional reading, and the like. But where do these organizations train businessmen to develop a Christian understanding of economic theory, capitalism, business ethics, or moral issues in the employer/employee relationship?

Our children can attend virtually any university and major in any subject they wish. But in a four-year course of study they will almost never interact with a Christian thinker in their field or with Christian ideas relevant to their course content. Why? No doubt, many reasons could be given. But clearly, one reason is that the cream rises to the top. If there are few Christian intellectuals who write college textbooks from a Christian perspective, it must be because our evangelical culture is simply not producing such people because we do not value the intellectual life. After all, the purpose of college for many is to get a job, and course work is considered secular, not sacred. What is important for our children is that they stay pure in college and, perhaps, witness, have a quiet time, and pray regularly. Obviously, these are important. But for a disciple, the purpose of college is not just to get a job. Rather, it is to discover a vocation, to identify a field of study in and through which I can serve Christ as my Lord. And one way to serve Him in this way is to learn to think in a Christian manner about my major. A person's Christianity doesn't begin at a dorm Bible study, when class is over; it permeates all of one's life, including how one thinks about the ideas in one's college major.

The church must train high school students for the intellectual life they will encounter at college. As theologian Carl Henry put it, "Training the mind is an essential responsibility of the home, the church, and the school. Unless evangelicals prod young people to disciplined thinking, they waste—even undermine—one of Christianity's most precious resources."[9] But if faith and reason are polar opposites, and if discipleship is private and sacred but college studies are public and secular, then training the intellect will not be valued as a part of teenage mentoring. That is why our discipleship materials often leave Christian young people vulnerable to atheistic college professors with an ax to grind. For such professors, shredding an intellectually unprepared undergraduate's faith is like shooting fish in a barrel.

We have seen that the church was attacked intellectually in the latter half of the nineteenth century and was not adequately prepared to respond to this attack in kind. Instead, with notable exceptions, the church withdrew from the world of ideas and the intellectual life and was thereby marginalized. As former president of the United Nations General Assembly Charles Malik has said, "I must be frank with you: the greatest danger confronting American evangelical Christianity is the danger of anti-intellectualism. The mind in its greatest and deepest reaches is not cared for enough."[10] This withdrawal and marginalization of the church has had devastating consequences for our attempt to produce vibrant, confident disciples and to penetrate our culture with a Christian worldview and the gospel of Christ. These consequences are most evident in three more areas.

*3. Weakened world missions.* One critical consequence of our first two anti-intellectual trends is the combined effect of weakening world missions. I once attended a meeting of missionaries from around the world, at which a national Christian leader from Central America stood up and passionately exhorted North American mission agencies to stop sending evangelists to his country because their efforts were producing Marxists bent on overthrowing the government. You could have heard a pin drop in that meeting, and confusion was written on everyone's face.

This leader went on to explain that the leading "Christian" thinkers in his country held to liberation theology, a form of Marxism draped in religious garb. Evangelical missionaries would lead people to Christ, but the liberals were attracting the thinking leaders among the converts and training them in Marxist ideology, which these liberals identified as the true center of biblical theology. The leader pleaded with North Americans to send more theologians and Bible teachers and to help set up more seminaries and training centers in his country because the need for intellectual leadership was great.

For some time, theological liberals have understood that whoever controls the thinking leadership of the church in a culture will eventually control the church itself. Once, I met a man from Fiji who was won to Christ by an evangelical missionary and who, subsequent to conversion, wanted to come to the United States for seminary training. Unfortunately, there was no money for this sort of "intellectual" development in the evangelical missions strategy there, but theological liberals gave him a scholarship to study at a liberal seminary in Texas. By the time I met him, he had given up his faith and was going back to Fiji with an extremely secular view of Christianity. His mission: to pastor a church! If evangelicals placed more value on the mind, we would give more to developing intellectual leadership around the world. Happily, some good things are now being done in this area, but we need to intensify our efforts in this regard, and this will happen only if we evangelicals come to value more fully Christ's admonitions to be good stewards of the intellectual life. Unfortunately, there remain two more deadly trends that have infected the church because of anti-intellectualism.

***4. Anti-intellectualism has spawned an irrelevant gospel.*** Today, we share the gospel primarily *as a means of addressing felt needs.* We give testimonies of changed lives and say to people that if they want to become better parents or overcome depression or loneliness, then Christ is the answer for them. As true as this may be, such an approach to evangelism is inadequate for two reasons. First, it does not reach people

HOW WE LOST THE CHRISTIAN MIND ... / 25

who may be out of touch with their feelings. Consequently, if men in our culture are, in general, less in touch with their feelings than women, this approach will not reach men effectively. Second, it invites the response, "Sorry, but I don't have a need." Have you ever wondered why no one responded to the apostle Paul in this manner? If you look at his evangelistic approach in Acts 17:20, the answer becomes obvious. He based his preaching on the fact that the gospel is true and reasonable to believe. He reasoned with and tried to persuade people intelligently to accept Christ.

Now, if the gospel is true and reasonable to believe, then it is obvious that every person has a need for Christ's forgiveness and power, whether or not that person "feels" that need. The only response to the Pauline evangelistic approach is either to accept Christ or deny the truth of the gospel. The person approached is not let off the hook simply because he is out of touch with his feelings or doesn't recognize the "felt need." The fact that many respond to our evangelistic efforts by denying a need for Christ should tip us off to an important fact. If truth and reasonableness are not uppermost in our presentation of the gospel to a pagan culture already predisposed to regarding religion as a set of private feelings, then we'll consistently hear this response: "Well, that's fine for you if having those feelings helps you." Religion is now viewed by many as a placebo or emotional crutch precisely because that is how we often pitch the gospel to unbelievers.

I wish I could stop here. But again, there's another trend in evangelicalism that we must place at the feet of anti-intellectualism.

*5. A loss of boldness in confronting the idea structures in our culture with effective Christian witness.* Now this is a mouthful, but anti-intellectualism has drained the church of its boldness in witnessing and speaking out about important issues in the places where ideas are generated. And for those who do have such courage, anti-intellectualism has created a context in which we Christians often come off as shallow, defensive, and reactionary, instead of thoughtful, confident, and articulate.

One evening a couple came to our home for dinner. During the meal the husband said almost nothing (except "Pass the chicken!"). Despite repeated attempts to engage him, the conversation took place primarily among the two wives and me. However, as dessert was being served, the topic of conversation turned to motorboats, and from that point on we could hardly get a word in edgewise. Why? Boats were the man's hobby. He owned two of them, knew how to build one from scratch, and truly was an expert on the subject. He had the courage to speak up because he knew what he was talking about; he did not need to be defensive when someone differed with his viewpoint because he was confident about his knowledge.

I have trained people to share their faith for over forty years. I can tell you from experience that when people learn what they believe and why, they become bold in their witness and attractive in the way they engage others in debate or dialogue. While pastoring a church in Baltimore, I once taught a twelve-week class on Christian apologetics. The course cost fifty dollars to take, required two textbooks, and had several homework assignments, including two papers. When the sixth week ended, a man named Bob came up to me after class and, with tears running down his cheeks, expressed his gratitude for the high academic standards and requirements in the class. I asked him why he was grateful about this. I will never forget his response. He told me he had worked at the same place for ten years but had never shared his faith with anyone because he was afraid someone would ask him a question, he would not know the answer, and his inadequate preparation would embarrass him and the Christian faith. But at his workplace the week before this particular class, he had shared his faith with three workers because for the first time he felt he had some answers, and his boldness was strengthened by that conviction. Being a Christian is no different from caring about boats in this regard. There is nothing magic about being confident, articulate, and bold in either area. Knowing what you're talking about may be hard work, but it clearly pays off.

Anti-intellectualism has not merely impacted the lives of believers within the bosom of Christ. It has had serious repercussions in the culture at large. As anti-intellectualism has softened our impact for Christ, so too has it contributed to the secularization of the culture. If the salt loses its saltiness, the meat will be impacted. In the aftermath of the Scopes trial in 1925, conservative Christianity was largely dismissed as an embarrassment among intellectual and cultural movers and shakers.[11] As a result, we now live in one of the most secular cultures in history.

## THE EMERGENCE OF A SECULAR CULTURE IN WHICH THE CHURCH IS CALLED TO LIVE AND MINISTER

### Culture Is Secular

Modern American culture is largely secular in this sense: Most people have little or no understanding of a Christian way of seeing the world, nor is a Christian worldview an important participant in the way we as a society frame and debate issues in the public square. Three of the major centers of influence in our culture—the university, the media, and the government—are largely devoid of serious religious discussion. In fact, it is not unfair to say that university, media, and governmental leaders are often illiterate about how Christians see the world and why. This is evident, for example, in those rare cases when the major television news media try to feature a Christian perspective on abortion, the state, or anything else. Usually, Christians watching the program feel misrepresented and misunderstood. More often than not, however, Christian perspectives are simply ignored and not covered at all.

If a Martian were watching television before coming to earth, he would get the idea that Americans are irreligious. Secularists tolerate religion as long as it remains a privatized perspective relative to a subgroup in society and as long as Christians don't assert that their views are objectively true and defend them articulately. R. C. Sproul,

John Gerstner, and Arthur Lindsley have accurately captured this
secular attitude toward Christianity:

> The church is safe from vicious persecution at the hands of the
> secularist, as educated people have finished with stake-burning
> circuses and torture racks. No martyr's blood is shed in the secular
> west. So long as the church knows her place and remains quietly at
> peace on her modern reservation. Let the babes pray and sing and
> read their Bibles, continuing steadfastly in their intellectual retar-
> dation; the church's extinction will not come by sword or pillory,
> but by the quiet death of irrelevance. But let the church step off the
> reservation, let her penetrate once more the culture of the day and
> the . . . face of secularism will change from a benign smile to a
> savage snarl.[12]

## Secularism Is Primarily a View About Knowledge

The primary characteristic of modern secularism is its view of the nature
and limits of knowledge. It is critical to understand this because if
knowledge gives one power—we give surgeons and not carpenters the
right to cut us open precisely because surgeons have the relevant knowledge not possessed by carpenters—then those with the cultural say-so
about who does and doesn't have knowledge will be in a position to
marginalize and silence groups judged to have mere belief and private
opinion.

For many secularists, knowledge is obtained solely by means of
the senses and science. Something is true and reasonable to believe to
the degree that it can be tested by the five senses—it can be seen,
heard, touched, tasted, or felt. Seeing is believing. Likewise, knowledge is identical to *scientific* knowledge. If you can prove something
scientifically, then it is culturally permissible or even obligatory to
believe it. Science is the measure of all things, and when a scientist
speaks about something, he or she speaks *ex cathedra*. For example, if
theological arguments imply homosexuality is in some sense a choice

over which one is responsible, and science makes a "claim" to the contrary, which one will win in public debate? We often hear it said that "if your religious beliefs work for you, that's great, but don't impose them on others." However, no one would say that a scientist is imposing anything on anyone when he says that water is $H_2O$ or that $2 + 2 = 4$. Nor would these claims be viewed as private opinions whose sole value was their usefulness for those who believe them. Why? Because only science supposedly deals with facts, truth, and reason, but religion and ethics allegedly deal with private, subjective opinions.

I have no bone to pick with legitimate science. Indeed, it has been argued repeatedly that science was born in Christian Europe precisely because Christian theology helped provide worldview justification for its assumptions.[13] *What I do reject is the idea that science and science alone can claim to give us knowledge.* This assertion—known as scientism—is patently false and, in fact, not even a claim of science but rather a philosophical view about science. Nevertheless, once this view of knowledge was widely embraced in the culture, the immediate effect was to marginalize and privatize religion by relegating it to the back of the intellectual bus.[14] To verify this, one need only compare the number of times scientists, as opposed to pastors or theologians, are called upon as experts on the evening news.

If knowledge and reason are identical with what can be tested scientifically or with scientific theories that a majority of scientists believes to be correct, then religion and ethics will no longer be viewed as true, rational domains of discourse because, supposedly, religious or ethical claims are not scientifically testable. This line of thought has led to several trends in society whose combined influence is to hinder ideal human flourishing as God intended it to be. It is similar to the sort of cultural milieu that spawned Stalinism in the Soviet Union and Nazism in pre-World War II Germany, with all of their attendant evils and tragic loss of human life and dignity. As G. K. Chesterton bemoaned, once people stop believing in God, the problem is not that they will believe nothing; rather, the problem is that they will believe anything. This is just what we are seeing happen in our secular culture bereft of the presence of an engaged, articulate evangelical community.

## Secular Views of Knowledge Are Responsible for Unfortunate Social Trends

Scientism is responsible for a number of unfortunate contemporary trends in society.

*1. In our scientifically oriented culture, traditional understandings of morality and related notions are considered passé.* The primary trend in ethical thinking today is toward *moral* and *religious relativism*. As I have already said, if ethics and religion are not scientifically testable, then many today will think they are mere "expressions of belief" that are true only for those who believe them. Science claims to deal only with fact; religion and ethics supposedly deal with feelings and privatized values. Therefore, religion and ethics are considered merely subjective notions in modern society.

Another modern trend is a change in what we mean by the *good life*. From Old Testament times and ancient Greece until this century, the good life was widely understood to mean a life of intellectual and moral virtue. The good life is the life of ideal human functioning according to the nature that God Himself gave to us. According to this view, prior to Creation God had in mind an ideal blueprint of human nature from which He created each and every human being. Happiness (Greek: *eudaimonia*) was understood as a life of virtue, and the successful person was one who knew how to live life well according to what we are by nature due to the creative design of God. When the Declaration of Independence says we are endowed by our Creator with certain inalienable rights, among them the right to pursue happiness, it is referring to virtue and character.[15] So understood, happiness involves suffering, endurance, and patience because these are important means to becoming a good person who lives the good life.

*Freedom* was traditionally understood as the power to do what one ought to do. For example, some people are not free to play the piano or to say no to lust because they have not undergone the training necessary to ingrain the relevant skillful habits. Moreover, since community is possible only if people accept as true a shared vision of the good life, it is easy to see why a sense of community and public virtue could be sustained given this understanding of the good life, happiness, and freedom.

Traditionally, *tolerance* of other viewpoints meant that even though I think those viewpoints are dead wrong and will argue against them fervently, nevertheless, I will defend your right to argue your own case. Just as importantly, I will treat you with respect as an image bearer of God, even though your views are abhorrent to me. Finally, while *individual rights* are important, they do not exhaust the moral life because virtue and duty are more central than rights to the moral life properly conceived.

**2. The traditional view is neither scientifically testable nor easily compatible with evolution.** Unfortunately, this traditional understanding of the good life, freedom, community, and tolerance is not scientifically testable. Moreover, Darwin's theory of evolution caused many to lose their belief in the *existence* of natures, human or otherwise. As Harvard zoologist Ernst Mayr has said:

> The concepts of unchanging essences and of complete discontinuities between every eidos (type) and all others make genuine evolutionary thinking impossible. I agree with those who claim that the essentialist philosophies of Aristotle and Plato are incompatible with evolutionary thinking.[16]

This belief has, in turn, led evolutionary thinkers like David Hull to make the following observation:

> The implications of moving species from the metaphysical category that can appropriately be characterized in terms of "natures" to a

category for which such characterizations are inappropriate are extensive and fundamental. If species evolve in anything like the way that Darwin thought they did, then they cannot possibly have the sort of natures that traditional philosophers claimed they did. If species in general lack natures, then so does *Homo sapiens* as a biological species. If *Homo sapiens* lacks a nature, then no reference to biology can be made to support one's claims about "human nature." Perhaps all people are "persons," share the same "personhood," etc., but such claims must be explicated and defended *with no reference to biology*. Because so many moral, ethical, and political theories depend on some notion or other of human nature, Darwin's theory brought into question all these theories. The implications are not entailments. One can always dissociate *"Homo sapiens"* from *"human being,"* but the result is a much less plausible position.[17]

Note Hull's comment that if a person or group dissociates the species-specific designation "Homo sapiens" from the designation "human being," with all of its attendant moral and theological implications, then that person or group has a "less plausible position." Why? Why should that which we see, hear, feel, taste, or touch (or observe through scientific method) have sway over any cultural debate, since Hull's entire conclusion rests on the giant "if" — "if species evolve in anything like the way that Darwin thought they did . . ."? Yet, as we'll see in the next section, we have allowed secular thinkers to frame the debate, and the Christian voice has been muffled at best.

***3. Secular ideas have replaced the traditional view.*** What Mayr and Hull are saying is that if naturalistic evolution is the story of how we came to be, then there is no human nature answering to a divine blueprint and no good life that expresses that nature. There are only accidentally formed individual human beings who are free to create whatever version of happiness they wish. According to the modern view, the good life is the satisfaction of any pleasure or desire that someone freely and autonomously chooses for himself or herself. The successful person is the individual who has a life of pleasure and can obtain enough consumer goods to satisfy his or her desires. Freedom is the right to do what I want, not the power to do what I by nature ought to. Community gives way to individualism with the result that narcissism—an inordinate sense of self-love and self-centered involvement—is an accurate description of many people's lives. If I am free to create my own moral universe and version of the good life, and there is no right or wrong answer to what I should create, then morality—indeed, everything—ultimately exists to make me happy. When a person considers abortion or physician-assisted suicide, the person's individual rights are all that matter. Questions about virtue or one's duty to the broader community simply do not arise.

Tolerance has come to mean that no one is right and no one is wrong and, indeed, the very act of stating that someone else's views are immoral or incorrect is now taken to be intolerant (of course, from this same point of view, it is all right to be intolerant of those who hold to objectively true moral or religious positions). Once the existence of knowable truth in religion and ethics is denied, authority (the right to be believed and obeyed) gives way to power (the ability to force compliance), reason gives way to rhetoric, the speech writer is replaced by the makeup man, and spirited but civil debate in the culture wars is replaced by politically correct special-interest groups who have nothing left but political coercion to enforce their views on others. While the Christian faith clearly teaches that believers are to be involved as good citizens in the state, nevertheless, it is obvious why so many secularists are addicted to politics today because political power is a surrogate for a Higher Power. As Friedrich Nietzsche said, once God died in Western culture—that is, once the concept of God no longer informed the major idea-generating centers of society turned secular—there would be turmoil and horrible secular wars unchecked by traditional morality because the state would come to be a surrogate god for many.

Finally, individual rights have come to dominate our public discussion of moral issues. The public square—those aspects of society where all citizens must interface regardless of personal views; for example, public schools and government—has become naked: religious, moral, and political debate therein is no longer informed by a clear, robust vision of the moral life shared by most citizens and taken to be true and rational. Once objective duty, goodness, and virtue were abandoned under the guise of scientism and secularism, the only moral map that could replace objective morality is what Daniel Callahan has called minimalistic ethics—anything is morally permissible provided only that you do not harm someone else.[18]

Individual rights are important, and, for the Christian, they are grounded in the image of God and not in the state. In other words, the Christian believes that human rights are derived from the image of God in us; they do not ultimately come from the state. But there are more fundamental questions of virtue and duty that are relevant to the overall development of a moral outlook. For example, the abortion debate should not be framed primarily as a debate about the right to life versus the right to choice. Basically, it should be discussed in terms of this question: What does a woman or a community committed to moral virtue and duty do when faced with the question of abortion? The tenor of the debate changes drastically when issues of virtue and duty to others is brought to the foreground and rights are relegated to a secondary position in the moral context.

Until Christians can do a better job of seeing these issues and articulating them in terms of objective duty and virtue, the Jack Kevorkians will continue to win the "debate" (if that is what we should call the media rhetoric that surrounds the framing of moral dilemmas), precisely because the Kevorkians are on the side of individual rights. If the only morally relevant question to ask a patient is whether or not he freely and competently chooses physician-assisted suicide, then we are left with no moral categories in which to introduce more basic questions of duty and virtue. And this is where our secular society is at present, given its commitment to scientism that emerged in no small measure because a marginalized and inarticulate church withdrew into privatized religion as she welcomed the Trojan horse of anti-intellectualism within her walls.

## THE CONTEMPORARY THREEFOLD WORLDVIEW STRUGGLE

On Sunday morning May 9, 2004, I was in the Seattle airport waiting to board my flight home. Having finished a weekend of speaking, I wanted to relax, so I picked up a copy of *The Seattle Times* and made a beeline for the sports page. Before I got there, the lead editorial in the opinion section caught my eye. It was entitled "A Nation Divided" and in it Joel Kitkin argued that America is more divided today than at any time since the Civil War.[19] America is two nations, he claimed, and the fundamental dividing line is not political, economic, or racial. Rather, it is "a struggle between contrasting and utterly incompatible worldviews"—a secular perspective championed by the universities, Hollywood, and the major media, and ethical monotheism, whose center of gravity—are you ready for this?—is evangelical churches.

In my view, Kitkin was painting with too broad a brush, and he overgeneralized to make his point. But his fundamental idea seems to me to be correct. The secularized perspective is constituted by two worldviews—naturalism and postmodernism—that agree with each other against ethical monotheism, of which Christianity is the main version, about one important point: *There is no nonempirical knowledge, especially no theological or ethical knowledge.* I assume you are reasonably familiar with a Christian worldview, so in this section, I shall briefly sketch a picture of the other two and reinforce the main challenge they present to Christianity.

### Scientific Naturalism

Just what is scientific naturalism (hereafter, naturalism)? Succinctly put, it is the view that the spatio-temporal universe of physical objects, properties, events, and processes that are well established by scientific forms of investigation is all there is, was, or ever will be.

There are three major components of naturalism. First, naturalism begins with an epistemology, a view about the nature and limits of knowledge, known as scientism. Scientism comes in two forms: strong and weak. Strong scientism is the view that the only thing we can know is what can be tested scientifically. Scientific knowledge exhausts what can be known, and if some belief is not part of a well-established scientific theory, it is not an item of knowledge. Weak scientism allows some minimum, low-grade degree of rational justification for claims in fields outside of science, such as ethics. But scientific knowledge is taken to be so vastly superior to other forms of reasonable belief, that if a good scientific theory implies something that contradicts a belief in some other discipline, then the other field will simply have to adjust itself to be in line with science.

Second, naturalism contains a creation story—a theory, a causal story, about how everything has come-to-be. The central components of this story are the atomic theory of matter and evolution. The details of this story are not of concern here, but two broad features are of critical importance. (1) The explanation of macrochanges in things (a macrochange is a change in some feature of a normal-sized object that can be detected by simple observation, such as the change in a leaf's color) in terms of microchanges (changes in small, unobservable entities at the atomic or subatomic level). Chemical change is explained in terms of rearrangements of atoms; phenotype changes are due to changes in genotypes. Causation is from bottom-up, micro to macro. We explain why heating water causes it to boil in terms of the excitation of water molecules, and so on. (2) All events that happen are due to the occurrence of earlier events plus the laws of nature, regardless of whether the laws of nature are taken to be deterministic or probablistic.

Third, naturalism has a view about what is real: physical entities are all there are. The mind is really the brain, free actions are merely happenings caused in the right way by inputs to the organism along with its internal "hardware" states, and there is no teleology or purpose in the world. History is just one event following another. The world is simply one big cluster of physical mechanisms affecting other physical mechanisms.

## Postmodernism

Postmodernism is a loose coalition of diverse thinkers from several different academic disciplines, so it is difficult to characterize postmodernism in a way that would be fair to this diversity. Still, it is possible to provide a fairly accurate characterization of postmodernism in general, since its friends and foes understand it well enough to debate its strengths and weaknesses.[20]

Postmodernism is both an historical, chronological notion and a philosophical ideology. Understood historically, postmodernism refers to a period of thought that follows, and is a reaction to, the period called *modernity*. Modernity is the period of European thought that developed out of the Renaissance (fourteenth–seventeenth centuries) and flourished in the Enlightenment (seventeenth–nineteenth centuries) in the ideas of people like Descartes, Locke, Berkeley, Hume, Leibniz, and Kant. In the chronological sense, postmodernism is sometimes called "post modernism." So understood, it is fair to say that postmodernism is often guilty of a simplistic characterization of modernity, because the thinkers in that time period were far from monolithic. Indeed, Descartes, Hume, and Kant have elements in their thought that are more at home in postmodernism than they are in the so-called modern era. Nevertheless, setting historical accuracy aside, the chronological notion of postmodernism depicts it as an era that began and, in some sense, replaces modernity.

As a philosophical standpoint, postmodernism is primarily a reinterpretation of what knowledge is and what counts as knowledge. More broadly, it represents a form of cultural relativism about such things as reality, truth, reason, value, linguistic meaning, the self, and other notions. On a postmodernist view, there is no such thing as objective reality, truth, knowledge, value, reason, and so forth. All these are social constructions, creations of linguistic practices and, as such, are relative not to individuals but to social groups that share a narrative. Roughly, a narrative is a perspective such as Marxism, atheism, or Christianity that is embedded in the group's social and linguistic practices. Important postmodern thinkers are Friedrich Nietzsche, Ludwig Wittgenstein, Jacques Derrida, Thomas Kuhn, Michel Foucault, Martin Heidegger, and Jean-Francois Lyotard. Some postmodernists are thorough-going relativists, though most allow that the hard sciences provide reliable knowledge of reality.

### Focusing on the Main Lesson

Given these two worldviews, we see again that the central defining feature of our secular culture is this: *There is no nonempirical knowledge, especially no theological or ethical knowledge.* Science and science alone carries authority in culture because the alleged possession of knowledge gives people authority, and science and science alone is perceived to have knowledge. Outside science—especially in theological, ethical, or political discussions—the makeup man is more important than the speechwriter (feeling and image are more important than reason, knowledge, and truth).

Let me illustrate how this view of knowledge carries authority today. A few years ago, *Time* magazine did a cover story on how the universe is going to end.[21] It said, basically, that scientists now know that the universe will eventually reach a point where it's going to wind down, and it will run out of heat, light, and motion. So there won't be any heat; there won't be any light; and there won't be any motion. Now it never occurred to any of these scientists that if things are winding down, they had to be wound up. And if things have to be wound up, there must be a winder-upper, but that's a line of thought for another occasion. For present purposes, the importance of the article was this claim: For centuries, millennia, it said, we've wanted to know how all this would end. Unfortunately, the only place we could turn was religion and philosophy, which amount to idle speculation. Now, for the first time in the human race, science has moved into this area of inquiry, and for the first time, we now have knowledge in answer to our questions.

This claim conveyed that science gives answers but that religion, ethics, politics, and things like that merely provide faith or mere belief of some kind.

Here's another example from The California Framework of this view of knowledge. This is the State of California's guidelines for teaching evolution in the public schools. You can pick this up in any elementary, junior high, or high school principal's office anywhere in the state of California. Here is what it says:

> At times, some students may insist that certain conclusions of science cannot be true because of certain religious or philosophical beliefs they hold. It is appropriate, if that happens, for the teacher to express the following: "I understand you may have personal reservations about accepting the scientific evidence, but it is scientific knowledge about which there is no reasonable doubt amongst scientists in their field, and it is my responsibility to teach it because it is part of our common intellectual heritage."[22]

When the average Christian reads this, he or she walks away thinking that the primary matter of concern is the Framework's statement about creation and evolution. However, the key issue is not about creation/evolution. It is about the Framework's view of knowledge, specifically, the limitation of knowledge to the hard sciences. Observe the descriptors used of science: "scientific evidence," "scientific knowledge," "no reasonable doubt," "common intellectual heritage." Contrast these descriptors with the descriptors used for a religious claim: "personal reservation," "beliefs they hold." It is easy to see the difference between the way science is being conveyed here as a source of knowledge, and Christianity and religious claims, which are a source of "personal reservation," personal feeling.

The current worldview struggle raises a question: Do we, the disciples of Jesus, possess through Scripture and other means a reliable source of knowledge of reality, or do we not? To answer this question, we will need to get clear on what knowledge is and is not. And that will be part of the task of the next chapter.

## WHAT SHOULD I DO TO LIVE FOR CHRIST IN THIS HOUR OF CRISIS?

If you are like I am, your heart may be saddened by what you have read in this chapter. As disciples of Jesus Christ, we must ask how we can become the kind of people we need to be to bring honor to Christ, to help turn the culture toward Him, and to be lights in the midst of darkness for our families, friends, churches, and communities. There is no simple answer to this question, but one thing is crystal clear: We must rededicate ourselves to being deeply spiritual people of whom it can truly be said that "Christ is formed in you" (Galatians 4:19). And, given the times in which we live, we must also obey Jesus' admonition to be as "wise as serpents, and harmless as doves" (Matthew 10:16, KJV). Surrounded by a fragmented culture, how do we become deeply spiritual people who are wise and savvy, yet innocent and pure? How do we raise children, develop good marriages, serve as role models at work, and make an attractive impact on our communities?

More than ever before, we need what the Old Testament calls wisdom. In later chapters we'll talk more about the biblical view of wisdom, but for now I want to make something very clear: The spiritually mature person is a wise person. And a wise person has the savvy and skill necessary to lead an exemplary life and to address the issues of the day in a responsible, attractive way that brings honor to God. As we will see throughout this book, wisdom is the fruit of a life of study and a developed mind. Wisdom is the application of knowledge gained from studying both God's written Word and His revealed truth in creation. *If we are going to be wise, spiritual people prepared to meet the crises of our age, we must be a studying, learning community that values the life of the mind.* The rest of this book develops the case for why this is so and presents resources for making it a reality in your own sojourn and in the life of your church. Clearly, to become spiritually formed in Christ, a person of wisdom, requires that we follow Christ's teaching in this critical area—and it was He who taught us to love the Lord our God with all our minds.

## SUMMARY

In closing, I want to repeat that I am neither adequate for, nor do I have space to conduct, a full analysis of what has happened to the culture and the church. Obviously, more is going on here than a changed perspective of the intellectual life. But we as Christians must face the main fact of this chapter, to wit: Due to certain forces in the 1800s, conservative American Christianity responded to intellectual attack by withdrawing from public discourse and developing an anti-intellectual view of the Christian faith. This response created both a marginalized church with a softened impact for Christ and a secular culture.

English professor Carolyn Kane wrote an article in *Newsweek* about the loss of thinking in American culture generally. After putting her finger squarely on the problem, Kane identified her solution in front of both God and the *Newsweek* readership: "But how can we revive interest in the art of thinking? The best place to start would be in homes and churches of our land."[23] It is striking that she did not appeal to government, or for more money for public schools or better college facilities. Instead, she identified the church as the key factor. Perhaps Kane has a better grasp of the importance of the intellectual life in the Christian faith than many of us do. Perhaps she has read enough Scripture to know that the church was meant to be and has often been the instrument of reason in society. In the next chapter, we will see what Scripture tells us about the role of reason in the Christian life.

# CHAPTER TWO

# SKETCHING A BIBLICAL PORTRAIT OF THE LIFE OF THE MIND

In graduate school, one of my professors was a radical skeptic and relativist who went out of his way to debunk anything that had to do with Christianity. The professor was a well-known scholar whose ideas influenced hundreds of thousands of people since he regularly contributed a guest editorial to a widely read newspaper. One year after my graduation I learned that this professor had been raised in an evangelical home and church and, in fact, had been the leader of his high school youth group. Because he was bright, he developed certain intellectual doubts as a teen. When he approached the elders and pastors of his church, they failed to answer his questions. Unfortunately, they also gave him the message that faith does not require answering intellectual queries and that his problem was really spiritual and not intellectual. Needless to say, this approach did not help him in his Christian journey.

Contrast this story with Saint Augustine's (AD 354–430) description of his own conversion. Prior to his conversion, Augustine was a member of a religious cult called Manichaeanism. Being bright, Augustine had intellectual doubts about Manichaeanism, but no fellow members of the sect could answer his questions. Instead, they kept telling him to wait for the arrival of Faustus, a leading Manichaean teacher. But when Faustus came, Augustine was bitterly disappointed to find out that he relied on rhetorical skills and eloquence of speech to persuade people of the Manichaean point of view, yet his answers were shallow and poorly reasoned. Eventually, Augustine abandoned Manichaeanism. Thankfully, over the next few years, Augustine came across two Christian leaders—Ambrose and Pontitianus—who intelligently discussed with him different issues concerning the faith. This profoundly influenced Augustine and helped him on his way toward conversion.[1]

What is the difference in these two stories? Ambrose and Pontitianus exhibited a more *biblical* appreciation of the role that reason plays in Christian life and ministry than did the leaders in my professor's church. Now don't get me wrong on this, those elders were right about the Christian's desire to be like God and to live a deep and fruitful Christian life. And no doubt the leaders in my professor's church had these desires. Unfortunately, sincerity is not enough for powerful Christian ministry. We must also have an accurate biblical understanding of what we are to be about. In this chapter, I want to show that the importance of reason and a Christian intellectual life is clearly taught in Scripture. My purpose is not to proof-text my claims by merely tacking a few verses onto my thesis here and there. Rather, my passion is to paint a picture, to sketch out a vision of what the Christian way is like and illustrate how important a life of study and thought is to flourishing in that way. This chapter weaves together strands of evidence into a tapestry to show that Augustine and his friends had it right: *According to the Bible, developing a Christian mind is part of the very essence of discipleship unto the Lord Jesus.*

Since I will be saying a lot about reason in this chapter, it is important from the start to clarify what I mean by it. Obviously, I do not mean by the term something that is opposed to faith or revelation. By "reason" I mean all our faculties relevant to gaining knowledge and justifying our beliefs about different things. We all possess a number of different human faculties. For example, through my *senses* I know there is a computer before me and it is colored gray. Through my *memory* I know I had coffee this morning. Through my *logical abilities* I know that if a tree is taller than a car and a car is taller than a dog, then a tree is taller than a dog. Through my *moral faculty* I know kindness is a virtue and torturing babies is wrong. By reason, I simply mean the faculties, in isolation or in combination, I use to gain knowledge and justify my beliefs.

In this chapter, I want to show that the careful cultivation of reason should be a high value for the Christian community. To do this, we will look at biblical teaching about reason and the Christian mind. Let us begin in earnest, then, and see what the Bible says about the importance of the intellect.

## A BIBLICAL SKETCH OF THE VALUE OF REASON
### The Nature of the God of the Bible

Our Lord is a God of reason as well as of revelation. The Bible teaches, for example, that among God's attributes is omniscience: God is perfect in knowledge and, in fact, knows everything both actual and possible (1 Samuel 23:11-13; Job 37:16; 1 John 3:20). The Son of God became incarnate as the *Logos* (Greek: "the word"), which some take to represent and emphasize this reasoned, omniscient aspect of God's character, that is, the divine reason or wisdom that is made manifest and understandable in the God-man Jesus Christ.

There are other examples of God's nature that demonstrate a biblical harmony with reason. For example, God exhibits wise intelligence in choosing the best goals and the best means of accomplishing them. So wise is He that Scripture calls Him "the only wise God" (Romans 16:27). He is the God of truth who cannot lie (Titus 1:2) and who is completely reliable (Romans 3:4; Hebrews 6:18). His very word is true (John 17:17), and His church—not the university—is the pillar and support of the truth (1 Timothy 3:15). He invites His creatures to come and reason together with Him (Isaiah 1:18) by bringing a legally reasoned case against His actions to which He will respond (Ecclesiastes 6:10; Jeremiah 12:1; 20:12).

What a contrast the God of the Bible is with the god of Islam, who is so transcendent that his ways are inscrutable (beyond understanding)! How different He is from the irrational, fickle, finite deities of the Greek pantheon or other polytheistic religions! These mythological "gods" exhibit the folly of human emotion and the danger of ignoring revelation. The God of the Bible requires teachers who diligently study His Word and handle it accurately (compare 2 Timothy 2:15 and 1 Timothy 4:15-16). He demands of His evangelists that they give rational justification to questioners who ask them why they believe as they do (1 Peter 3:15). On one occasion His chief apostle, Paul, emphasized that his gospel preaching was by way of "words of sober truth" (Acts 26:25, NASB) when Festus charged that his great learning was driving him mad (Acts 26:24). No anti-intellectualism here! By contrast, the monistic religions of the East promote gurus who offer koans, paradoxes like the sound of one hand clapping, upon which to meditate in order to free the devotee from dependence on reason and enable him to escape the laws of logic. The Buddhist is to leave his mind behind, but the Christian God requires transformation by way of the mind's renewal (Romans 12:1-2).

Is it any wonder that we Christians started the first universities and have planted schools and colleges everywhere our missionaries have gone? Is it any wonder that science began in Christian Europe because of the belief that the same rational God who made the human mind also created the world so the mind would be suited to discern the world's rational structure placed there by God? God is certainly not a cultural elitist, and He does not love intellectuals more than anyone else. But it needs to be said in the same breath that ignorance is not a Christian virtue if those virtues mirror the perfection of God's own character.

### How the Bible as Revelation Points Us to a Christian Mind

We have now revisited what the Scriptures say about the nature of God Himself and briefly contrasted the biblical portrait of God with other religious worldviews (Islam, Eastern pantheism, polytheism). We've seen that only the God of the Bible has a natural affinity for reason and rationality in humans (we are, after all, created in His image). Now let us look at how God's revelation of Himself in the Scriptures points us further toward the importance of developing a Christian mind.

*1. Revelation is truth.* When the God we love chose to reveal Himself, He did so in creation itself and in more specific, special ways—most importantly, in the Scriptures and Jesus Christ. For now I want to focus on the nature of the Bible as a revelation from God and see what implications this may have for the importance of the mind. The central biblical terms for revelation—*galah*[2] (Hebrew), *apocalupto, phaneroo* (Greek)—express the idea of revealing, disclosing, making manifest or known. When we affirm that the Bible is a revelation from God, we do not simply assert that God as a person is known in and through it. We also mean that God has revealed understandable, objectively true propositions. The Lord's Word is not only practically useful, it is also theoretically true (John 17:17). God has revealed *truth* to us and not just Himself. This truth is addressed to our minds and requires an intellectual grasp to understand and then apply.

*2. How does the Holy Spirit help us understand the Bible?* Because of the Bible's nature, serious study is needed to grasp what it says. Of course, Scripture contains easily grasped portions that are fairly straightforward. But some of it is very difficult, intellectually speaking. In fact, Peter once said that some of Paul's writings were intellectually challenging, hard to understand, and easily distorted by untaught (that is, uneducated in Christian theology) and unstable people (2 Peter 3:16). Anyone who has tried to grasp the theological depths of Romans or Ephesians will say "Amen!" to that. The more a person develops the mind and the understanding of hermeneutics (the science of interpreting the Scriptures), the more he or she will be able to understand the meaning and significance of the Scriptures.

Unfortunately, many today apparently think that hard intellectual work is not needed to understand God's propositional revelation to us. Instead, they believe that the Holy Spirit will simply make known the meaning of a text if implored to do so. Tragically, this represents a misunderstanding of the Spirit's role in understanding the Scriptures. In my view, the Spirit does not help the believer understand the meaning of Scripture. Rather, He speaks to the believer's soul, convicting, comforting, opening up applications of His truth through His promptings. There are three passages typically used to justify the idea that the Spirit helps us understand the meaning of a scriptural text: 1 Corinthians 2:14-15, John 14:26, and 1 John 2:27. Let's unpack these biblical bags.

First Corinthians 2:14-15 reads as follows:

> But a natural man does not accept the things of the Spirit of God, for they are foolishness to him; and he cannot understand them, because they are spiritually appraised. But he who is spiritual appraises all things, yet he himself is appraised by no one. (NASB)

The context of the passage is a discussion of the disunity in the Corinthian church, the manner in which Paul came to them, and the spiritual state in which he discovered them. There are three keys for interpreting the verse. First, the word for "accept" is *dechomai*. The more frequently used word in Greek with a similar meaning is *lambano*, which means simply "to receive." *Dechomai* sometimes has a slightly different shade of meaning, namely, "to receive *willingly*." It is used in 2 Corinthians 8:17 to refer to Titus's acceptance of Paul's request to visit Corinth. The term has nothing to do with Titus grasping Paul's request intellectually. It expresses his willingness and openness to accept it. So in our passage, the natural man—the unbelieving person—does not receive *willingly* the things of God.

In 1 Corinthians 2:14, what are the "things of the Spirit of God" that the unbeliever does not receive willingly? The context indicates that Paul has in mind the very words and meanings of Holy Scripture. Paul is concerned to preserve the unity in the Corinthian church, and he does this by defending the divine authority of the apostles' message, including his own "words of wisdom" to mature believers. In 1 Corinthians 2:10, Paul assures his readers that the apostles' words of wisdom were revealed to them by God's Spirit. Even more, Paul says in verse 13, God's Spirit took the thoughts and ideas He had revealed to the apostles and combined them with just the right words necessary to convey these thoughts! It is these inspired words of the Scriptures that the unbeliever resists.

Second, the word for "understand" is *ginosko* in the Greek text and has the sense of "discerning as true and good" or "to know experientially by entering into." It does not mean simply to grasp something *cognitively*. It is in this experiential sense that the Bible says a man "knows" his wife in sexual intercourse. Third, the term for "appraised" is *anakrino*, which means "to spiritually appraise or sift something." It is used in Acts 17:11 of the Bereans, who tried to assess whether or not Paul's understanding of the Old Testament was good and acceptable. Note that the Bereans had to already possess an intellectual grasp of Paul's teachings before they could assess them. Combining these three insights, we see that 1 Corinthians 2:14-15 tells us that the Spirit aids the believer in being open to Scripture, in entering into it experientially, and in finding it good and acceptable. The Spirit helps us apply the significance of the text, but He does not teach us the cognitive meaning of the text. He leaves that up to us.

John 14:26 reads this way: "But the Helper, the Holy Spirit, whom the Father will send in My name, He will teach you all things, and bring to your remembrance all that I said to you" (NASB). This passage does not affirm that the Holy Spirit will teach the meaning of Scripture to believers. It promises to the apostles that the Spirit will inspire them and aid them in remembering the words of Jesus. The context makes this clear. Several verses (John 14:1,25,28-29; 16:16; 17:12-14,26) show that the disciples themselves are being spoken of and not believers in general. John 17:20 is conclusive evidence of this: "I do not ask on behalf of these alone, but for those also who believe in Me through their word" (NASB). Here Jesus makes a distinction between the disciples who are present and whom He is addressing ("you" in John 14:26 and "these alone" in 17:20) and believers in general ("those also who believe in Me through their word").

In 1 John 2:27 we are told that "you have no need for anyone to teach you; but as His anointing teaches you about all things, and is true and is not a lie, and just as it has taught you, you abide in Him" (NASB). Some take this to say that the Holy Spirit teaches the believer the truths of Scripture and that there is no need for a teacher—directly or in the form of commentaries—to understand the Bible. Common sense tells us this cannot be the correct way to take the passage, for two reasons. First, if we don't need a teacher, we wouldn't need John to teach us that we don't need a teacher! We would already know this by the "anointing!" Second, the disposition of the entire New Testament is that God has given His people gifted teachers who are to work diligently at their teaching (for example, Ephesians 4:11).

More specifically, John is addressing a historical situation in which Gnostic-like teachers were claiming special, secret insight into the Bible, a sort of specially illumined wisdom of which they were gatekeepers in much the same way some people today appeal to the Spirit to validate their biblical interpretations! John is saying that since the believers have been baptized (anointed) into the body of Christ by the Spirit, they have no need of some additional, special, secret knowledge only given to certain teachers. John is not making a statement about the need for teachers generally.

I don't want to belabor the point about the Spirit and biblical interpretation, but it is crucial to grasp the implications of what I am saying. When cultists come to my door, I often point out that they take passages out of context. To prove my charge I ask them to state the historical setting, main theme, and basic structure of just one of the sixty-six books of the Bible. It would be unfair to expect someone to do this for all the books, but if someone is in the habit of studying Scripture properly and with an eye on context, then over the years that person should have a growing ability to do this. I have never once had a cultist answer this question.

Could you do it? If the answer is no, you should ask yourself whether your approach to the Bible is adequate. I fear that our inaccurate emphasis on the Holy Spirit's role in understanding Scripture has become an easy shortcut to the hard work of building a personal library of study tools and using them. As Gallup poll after Gallup poll has shown, the result of our inaccurate emphasis on the Spirit, along with our intellectual laziness, is that modern Christians are largely illiterate about the content of their own religion and feel inadequate because of it. We need local churches dedicated to the task of training believers to think theologically and biblically. We must develop intelligent Christians; that is, Christians who have the mental training to see issues clearly, make important distinctions carefully, and weigh various factors appropriately. If we are not really planning to see this happen, then at the end of the day, what we are really saying is that a deep understanding of the Scripture, creeds, and theology of Christianity just doesn't matter that much. But as we'll see in the next section, the Scriptures themselves attest to the importance of our minds in our spiritual formation in Christ. Let's look at the most critical texts in the New Testament in this regard.

### Three Important Texts

Any disciple of Jesus who is doing his or her best to raise children, nurture other believers, or grow in the Christian way needs a plan for making certain progress in these endeavors. And any plan must take into account three critical New Testament texts: Paul's most important statement of Christian dedication in Romans 12:1-2, Jesus' summary of the Old Testament in Matthew 22:37-39, and Peter's imperative for flourishing courageously in a hostile, unbelieving environment in 1 Peter 3:15.

**1. Romans 12:1-2.** Because of its special relevance to the topic of chapter 3, I will defer in-depth treatment of Romans 12:1-2 to the next chapter. For our purposes here, let's simply look at the text and relate it to our overall understanding of the importance of the Christian mind and what the Scriptures are teaching us:

> Therefore I urge you, brethren, by the mercies of God, to present
> your bodies a living and holy sacrifice, acceptable to God, which is
> your spiritual service of worship. And do not be conformed to this

world, but be transformed by the renewing of your mind, so that you may prove what the will of God is, that which is good and acceptable and perfect. (NASB)

Now these words of Paul's are familiar to many, but the critical point of verse 2 is that we cannot "prove," that is, "make known to ourselves and to others," what God's will is *without the renewing or transformation of our minds*. This brings the mind to the spiritual stage, front and center! We all want to know God's will, but this text is telling us we can't unless we present our bodies, including our soul and minds, to the Lord for transformation and renewal! We'll look at this in more depth in the next chapter, but for now, be aware of this important insight: by "presenting our bodies," Paul means we must be available to do the hard work of understanding what God has said in His Word and take the time to study it in order to have our minds transformed!

*2. Matthew 22:37-39.* In Matthew 22:35-40, an expert in Mosaic Law challenged Jesus to summarize the entire Old Testament. In order to answer this question, Jesus must have studied the Old Testament thoroughly. Remember, even though He was God, He was also human, and during most of His earthly life He hid and subordinated His divine nature to His Father and lived as a genuine human being. The Scriptures tell us He grew in knowledge, learned things, and so forth. His now-famous answer to the lawyer included these words: "You shall love the Lord your God with all your heart, and with all your soul, and with all your mind" (verse 37, NASB). In other words, God is worthy of being loved with every single facet of human personality, not simply with one or two aspects of our nature. Note carefully that Jesus included an intellectual love for God with the mind.

What would it look like for a church, a parent, a teen, or any individual disciple to try to nurture an intellectual love for God in himself and others? We will look more fully at this question in later chapters, but for now I want to press home that answering this question is the duty of any disciple of Jesus. We get a hint at what might be included in loving

God with the mind in the context preceding Jesus' answer. In Matthew 22:23-33 a group of Sadducees (who did not believe in the resurrection of the dead) tried to trap Jesus with an intellectual argument involving a story of a woman who had successively been married to seven brothers. Whose wife will she be in the resurrection? they asked. Jesus' options seemed to be: (1) deny the resurrection, (2) accept polygamy and adultery by affirming her marriage to all seven in heaven, or (3) unfairly and arbitrarily limit her marriage to one brother only.

It is interesting to note that Jesus did something His followers should emulate: He *intelligently* answered the Sadducees' question! First, He addressed the surface issue by denying the necessary condition for the Sadducees' argument to get off the ground; that is, He denied that there is marriage in heaven. He then went for the deeper issue about the resurrection, and His strategy is instructive. He cites what on the surface appears to be a verse inadequately related to the issue of resurrection: "'I am the God of Abraham, and the God of Isaac, and the God of Jacob[.]' He is not the God of the dead but of the living" (verse 32, NASB). As a young Christian, I was puzzled by Jesus' response because I myself could have cited better verses than this one—for example, Daniel 12:2, which explicitly affirms the resurrection. Or so I thought. Jesus' genius is revealed when we recognize that He had studied Sadducean theology and knew that they did not accept the full authority of the prophets, including Daniel. He also knew that the very passage He used was one of the very defining verses for the entire Sadducean party! His argument hinged on the tense of the Hebrew verb. Jesus does not say, "I *was* the God of Abraham, etc.," but, "I *am* (continue to be) the God of Abraham, etc.," a claim that could be true only if Abraham and others continued to exist.

For our purposes, two things are important about the narrative. First, Jesus revealed His intellectual skills in debate by: (1) showing His familiarity with His opponents' point of view; (2) appealing to common ground (a text all the disputants accepted) instead of expressing a biblical text He accepted but they rejected (Daniel 12:2); and (3) deftly using the laws of logic to dissect His opponents' argument and refute it powerfully. Second, because it forms the immediately preceding context for Matthew 22:37-39, this incident may inform at least part of what it means to love God intellectually: to be prepared to stand up for God's truth and honor when they are challenged and to do so with carefully thought-out answers.

**3. *1 Peter 3:15.*** The need to have answers to people's questions is the core of our third passage: "And do not fear their intimidation, and do not be troubled, but sanctify Christ as Lord in your hearts, always being ready to make a defense [*apologia*] to everyone who asks you to give an account [*logos*] for the hope that is in you, yet with gentleness and reverence" (1 Peter 3:14-15, NASB). Two key words are central to Peter's meaning: *apologia* and *logos*. The word *apologia* means "to defend something," for example, offering positive arguments for and responding to negative arguments against your position in a courtroom. It is important to recognize that this is exactly how the apostle Paul did evangelism (Acts 14:15-17; 17:2,4,17-31; 18:4; 19:8). He persuaded people to become Christians by offering rational arguments on behalf of the truth of the gospel. He even cited approvingly two pagan philosophers, Epimenides and Aratus (Acts 17:28), as part of his case for the gospel. In 1 Peter 3:15, the apostle does not suggest that we be prepared to do this, he *commands* it.

The word *logos* means "evidence or argument which provides rational justification for some belief." In his dialogue *Theaetetus*, Plato attempted to define knowledge. According to Plato, if you know something, what you know must at least be true and you must believe it. If you said you knew it was raining outside, but either it was not raining outside or you did not even believe it was, others would rightly be puzzled at your claim to knowledge. But as Plato pointed out, knowledge is more than just true beliefs. We all have many true beliefs that don't count as knowledge. If someone hits you on the head and, as a result, somehow you form the true belief that a methane molecule has four carbon atoms in it, no one would claim that you knew this to be the case, especially compared to a scientist who had spent five years studying methane. You and the scientist both have true beliefs about methane, but he has knowledge and you don't. What is the difference? Plato says the scientist has a true belief plus *logos* (evidence) and you fail to have logos. The scientist has good reasons that justify his true belief, you have a blind faith that just happens to be true. Applied to our passage, Peter is saying that we are to be prepared to give rational arguments and good reasons for why we believe what we believe, and this involves the mind. Peter's reference to gentleness and reverence implies that we are to argue but not be argumentative.

Have you been afraid to stand up for Christ when the opportunity presented itself? Or when you have done so, have you come off as shallow, reactionary, and defensive? If so, there is nothing magical about changing your life in this area. First, as with every other area of life, you have to study hard and gain an intellectual grasp of the issues so you can be confident and courageous. Second, you need to be sure that Jesus Christ is the Lord of your life; that is, you are to serve His name, not make one for yourself. This was Peter's counsel to fearful believers being intimidated by powerful forces outside the church.

Before we leave this passage, I cannot resist making one more observation. In Acts 4:13 we read that certain Jewish elders and rulers noted that Peter and John were uneducated and unlearned. Some have taken this to have anti-intellectual implications for Christian life and witness. However, the Jewish leaders did not mean that Peter and John were irrational or intellectually unskilled. Rather, they meant that Peter and John had not undergone formal rabbinic training. There are no implications whatever from this verse about the value of education per se. Moreover, this was said of Peter at the beginning of his ministry. When he wrote his first epistle some thirty years later, he had changed. Many liberals deny that Peter could have written 1 Peter because it is written in a highly educated, intellectual Greek style unlikely to be within the purview of a simple fisherman. However, it is more likely that Peter took his own advice (1 Peter 3:15) and, from the time of Acts 4:13 to the time he wrote his epistle, devoted himself to intellectual cultivation as a part of his discipleship unto the Lord Jesus. By the time the opportunity presented itself for him to address a dispersed group of Greek Christians, some of them well-educated, he was up to the task. Even if we grant that Silvanus polished Peter's style (compare 1 Peter 5:12), there were limits to the degree that a scribe could exercise such polishing, and Peter's grammar would have been better than average and certainly an improvement over the Greek linguistic skills of a typical fisherman. Moreover, the care and precision of the argument of 1 Peter reveals a carefully trained mind.

## CHRISTIANITY AND KNOWLEDGE

Do we, the disciples of Jesus, possess through Scripture and other means a reliable source of knowledge of reality, or do we not? This is an important question. The possession of knowledge—especially religious and moral knowledge—is essential for a life of flourishing. To answer this question we must, first, answer another question: What exactly is knowledge, and what does it mean to say Christian teaching provides it? Let's begin in earnest and see if we can find an answer to this query.

### Knowledge Defined

Here's a simple definition of knowledge: It is *to represent reality in thought or experience the way it really is on the basis of adequate grounds*. To know something (the nature of cancer, forgiveness, God) is to think of or experience it as it really is on a solid basis of evidence, experience, intuition, and so forth. Little can be said in general about what counts as "adequate grounds." The best one can do is to start with specific cases of knowledge and its absence in art, chemistry, memory, Scripture, and logic and formulate helpful descriptions of "adequate grounds" accordingly.

### Three Important Clarifications About Knowledge

Please note three important things.

*1. Knowledge has nothing to do with certainty or an anxious quest for it.* One can know something without being certain about it and in the presence of doubt or the admission that one might be wrong. Recently, I know that God spoke to me about a specific matter, but I admit it is possible I am wrong about this (though, so far, I have no good reason to think I am wrong). When Paul said, "This you know with certainty" (Ephesians 5:5, NASB), he clearly implied that one can know without certainty; otherwise, the statement would be redundant. Why? If I say, "Give me a burger with pickles on it," I imply that it is possible to have a burger without pickles. If, contrary to fact, pickles were simply essential ingredients of burgers, it would be redundant to ask for burgers with pickles. The parallel to "knowledge with certainty" should be easy to see. When Christians claim to have knowledge of this or that, for example, that God is real, that Jesus rose from the dead, that the Bible is the Word of God, they are not saying that there is no possibility that they could be wrong, that they have no doubts, or that they have answers to every question raised against them. They are simply saying that these and other claims satisfy the definition given above.

**2. One can know something without knowing how one knows it.** If one always has to know how one knows something before one can know it, one would also have to know how one knows how one knows something, and so on to infinity. Life is too short for such lengthy regresses and, thankfully, we often just know things without having any idea how we do. Thus, a person could know he or she has experienced the presence of God without being able to tell a skeptic how he or she knows this. When Christians claim to know this or that, they are not saying that they always know how they know the things they do. For example, many Christians have had experiences in which they *knew* that God was guiding them in a certain way, but they may not have been able to say exactly how they knew this. Now, it is often the case that some in the Christian community—for example, experts in New Testament studies or philosophy—do, in fact, know how we Christians know certain things. But it is not necessary for the average believer to have this information before they are within their rights to claim to know God is real and so forth.

**3. One can know without knowing that one knows.** Consider Joe, an insecure yet dedicated high school student, who is about to take his history final. He has studied thoroughly and knows the material, but when a friend asks him if he is prepared for the test, he says, "no." In this case, Joe actually knows the material, but he doesn't know he knows it. Thus, he lacks confidence. Today, cultural elites in the media and university tell us that we cannot know that God is real, and so on. As a result, while many Christians actually do know various things relevant to Christianity, they lack confidence because they do not know that they have this knowledge.

### Three Kinds of Knowledge

In addition to these three observations about knowledge, there are three different kinds of knowledge.

**1. Knowledge by acquaintance.** This happens when we are directly aware of something, for example, when I see an apple directly before me or pay attention to my inner feelings, I know these things by acquaintance. One does not need a concept of an apple or knowledge of how to use the word *apple* in English to have knowledge by acquaintance with an apple. A baby can see an apple without having the relevant concept or linguistic skills. *Knowledge by acquaintance is sometimes called "simple seeing," being directly aware of something.* Sometimes Christians know God by directly experiencing His presence, forgiveness, and so on.

**2. Propositional knowledge.** This is knowledge that an entire proposition is true. For example, knowledge that "the object there is an apple" requires having a concept of an apple and knowing that the object under consideration satisfies the concept. *Propositional knowledge is justified true belief; it is believing something that is true on the basis of adequate grounds.* The Bible is our ultimate, final source of propositional knowledge about the doctrines of Christianity.

**3. Know-how.** *This is the ability to do certain things*, for example, to use apples for certain purposes. We may distinguish mere know-how from genuine know-how or skill. The latter is know-how based on knowledge and insight and is characteristic of skilled practitioners in some field. Mere know-how is the ability to engage in the correct behavioral movements, say by following the steps in a manual, with little or no knowledge of why one is performing these movements. Biblical know-how directed at living life well is called wisdom.

Because knowledge by acquaintance is so important, let me elaborate on it a bit further. This sort of knowledge is knowledge by simple seeing—when one directly experiences something. One can think of a tree, God, or whether or not one is angry, but these are all different from directly being aware of the tree, God, or one's inner state of anger. Knowledge by acquaintance is an important foundation for all knowledge, and in an important sense, experience or direct awareness of reality is the basis for everything we know. *Experience is more basic than ultimate worldview presuppositions and, in fact, the evidence of experience provides data for evaluating rival worldviews or interpretations of some event.*

One should not limit what one can see or directly be aware of to the five senses. One can also be directly aware of one's own soul and inner states of thoughts, feelings, desires, beliefs, and so forth by introspective awareness of one's inner life. One can be directly aware of God and His presence in religious experience, of His speaking to one in guidance, of the Spirit's testimony to various things, and so forth. From Plato to the present, many philosophers have believed, correctly in my view, in what is called *rational awareness*, the soul's ability to directly be aware of aesthetic and moral values, numbers and the laws of mathematics, the laws of logic, and various abstract objects such as humanness, wisdom, and so forth. *The important thing to note is that we humans have the power to "see," to be directly aware of, to directly experience a wide range of things, many of which are not subject to sensory awareness with the five senses.*

To "*simply* see" an apple (or experience God in contemplative prayer) is to be directly aware of it. To *see something **as** an apple* (or God) requires that one has acquired the concept of being an apple (perhaps from repeated exposure to simply seeing apples) and applies it to the object before one. To *see **that*** an object is an apple (or God), one must have the entire thought in one's mind, "The object before me is an apple," and judge that the object genuinely corresponds to that thought. All three have relevance to mystical experience and awareness of God.

Given the reality and nature of knowledge by acquaintance, it follows that knowledge does not begin with presuppositions, language, concepts, one's cultural standpoint, worldview, or anything else. It starts with awareness of reality. *Seeing as* and *seeing that* require that one has presuppositions, concepts, and so forth. One's presuppositions and so forth will *influence* how we see things *as such and such*, for example, as a healing from God, and one's worldview will *influence* our *seeing **that*** or *judging **that*** *such and such*, for example, seeing/judging that this event is a miraculous healing. But one's worldview does not *determine* the way we see or judge things. That's far too strong. Influence is one thing; determination is another. Failure to make this distinction has contributed to confusions I will address later.

And because we have direct acquaintance with the world itself prior to *seeing as* (applying a concept to something) or *seeing that* (judging that an entire proposition is true), we can compare the way we see things or judge things with the things themselves, and thereby we can adjust our worldview. For example, because we actually see the person get well, we can verify or disconfirm that we are right to see the event as or to judge it as a miracle from God. Knowledge by acquaintance gives us direct access to reality as it is in itself, and we actually know this to be the case in our daily lives.

### The Biblical Emphasis on Knowledge

The possession of knowledge is crucial for life. Knowledge provides truth about reality along with the skillful ability to interact with reality. It is so important that Hosea 4:6 categorically asserts that "my people are destroyed for lack of knowledge. Because you have rejected knowledge, I also will reject you from being My priest. Since you have forgotten the law of your God, I also will forget your children" (NASB).

Note carefully that Hosea did not say the people had rejected faith. It was far worse than that. They had rejected the only appropriate ground for faith—knowledge. It comes as a surprise to people that Scripture has as much or more to say about knowledge than faith. Consider the following passages (emphasis added) about the scriptural importance of knowledge:

> Now I *know* that the LORD is greater than all other gods, for he did this to those who had treated Israel arrogantly. (Exodus 18:11)

> *Acknowledge* [lit., know] and take to heart this day that the LORD is God in heaven above and on the earth below. There is no other. (Deuteronomy 4:39)

> *Know* that the LORD has set apart the godly for himself; the LORD will hear when I call to him. (Psalm 4:3)

> The lips of the righteous *know* what is fitting. (Proverbs 10:32)

> Then all mankind *will know* that I, the LORD, am your Savior, your Redeemer, the Mighty One of Jacob. (Isaiah 49:26)

> You are in error because you *do not know* the Scriptures or the power of God. (Matthew 22:29—a fine combination of propositional and experiential knowledge)

> If anyone chooses to do God's will, he *will find out* [lit., will know] whether my teaching comes from God or whether I speak on my own. (John 7:17)

> This is the disciple who testifies to these things and who wrote them down. We *know* that his testimony is true. (John 21:24)

> We *know* that the law is spiritual. (Romans 7:14)

> We *know* that the whole creation has been groaning as in the pains of childbirth right up to the present time. (Romans 8:22)

And we *know* that in all things God works for the good of those who love him, who have been called according to his purpose. (Romans 8:28)

Always give yourselves fully to the work of the Lord, because you *know* that your labor in the Lord is not in vain. (1 Corinthians 15:58)

Now we *know* that if the earthly tent we live in is destroyed, we have a building from God, an eternal house in heaven, not built by human hands. (2 Corinthians 5:1)

We *know* that the law is good if one uses it properly. (1 Timothy 1:8)

We *know* that we have come to *know* him if we obey his commands. (1 John 2:3 — a matchless example of propositional knowledge, personal knowledge, and moral ground)

### Scripture on the Value of Extrabiblical Knowledge

A picture is emerging from our glance at Holy Scripture, a portrait of the mature Christian life in which the intellectual life, the careful development of our faculty of reason, is an essential, valuable component. The spiritual journey is certainly more than loving God with our minds, but just as surely, that journey is at least a life of such intellectual devotion. As we grow in our love for God and seek to be like Him, we make it our intention to become as well-informed and knowledgeable as we can, given that our intellectual development must be balanced with devotion to growth in other aspects of our human selves.

***1. The Scriptures show us the value of extrabiblical knowledge for a life of wisdom.*** The Bible has a lot to say about wisdom, and reverence for God is where it begins (Proverbs 1:7). But such reverence alone will not bring wisdom. Wisdom results when a respectful heart is united with a disciplined mind. Knowledge is the fruit of study, and knowledge is necessary for wisdom.

Holy Scripture is the central object of study in loving God with the mind. However, it is not the only object of such study. God has revealed

Himself and various truths on a number of topics outside the Bible. As Christians have known throughout our history, common sense, logic, and mathematics—along with the arts, humanities, sciences, and other areas of study—contain important truths relevant to life in general and to the development of a careful, life-related Christian worldview. According to the Bible, wisdom comes from studying ants as well as learning Scripture (Proverbs 6)!

In 1756, John Wesley delivered an address to a gathering of clergy on how to carry out the pastoral ministry with joy and skill. In his address, Wesley cataloged a number of things familiar to most contemporary believers—the cultivation of a disposition to glorify God and save souls, a knowledge of Scripture, and similar notions. However, at the very beginning of his list, Wesley focused on something seldom expressly valued by most pastoral search committees: "Ought not a Minister to have, First, a good understanding, a clear apprehension, a sound judgment, and a capacity of reasoning with some closeness?"[3] Time and again throughout the address, Wesley unpacked this remark by admonishing ministers to know what would sound truly odd and almost pagan to the average person in the pew today: logic, metaphysics, natural theology, geometry, and the ideas of important figures in the history of thought (philosophy, history, literature). For Wesley, study in these areas (especially philosophy and geometry) helped train the mind to think precisely, a habit of incredible value, he asserted, when it comes to thinking as a Christian about theological themes or scriptural texts. For Wesley, the study of extrabiblical information and the writings of unbelievers was of critical value for growth and maturity. As he put it elsewhere, "To imagine none can teach you but those who are themselves saved from sin, is a very great and dangerous mistake. Give not place to it for a moment."[4]

Wesley's remarks were not unusual in his time. A century earlier, the great Reformed pastor Richard Baxter was faced with lukewarmness in the church and unbelief outside it. In 1667 he wrote a book to meet these needs, and in it he used philosophy, logic, and general items of knowledge outside Scripture to argue for the existence of the soul and the life to come.[5] The fact that Baxter turned to philosophy and extra-biblical knowledge instead of therapy or praise hymns is worth pondering. Over a millennium earlier, Augustine summarized the view of many early church fathers when he said that "We must show our Scriptures not to be in conflict with whatever [our critics] can demonstrate about the nature of things from reliable sources."[6] Philosophy and extrabiblical knowledge were the main tools Augustine used in this task. In fact, it is safe to say that throughout much of church history, Scripture and right reason were considered twin allies to be prized and used by disciples of Jesus.

In valuing extrabiblical knowledge, our brothers and sisters in church history were merely following common sense and Scripture itself. Repeatedly, Scripture acknowledges the wisdom of cultures outside Israel; for example, Egypt (Isaiah 19:11-13), the Edomites (Jeremiah 49:7), the Phoenicians (Zechariah 9:2), and many, many others. The remarkable achievements produced by human wisdom are acknowledged in Job 28:1-11. The wisdom of Solomon is compared to that of the "men of the east" and Egypt in order to show that it surpassed that of people with a longstanding, well-deserved reputation for wisdom (1 Kings 4:29-34). Paul approvingly quotes pagan philosophers (Acts 17:28) and Jude cites the noncanonical book *The Assumption of Moses* in Jude 9. The book of Proverbs is filled with examples in which knowledge, even moral and spiritual knowledge, can be gained from studying things (for example, ants) in the natural world. Once Jesus taught that we should know we are to love our enemies, not on the basis of an Old Testament text, but from careful reflection on how the sun and rain behave (Matthew 5:44-45). We can and must cultivate the Christian mind, but in that tilling we must include the study of the works of extrabiblical knowledge.

*2. Scripture teaches us the value of the natural moral law.* Two specific aspects of scriptural teaching about extrabiblical knowledge are worthy of special note. First, Scripture repeatedly acknowledges the existence of natural moral law: true moral principles rooted in the way God made things, addressed to humans as humans (instead of to man as a believing member of the kingdom of God) and knowable by all people independently of the Bible (Job 31:13-15; Romans 1–2).[7] Among other things, what this means is that believers need not appeal to Scripture in arguing for certain ethical positions, say, in the abortion debate.

Indeed, in my own view, the church is to work for a just state, not a Christian state or theocracy.[8] We are not to place the state under Scripture. But if this is true, where is the source of moral guidance for the state to be just and to punish wrongdoers as Romans 13:1-7 teaches? The answer is the natural moral law. God has revealed enough of His moral law in creation for the state to do its job. The church may *preach* to unbelievers what Scripture says about some topic, but when believers *argue* for their views in the public square or *defend* them against those who do not accept the Scriptures, they should use general principles of moral argument and reasoning.

This is precisely what the prophet Amos did. In Amos 1 and 2, he denounced the moral behavior of several people-groups outside of Israel, and he never once appealed to Scripture. Instead, he was content to rest his case with an appeal to self-evident moral principles in the natural law, which he assumed were known by those without Scripture. But when he turned to rebuke the people of Israel, for the first time he said that they had violated the "law of the LORD" (Amos 2:4), knowing that they had a familiarity with Holy Scripture. Amos appealed to common ground in all these cases, just as Jesus did in reasoning with the Sadducees (Matthew 22:23-33) and Paul in evangelizing the Greeks (Acts 17:16-31).

***3. Scripture shows the value of being qualified to minister from a position of influence.*** The second aspect of scriptural teaching about extrabiblical knowledge is, Scripture shows people qualified to minister in God's name in situations that required them to have intellectual skills in extrabiblical knowledge. In Daniel 1:3-4; 2:12-13; 5:7, we see Daniel and his friends in a position to influence Nebuchadnezzar, king of

Babylon, only because they showed intelligence in every branch of wisdom. These men had studied and learned Babylonian science, geometry, and literature. And because of this, they were prepared to serve when the occasion presented itself.

I remember being in a meeting with Dr. Bill Bright, founder of Campus Crusade for Christ, shortly after Ronald Reagan had been elected president. Dr. Bright came into the meeting late because Reagan had called to ask him to confer with other evangelical leaders in order to suggest a list of qualified evangelicals to serve in his presidential cabinet. With sadness in his heart, Dr. Bright said that after numerous phone conversations with other evangelical leaders, they had concluded that there simply were not many evangelicals with the intellectual and profes-sional excellence for such a high post. C. Everett Koop was all they could think of and, as we now know, Koop got the position of surgeon general. Had evangelicals valued the study of extrabiblical knowledge the way Daniel and his friends did, things may have turned out quite differently.

How, then, should this attitude toward extrabiblical intellectual training inform parents and youth groups when they prepare Christian teenagers to go to college and tell teens why college is important? According to various studies, increasing numbers of college freshmen, on the advice of parents, say their primary goal in going to college is to get a good job and ensure a secure financial future for themselves. This parallels a trend in the same students toward valuing a good job more than developing a meaningful philosophy of life. Given this view of a college education, it is clear why the humanities have fallen on hard times. It is equally clear why the level of our public discourse on topics central to the culture wars is so shallow, since it is precisely the humani-ties that train people to think carefully about these topics.

What is not so clear is why Christians, with a confidence in the providential care and provision of God, would follow the secular culture in adopting this approach to college. How different this approach is compared to the value of a college education embraced by earlier generations of Christians: A Christian goes to college to discover his vocation—the area of service to which God has called him—and to develop the skills necessary to occupy a section of the cultural, intellectual domain in a manner worthy of the kingdom of God. A believer also goes to college to gain general information and the habits of thought necessary for developing a well-structured soul suitable for a well-informed, good citizen of both earthly and heavenly kingdoms. If the public square is naked, it may be because Christians have abandoned the humanities due to a sub-biblical appreciation for extra-biblical knowledge.

We have just looked at three important arguments that show the value of extrabiblical knowledge and the baptism of such knowledge by the Scriptures themselves. So, why do Christians continue to ignore the value of the life of the mind in the face of all this evidence? Let's look briefly at five barriers to reason.

### Biblical Resistance to the Intellectual Life

In spite of the multifaceted case for the centrality of a well-developed Christian mind to the Christian life, you still may be hesitant to accept its value. I will address these sources of resistance in chapter 4, but here I want to demolish five misconceptions that in one way or another wage war on the Christian mind by distorting what Scripture says on this topic.

*1. The distortion of 1 Corinthians 1–2.* Two frequently cited but misunderstood texts relevant to the Christian mind are 1 Corinthians 1–2 and Colossians 2:8. In 1 Corinthians 1 and 2, Paul argues against the wisdom of the world and reminds his readers that he did not visit them with persuasive words of wisdom. Some conclude from this that human reasoning and argument are futile, especially when applied to evangelism. There are several problems with this understanding of the passage. For one thing, if it is in fact an indictment against argumentation and reasoning, then it contradicts Paul's own practices in Acts and his explicit appeal to argument and evidence on behalf of the Resurrection in the very same epistle (1 Corinthians 15).

Second, this passage is more accurately seen as a condemnation of the false, prideful use of reason, not of reason itself. It is *hubris* (pride) that is in view, not *nous* (mind). God chose foolish (*moria*) things that were offensive to human pride, not to reason properly used. For example, the idea of God being crucified was so offensive that the Greek spirit would have judged it to be morally disgusting.

The passage may also be a condemnation of Greek rhetoric. Greek orators prided themselves in possessing "persuasive words of wisdom," and it was their practice to persuade a crowd of any side of an issue for the right price. They did not base their persuasion on rational considerations but on speaking ability, thus bypassing issues of substance. Paul is most likely contrasting himself with Greek rhetoricians. If so, then Paul is arguing against evangelists who spend all of their time working on their speaking techniques yet fail to address the minds of unbelievers in their gospel presentations!

Paul could also be making the claim that the content of the gospel cannot be deduced by pure reason from some set of first principles. No one could start off with an abstract concept of a first mover and deduce that a crucifixion would happen from this information alone. Thus, the gospel could never have been discovered by pure deductive reason from self-evident first principles, but had to be revealed by the biblical God who acts in history. Paul was insistent that the intellect could assess whether or not there was sufficient evidence to judge that God had so acted (1 Corinthians 15). So we cannot conclude from this passage that using reason is futile.

**2. The distortion of Colossians 2:8.** In this passage, Paul says, "See to it that no one takes you captive through hollow and deceptive philosophy, which depends on human tradition and the basic principles of this world rather than on Christ." Some take this to be a command to avoid secular studies, especially philosophy. However, upon closer inspection of the structure of the verse, it becomes clear that philosophy in general was not the focus. Rather, it is a certain sort of philosophy — hollow and deceptive philosophy.

In the context of Colossians, Paul was warning the church not to form and base doctrinal views according to a philosophical system hostile to orthodoxy. His remarks were a simple warning not to embrace heresy; in context, they were not meant to represent his views of philosophy as a discipline of study. In fact, one of the best ways to avoid hollow and deceptive philosophy is to study philosophy itself, so you can learn to recognize truth from error, using Scripture and right reason as a guide. *This is exactly what Paul himself did.* Colossians reveals an apostle who was entirely familiar with the type of proto-Gnostic philosophy threatening Colossian believers, who possessed a thorough knowledge of that philosophical system and an ability to point out its inadequacy. And remember, Paul himself cited pagan philosophers approvingly in Acts 17:28. Neither of these texts should dampen our enthusiasm to cultivate a Christian mind or use reason in our Christian walk.

**3. The doctrine of depravity doesn't mean reason is irrelevant.** Some argue that the human intellect is fallen, depraved, darkened, and blinded, and therefore human reason is irrelevant or suspect when it comes to becoming or growing as a Christian. Now, even if this point is granted in the case of evangelizing unbelievers, it doesn't follow that Christians should not use or cultivate their intellects once they have become disciples. Moreover, from the fact that reasoning alone will not bring someone to Christ, it does not follow that we should not persuade or reason with people. Preaching alone will not save people without the Spirit's work, but we still preach and work on our messages. We should do the same thing with our use of reason in evangelism.

The will is fallen and depraved too, but God still commands people to make a choice to believe. The doctrine of total depravity does not mean that the image of God is effaced, that sinners are as evil as they could possibly be, or that the intellect, emotions, and will are gone or completely useless. Rather, total depravity means that the entire person, including the intellect, has been adversely affected by the Fall and is separate from God. The sinner alone cannot extricate himself from this condition and cannot merit God's favor or commend himself to God on the basis of his own righteousness. Further, the entire personality is corrupt but not inoperative, and every aspect of our personality has a natural inclination to run in ways contrary to God's ways. However, none of this means that reason, considered in itself, is bad.

*4. Distorting the nature of faith as a matter of the heart, not the head.* As we have already seen, some think faith is opposed to or should be separate from reason. This is sometimes supported by Jesus' own teaching about the importance of being like little children in order to enter the kingdom of God (Matthew 18:1-4). It is also justified by the idea that a relationship with God is a matter of the heart, not the head.

Unfortunately, the opinions just expressed do not capture the substance of biblical teaching. In Scripture, faith can be directed at different things — most frequently, at a statement or a person, especially God. To have faith in a statement means to let yourself be convinced of and, therefore, accept the statement as true. To have faith in God means to firmly rely on Him. Either way, *faith is relying on what you have reason to believe is true and trustworthy.* Faith involves the readiness to act as if something were so.

Throughout church history, theologians have expressed three different aspects of biblical faith: *notitia* (knowledge), *fiducia* (trust), and *assensus* (assent). *Notitia* refers to the data or doctrinal content of the Christian faith (Jude 3). *Assensus* denotes the assent of the intellect to the truth of the content of Christian teaching. Note that each of these aspects of faith requires a careful exercise of reason, both in understanding what the teachings of Christianity are and in judging their truthfulness. In this way, reason is indispensable for the third aspect of faith—*fiducia*—which captures the personal application or trust involved in faith, an act that primarily involves the will but includes the affections and intellect too.[9]

What about being like a little child and the importance of the heart over the head in the Christian life? In the context, Jesus' teaching about becoming like a little child had nothing to do with the intellect. It was directed against being self-sufficient and arrogant. To be a child in this sense is to be humble and willing to trust in or rely on others, especially God. The opposite of the child is a proud, stiff-necked person, not an intelligent, reasonable one. Further, the distinction between the head and the heart is very misleading. In Scripture, the term *heart* has several meanings. Most of the time it simply refers to the seat or center of the entire person, the total self, including intellect, emotion, and will. Sometimes it simply refers to the emotions or affections (Romans 1:24; Philippians 1:8). However, the term *heart* often actually refers to the mind itself (Romans 1:21; 2 Corinthians 4:6; 9:7; Ephesians 1:18). Therefore, it is safe to say that when the term heart is used in a verse, it most likely includes or explicitly refers to our mental faculty unless the context shows otherwise. Let's not allow hollow or false teaching to distort our understanding of the critical nature of the heart and move on in our development of a Christian mind.

**5. A grotesque distortion: Our response to God's way should be ignorance.** Finally, I sometimes hear two claims that express the idea that it is futile to use your reason or to emphasize its importance when it comes to the Christian way: God's ways and thoughts are higher than ours (Isaiah 55:9) and knowledge puffs people up and makes them arrogant (1 Corinthians 8:1). It should be clear what is wrong with these claims. The fact that God's thoughts are higher than ours means that we will never be able to fully grasp God's motives, purposes, or providential guidance in the world. But who in his right mind ever thought that we could gain such a thing! To admit this, however, says absolutely nothing about whether or not we should try to love God and serve Him better with our minds.

Regarding the arrogance that comes from knowledge, we need to keep two things in mind. First, Paul's statement is not against knowledge per se, but against a certain attitude toward it. The proper response to his warning is *humility*, not ignorance! Second, for every knowledgeable person who is arrogant, there is an unknowledgeable person who is defensive and proud as a cover-up for his or her lack of knowledge. Arrogance is not possessed solely by people who have developed their reasoning abilities.

## SUMMARY

We Christians have a desire deep within us to be like God and to bring honor to His name. But what are we to look like if we are to fulfill these desires? In this chapter, I have not tried to give a full answer to that question. But a picture has emerged from several strands of biblical evidence, and that picture clearly implies that a growing, vibrant disciple will be someone who values his intellectual life and works at developing his mind carefully.

Two of the most prominent Christian leaders of the twentieth century were an evangelist and a pastor: Billy Graham and John Stott. Both have expressed their deep commitment to reason and the intellectual life. In 1981, Billy Graham was asked if it bothered him that so many evangelicals seem to be theologically illiterate. He answered, "It bothers me terribly, as much as anything I can think of."[10] Later, as the October 20, 1996, issue of *Parade* magazine reports, Graham was asked what he would do differently if given the chance. He replied, "I would have studied more. I would have gotten my Ph.D. in anthropology."[11] In the same vein, British pastor John Stott was asked to reflect on fifty years of ministry and give advice to a new generation of Christian leaders. Upon reflection, here was his response:

> I'd want to say so many things. But my main exhortation would be this: Don't neglect your critical faculties. Remember that God is a rational God, who has made us in His own image. God invites and expects us to explore His double revelation, in nature and Scripture, with the minds He has given us, and to go on in the development of a Christian mind to apply His marvelous revealed truth to every aspect of the modern and post-modern world.[12]

Graham and Stott are expressing the very heart of New Testament religion. We neglect their admonitions to our own peril. In the next chapter, we will see exactly why the mind and its cultivation are so important for spiritual growth in God's kingdom.

# CHAPTER THREE

# THE MIND'S ROLE IN SPIRITUAL TRANSFORMATION

I have a confession to make. I am no fix-it man. In fact, one of my friends said that if I were considered a handyman, then Pee-wee Herman would be an NFL lineman! Ouch! Because of my mechanical ineptness, I usually call for help when something breaks down or needs to be installed. However, several summers ago, I worked up the courage to put in a ceiling fan. I break out in hives when I remember my first glance at the instructions (who writes these instructions, anyway?). I had to take it step-by-step, and I had absolutely no idea about the overall picture of what I was doing or why each step was located where it was. I finally got it in and it worked. Shortly thereafter, I tried to put in a second fan. Interestingly, it was as though I had never done one before. I couldn't remember a thing about how to do it, and I had to take it step-by-step just as I had the first time.

My father was very different. He was literally a mechanical wizard. He usually threw instructions away, and when he did look at them it was only for a moment, and then he followed his own skill and know-how. And if he did something once, he knew how to do it from then on. It stuck with him. Why was this the case with my dad but not with me? The answer is simple. The more you know about something, the more you're able to see when you look at it, the more you can remember about it, and the less tied you will be to following a mindless series of steps in working with what you know. My father simply knew how things work and I don't. He saw the world mechanically; I see the world as a bloomin', buzzin' confusion.

Learning to value, develop, deepen, and use your intellect in the overall process of spiritual transformation is a lot like being a fix-it man. In chapters 1 and 2, we examined the serious problems in society and the church due to an emergence of anti-intellectualism in the body of Christ. We also learned that there are solid biblical grounds for nurturing and developing our intellectual lives. But if this were all we had, we would be like a person tied to a step-by-step set of instructions. The information of chapters 1 and 2 would not stick very well, we would have to be reminded of it regularly, and we certainly would not see the world as a growing Christian thinker. What we need is an understanding of what the mind is and how it fits into the process of human transformation and spiritual growth. And that is what I want to discuss in this chapter.

## NEW TESTAMENT TRANSFORMATION AND OLD TESTAMENT WISDOM

That the mind is the crucial component in the spiritual journey cannot be accurately denied. The apostle Paul's writings are probably the most complete set of biblical instructions about what individual and corporate discipleship are and how they are to be attained. Arguably, the most important text he ever penned about spiritual transformation is Romans 12:1-2. In this wise and tender admonition, the devotional master, Paul, puts his finger on the very essence of how we grow to become like Jesus: "Do not conform any longer to the pattern of this world," he tells us, "but be transformed by the renewing of your mind" (verse 2). "Renewing" is *anakainosis* in the Greek, and its meaning is fairly straightforward: making something new. Later in this chapter we will appreciate how appropriate this term is for describing what happens to the mind when it incorporates new thoughts and beliefs. "Mind" is *nous* and means "the intellect, reason, or the faculty of understanding."

We are so familiar with this verse that some of its oddness or peculiarity is lost on us. But to see how truly peculiar this teaching is, think of what Paul could have said but did not. He could have said, "Be transformed by developing close feelings toward God," or "by exercising your will in obeying biblical commands," or "by intensifying your desire for the right things," or "by fellowship and worship," and so on. Obviously, all are important parts of the Christian life. Yet Paul chose to mention none of them in his most important précis of the spiritual life. Why is that? What is it about the mind that justifies Paul's elevation of it to such a position of prominence in religious life?

In the preceding verse, Paul reminds us that we should offer our bodies to God because this is the most reasonable way to express service to Him in light of His mercies toward us. Paul mentions the body and its members—our faces, hands, tongues, feet—for two reasons. First, the body is the vehicle through which we interact with the world. For example, to get groceries, it is not enough for me just to think about the grocery store. I have to move my body and go to the store! Likewise, it is not enough to think about showing love to my wife or to feel a desire inside to evangelize a friend. In both cases, I have to move my body—I smile, use my tongue to bless or communicate, and so forth.

Second, my habits dwell in my body and its members. Some people frown so much, gossip so often, or eat certain soothing foods so regularly that routines and habits get deeply woven into their bodies. In the right circumstances, their faces are habituated to frown, their tongues to talk, and their legs to walk to the refrigerator *without even thinking* about it. To change our habits and to interact differently with the world, we need to retrain our bodies to form new habits that replace the old ones.

But how do we gain the motivation, the insights, the perspective necessary to change? Anyone who has struggled with bad habits knows that you don't become transformed by just willing the old habits to go away. This is why preaching that centers too much on exhortation without instruction is ineffective. According to Paul, the key to change is the formation of a new perspective, the development of fresh insights about our lives and the world around us, the gathering of the knowledge and skill required to know what to do and how to do it. And this is where the mind comes in. Truth, knowledge, and study are powerful factors in the transformation of the self and the control of the body and its habits for a healthy life in the kingdom of God.

Paul's teaching about the centrality of the intellect for spiritual renewal was not new. The Old Testament is pregnant with this same idea in its teaching about the nature and role of wisdom in life. It summons us to think long, hard, and carefully because God has placed His stamp of reason all about us:

Do you know the ordinances of the heavens? . . .
Who has put wisdom in the innermost being
Or given understanding to the mind? (Job 38:33,36, NASB)

As James L. Crenshaw says, "Wisdom is a particular attitude toward reality, a worldview. . . . That worldview assumes . . . the one God embedded truth within all reality."[1]

The Old Testament proclaims that the same rational God who reveals Himself to the prophets also created the world as an orderly, understandable cosmos. And the Old Testament assures us that this God made our minds to be apt for gaining knowledge and understanding so as to avoid foolish living and ignorant beliefs. For those willing to pay the price of exercising their minds and studying diligently, there is knowledge and wisdom to be found in Scripture (Psalm 119); in the natural world and its operations (Isaiah 28:23-29); and in the accumulated insights embedded in the art, literature, and science of the different cultures of the world (Isaiah 19:11-13; Jeremiah 49:7; Daniel 2:12-13; 5:7).

But just as surely as the Old Testament places a value on wisdom and knowledge, it warns us that they only come to the diligent:

Make your ear attentive to wisdom,
Incline your heart to understanding. (Proverbs 2:2, NASB)

We are to

seek her [wisdom] as silver
And search for her as for hidden treasures. (2:4, NASB)

A wise life of virtue and knowledge comes to those who, with humility of heart and reverence for God, work hard at using their minds to study, to seek understanding, to capture truth.

But what is it about our makeup that requires us to use our minds in order to change? How does intellectual growth change the soul, and what is it about a well-formed mind that makes it so valuable for gaining a new way of seeing life?

In order to answer these questions, we will first examine the nature of the soul and the mind it contains and second investigate how the mind relates to other aspects of human personality. Here is the thesis of the chapter: *The mind is the soul's primary vehicle for making contact with God, and it plays a fundamental role in the process of human maturation and change, including spiritual transformation. In thought, the mind's structure conforms to the order of the object of thought. Since this is so, and since truth dwells in the mind, truth itself is powerful and rationality is valuable as a means of obtaining truth and avoiding error. Therefore, God desires a life of intellectual growth and study for His children.*

## THE STRUCTURE OF THE SOUL
### The Soul and the Body

During a family time one evening, my sixth-grade daughter, Allison, complained that if only she could see God, say, sitting in a chair, then prayer would be much easier. I pointed out that not only had she never seen God, neither had she ever seen me. She could see my body, but she could not see my I, my self, my ego, nor could she see my thoughts, feelings, and so forth. Persons, I told her, are invisible objects and, since God is too big to have a body, He is not perceivable in the same way a chair or a person's body is.[2]

That evening, I expressed to Allison the Christian understanding of human persons. Historically and biblically, Christianity has held to a dualistic notion of the human being. A human being is a functional unity of two distinct realities—body and soul.[3] More specifically, I *am* my soul and I *have* a body. The soul, while not by nature immortal, is nevertheless capable of entering an intermediate disembodied state upon death and, eventually, being reunited with a resurrected body. The formal name for this position is "substance dualism." The soul (which is the same thing as the self or the I) is that immaterial, invisible thing that makes me a conscious, living human being. The soul is what I am aware of when I engage in various acts of introspection in which I am aware of what is going on "inside" me. I go where my soul goes. If God took my soul and put it into your body and placed your soul into my body, we would have different bodies. If my soul leaves my body, I leave my body because I am my soul.

## *What Am I?*

During the Los Angeles riots following the Rodney King beating, a bystander said on a TV interview how surprised she was that people were acting like animals. What was unclear was why this should surprise anyone, given that we are taught all week long in public schools that this is exactly what we are—evolved animals. Our judgments about right and wrong, virtue and vice, and appropriate or inappropriate lifestyles depend largely upon what we take a human being to be. More personally, an individual's sense of well-being is in good measure a function of his or her self-concept. Thus, a proper grasp of what we are and how we function is foundational to a well-ordered society and a life well lived.

The Bible has a rich, deep anthropology expressed in terms like "soul," "spirit," "heart," and "mind."[4] Properly understood, they convey important insights about what we are and how we function. Terms in a language have a wide field of meaning. The term "red" can mean a color, being embarrassed, or being a communist. Caution should be exercised in grasping just exactly how the term is used in a specific context. For example, "my book is red" is not saying that my book is embarrassed or communist, even though these are correct meanings for "red" in other contexts.

Likewise, the biblical terms listed above have a wide variety of meanings. Sometimes they are used as synonyms, and on other occasions they have different nuances. We should be careful not to read all of the meanings associated with, say, "heart" into a specific passage.

Having said this, I want to sketch a brief portrait of the more important meanings of the biblical terms within our purview. When applied to the human being, the term "soul" sometimes stands for the total person, including the body (Genesis 2:7, KJV; Psalm 63:1). Frequently, however, the term refers to the total immaterial self, or "I," which can survive the destruction of the body (Matthew 10:28; John 12:25). It contains desires (2 Samuel 3:21) and emotions (Psalm 119:28), and the soul is what knows (Psalm 139:14) and exercises volition (Psalm 119:129; 130:6).

Sometimes "spirit" is used as a synonym for "soul." But "spirit" also refers to that aspect of human beings through which they relate to God (Psalm 51:10; Romans 8:16; Ephesians 4:23). "Heart" refers to the center of human personality (Proverbs 4:23), in which case it is equivalent to "soul." At other times, "heart" signifies the seat of volition and desire (Exodus 35:5; Deuteronomy 8:2; Romans 2:5), of feelings (Proverbs 14:30; 23:17), and of thought and reason (Deuteronomy 29:2-4; Psalm 90:12; Isaiah 65:17). Finally, the "mind" is that which reasons and thinks (Romans 14:5; Philippians 4:8; Colossians 3:2).

Does all this seem a bit complicated? Let's see if we can take these biblical terms, add some careful reflection, and develop a map of what is inside the soul.

## *What's Inside My Soul?*

The soul is a very complicated thing with an intricate internal structure that we need to understand if we are to appreciate the mind's role in spiritual transformation. In order to understand that structure, we need to grasp two important issues: *the different types of states within the soul and the notion of a faculty of the soul.* The soul is a substantial, unified reality that informs its body. The soul is to the body what God is to space—it is fully "present" at each point within the body. Further, the soul and body relate to each other in a cause-effect way. For example, if I worry in my soul, my brain chemistry[5] will change; if I exercise my will to raise my arm in my soul, the arm goes up. If I experience brain damage, this can cause me to lose the ability to remember certain things in my soul. And so forth. The soul also contains various mental states within it—for example, sensations, thoughts, beliefs, desires, and acts of will. This is not as complicated as it sounds. Water can be in a cold or a hot state. Likewise, the soul can be in a feeling or thinking state.

## The Five States of the Soul

The soul contains more states than the five I just mentioned, but it will be helpful to single these out and explain them more fully. A *sensation* is a state of awareness or sentience, a mode of consciousness—for example, a conscious awareness of sound, color, or pain. A visual sensation, like an experience of a tree, is a state of the soul, not a state of the eyeballs. The eyes do not see. I (my soul) see with or by means of the eyes. The eyes, and the body in general, are instruments, tools the soul uses to experience the external world. Some sensations are experiences of things outside me like a tree or table. Others are awarenesses of other states within me like pains or itches. Emotions are a subclass of sensations and, as such, forms of awareness of things. I can be aware of something angrily or lovingly or fearfully.

A *thought* is a mental content that can be expressed in an entire sentence and that only exists while it is being thought. Some thoughts logically imply other thoughts. For example, "All dogs are mammals" entails "This dog is a mammal." If the former is true, the latter must be true. Some thoughts don't entail but merely provide evidence for other thoughts. For example, certain thoughts about evidence in a court case provide evidence for the thought that a person is guilty. A *belief* is a person's view, accepted to varying degrees of strength, of how things really are. If a person has a belief (for example, that it is raining), then that belief serves as the basis for the person's tendency or readiness to act as if the thing believed were really so (for example, the person gets an umbrella). At any given time, one can have many beliefs that are not currently being contemplated. A *desire* is a certain felt inclination to do, have, or experience certain things. Desires are either conscious or such that they can be made conscious through certain activities, for example, through therapy. An *act of will* is a volition or choice, an exercise of power, an endeavoring to do a certain thing.

### The Faculties of the Soul Include the Mind and Spirit

In addition to its states, at any given time the soul has a number of capacities that are not currently being actualized or utilized. To understand this, consider an acorn. The acorn has certain actual characteristics or states—a specific size, shape, or color. But it also has a number of capacities or potentialities that could become actual if certain things happen. For example, the acorn has the capacity to grow a root system or change into the shape of a tree. Likewise, the soul has capacities. I have the ability to see color, think about math, or desire ice cream even when I am asleep and not in the actual states just mentioned.

Now, capacities come in hierarchies. There are first-order capacities, second-order capacities to have these first-order capacities, and so on, until ultimate capacities are reached. For example, if I can speak English but not Russian, then I have the first-order capacity for English as well as the second-order language capacity to have this first-order capacity (which I have already developed). I also have the second-order capacity to have the capacity to speak Russian, but I lack the first-order capacity to do so. Higher-order capacities are realized by the development of lower-order capacities under them. An acorn has the ultimate capacity to draw nourishment from the soil, but this can be actualized and unfolded only by developing the lower capacity to have a root system, then developing the still lower capacities of the root system, and so on.

When something has a defect (for example, a child who is colorblind), it does not lose its ultimate capacities. Rather, it lacks some lower-order capacity it needs for the ultimate capacity to be developed.

The adult human soul has literally thousands of capacities within its structure. But the soul is not just a collection of isolated, discrete, randomly related internal capacities. Rather, the various capacities within the soul fall into natural groupings called *faculties* of the soul. In order to get hold of this, think for a moment about this list of capacities: the ability to see red, see orange, hear a dog bark, hear a tune, think about math, think about God, desire lunch, desire a family. Now it should be obvious that the ability to see red is more closely related to the ability to see orange than it is to the ability to think about math. We express this insight by saying that the abilities to see red or orange are parts of the same faculty—the faculty of sight. The ability to think about math is a capacity within the thinking faculty. In general, *a faculty is a compartment of the soul that contains a natural family of related capacities.*

We are now in a position to map out the soul in more detail. All the soul's capacities to see are part of the faculty of sight. If my eyeballs are defective, then my soul's faculty of sight will be inoperative just as a driver cannot get to work in his car if the spark plugs are broken. Likewise, if my eyeballs work but my soul is inattentive—say I am daydreaming—then I won't see what is before me either. The soul also contains faculties of smell, touch, taste, and hearing. Taken together, these five are called sensory faculties of the soul. The will is a faculty of the soul that contains my abilities to choose. The emotional faculty of the soul contains my abilities to experience fear, love, and so forth.

Two additional faculties of the soul are of crucial importance. The *mind* is that faculty of the soul that contains thoughts and beliefs along with the relevant abilities to have such things. It is with my mind that I think, and my mind contains my beliefs. The *spirit* is that faculty of the soul through which the person relates to God (Psalm 51:10; Romans 8:16; Ephesians 4:23).[6] Before the new birth, the spirit is real and has certain abilities to be aware of God. But most of the capacities of the unregenerate spirit are dead and inoperative. At the new birth, God implants new capacities in the spirit. These fresh capacities need to be nourished and developed so they can grow.

Scripture tells us that we are fearfully and wonderfully made, and this insight applies to the soul as well as the body. As we have seen, the soul contains a rich set of faculties within it and each faculty contains a large number of specifically ordered abilities. As we learn more about how the soul functions, it becomes clear that the abilities present in a faculty of the soul can have an impact on other abilities within that very faculty. For example, a person can be so enslaved to eating that he or she cannot say no to ice cream if it is in the freezer. The person simply does not have the volitional ability to refrain. But the person may very well have the second-order ability to develop the ability to refrain. If the person works on this second-order ability—for example, by choosing to ask one's self regularly (especially just prior to a snack attack!) what comfort need is being met by eating ice cream and finding alternative ways to meet that need—he or she can develop the first-order ability to refrain. The various spiritual disciplines of fasting, solitude, and so on work in just this way. They allow people to develop spiritual abilities that would be unavailable to them by direct effort.

Sometimes the abilities within one faculty of the soul affect those in another faculty. If my emotional faculty is filled with feelings of racial hatred for a certain person, then I will not be able to see that person as valuable and precious, nor will I be able to think deeply about working for his or her welfare. The fact that one faculty can affect others explains why the new birth has the potential of transforming every aspect of one's personality. Just as a seed grows to maturity, so the new spiritual life implanted in the soul can grow in its capacities. When this happens, the strengthened, maturing spirit can exert an influence on other aspects of the self. Similarly, a problem in a different faculty of the soul may need therapeutic counsel before a spiritual capacity can be developed.

Further, the body can impact my various faculties and vice versa. If my eyes are defective, I will not be able to use my faculty of sight to see anything. If I am angry or anxious much of the time, I can deplete my brain chemistry and this, in turn, can contribute to depression.[7] Though we are unified selves, nevertheless, we are complicated beings in which the various faculties of the soul interact with each other and with the body in a number of different ways. The ancient Greeks and the Fathers of the church were right to believe that a virtuous, mature person is an individual with a well-ordered soul. With this in mind, let us look at why that specific faculty of the soul, the mind, is of such importance for spiritual transformation and maturity in virtue.

## THE MIND'S ROLE IN TRANSFORMATION
### Beliefs, Behavior, and Character

Beliefs are the rails upon which our lives run. We almost always act according to what we really believe. It doesn't matter much what we say we believe or what we want others to think we believe. When the rubber meets the road, we act out our actual beliefs most of the time. That is why behavior is such a good indicator of a person's beliefs. Let us look, then, at five aspects of belief that are critical to the shape of our minds.

*1. The content of a belief.* A belief's impact on behavior is a function of three of the belief's traits: its content, strength, and centrality. The *content* of a belief helps determine how important the belief is for our character and behavior. *What* we believe matters—the actual content of what we believe about God, morality, politics, life after death, and so on will shape the contours of our lives and actions. In fact, the contents of one's beliefs are so important that, according to Scripture, our eternal destiny is determined by what we believe about Jesus Christ.

Today, people are inclined to think that the sincerity and fervency of one's beliefs are more important than the content. As long as we believe something honestly and strongly, we are told, then that is all that matters. Nothing could be further from the truth. Reality is basically indifferent to how sincerely we believe something. I can believe with all my might that my car will fly me to Hawaii or that homosexuality is caused solely by the brain, but that fervency doesn't change a thing. As far as reality is concerned, what matters is not whether I like a belief or how sincere I am in believing it but whether or not the belief is true. I am responsible for what I believe and, I might add, for what I refuse to believe because the content of what I do or do not believe makes a tremendous difference to what I become and how I act.

**2. The strength of a belief.** There is, however, more to a belief than its content. There is also its *strength* and centrality for the person who believes it. We are all familiar with the idea of a belief having strength. If you believe something, that does not mean you are certain that it is true. Rather, it means that you are at least more than 50 percent convinced the belief is true. If it were fifty-fifty for you, you wouldn't really have the belief in question. Instead, you would still be in a process of deciding whether or not you should adopt the belief. A belief's strength is the degree to which you are convinced the belief is true. As you gain evidence and support for a belief, its strength grows for you. It may start off as plausible and later become fairly likely, quite likely, beyond reasonable doubt, or completely certain. The more certain you are of a belief, the more it becomes a part of your very soul, and the more you rely on it as a basis for action.

**3. The centrality of a belief.** You may be less familiar with this concept than with the previous two, but with a little reflection the idea of *centrality* is easy to grasp. The centrality of a belief is the degree of importance the belief plays in your entire set of beliefs, that is, in your worldview. The more central a belief is, the greater the impact on one's worldview were the belief given up. My belief that prunes are good for me is fairly strong (even though I don't like the belief!), but it isn't very central for me. I could give it up and not have to abandon or adjust very many other beliefs I hold. But my beliefs in absolute morality, life after death, and the Christian faith are very central for me—more central now, in fact, than just after my conversion in 1968. If I were to lose these beliefs, my entire set of beliefs would undergo a radical reshuffling—more so now than in, say, 1969. As I grow, some of my beliefs come to play a more central role in the entire way I see life.

**4. How we change beliefs.** In sum, the content, strength, and centrality of a person's beliefs play a powerful role in determining the person's character and behavior. But here is an apparent paradox about one's beliefs. On the one hand, Scripture holds us responsible for our beliefs since it commands us to embrace certain beliefs and warns us of the consequences of accepting other beliefs. On the other hand, experience teaches us that we cannot choose or change our beliefs by direct effort. For example, if someone offered you $10,000 to believe right now that a pink elephant was sitting next to you, you could not really choose to believe this in spite of having a good motive to do so!

Happily, there is a way out of this paradox: We can change our beliefs *indirectly*. If I want to change my beliefs about something, I can embark on a course of study in which I choose to think regularly about certain things, read certain pieces of evidence and argument, and try to find problems with evidence raised against the belief in question. More generally, by choosing to undertake a course of study, meditation, and reflection, I can put myself in a position to undergo a change in the content, strength, and centrality of my beliefs. (We will look more at these truths in chapters 4 and 5.) And if these kinds of changes in belief are what cause a change in my character and behavior, then I will be transformed by these belief changes. This is exactly why Paul tells us to be transformed by *the renewing of the mind*, because it is precisely activities of the mind that change these three aspects of belief, which, in turn, transform our character and behavior.

**5. How beliefs form the plausibility structure of a culture.** There is a critical corollary of this insight. I will never be able to change my life if I cannot even entertain the belief needed to bring about that change. By "entertain a belief" I mean to consider the *possibility* that the belief *might* be true. If you are hateful and mean to someone at work, you will have to change what you believe about the person before you will treat him or her differently. But if you cannot even entertain the thought that he or she is a good person worthy of kindness, you won't change.

There is a straightforward application here for evangelism. A person's plausibility structure is the set of ideas the person either is or is not willing to entertain as possibly true. For example, no one would come to a lecture defending a flat earth because this idea is just not part of our plausibility structure. We cannot even entertain the idea. Moreover, a person's plausibility structure is a function of the beliefs he or she already has. Applied to evangelism, J. Gresham Machen got it right when he said:

> God usually exerts that power in connection with certain prior conditions of the human mind, and it should be ours to create, so far as we can, with the help of God, those favourable conditions for the reception of the gospel. False ideas are the greatest obstacles to the reception of the gospel. We may preach with all the fervour of a reformer and yet succeed only in winning a straggler here and there, if we permit the whole collective thought of the nation or of the world to be controlled by ideas which, by the resistless force of logic, prevent Christianity from being regarded as anything more than a harmless delusion.[8]

If a culture reaches the point where Christian claims are not even part of its plausibility structure, fewer and fewer people will be able to entertain the possibility that they might be true. Whatever stragglers do come to faith in such a context would do so on the basis of felt needs alone, and the genuineness of such conversions would be questionable to say the least. This is why apologetics is so crucial to evangelism. It seeks to create a plausibility structure in a person's mind, "favourable conditions" as Machen puts it, so the gospel can be entertained by a person. To plant a seed in someone's mind in pre-evangelism is to present a person with an idea that will work on his or her plausibility structure to create a space in which Christianity can be entertained seriously. If this is important to evangelism, it is strategically crucial that local churches think about how they can address those aspects of the modern worldview that place Christianity outside the plausibility structures of so many.

Our modern post-Christian society is perilously close to regarding Christian claims as mere figments in the minds of the faithful. Speaking of fundamentalists after the Scopes trial in 1925, historian George Marsden observes that they could not "raise the level of discourse to a plane where any of their arguments would be taken seriously. Whatever they said would be overshadowed by the pejorative associations attached to the movement by the seemingly victorious secular establishment."[9] Tragically, as we move through the twenty-first century, our current context for proclaiming Christian truth is even worse than it was in the decades following 1925. During those decades, at least *argumentation* was considered relevant to making or accepting religious claims. But now, religious assertions are regarded as mere expressions of private belief or emotion, far below the level needed for argument itself to be considered at all relevant.

In summary, the plausibility, content, strength, and centrality of our beliefs play a key role in determining our character and behavior. And various activities of thought and study affect our beliefs and thereby impact our character and behavior. Because thoughts and beliefs are contained in the mind, intellectual development and the renewal of the mind transform our lives.

### The Mind's Role in Seeing, Willing, Feeling, and Desiring

**1. How three types of seeing feed our minds.** The mind plays an important role in determining what a person is able to see, will, feel, and desire. If this is true, then intellectual development can pay rich dividends in the changes that result in one's other faculties. In order to focus our thoughts about this topic, let us consider the mind's role in the process of seeing. Philosophers distinguish three different kinds of seeing.

Consider an ordinary case of seeing a dog. First, there is *simple seeing*: having the dog directly present to you in your visual field and noticing the dog. You don't need to have a concept of what a dog is to see one. For example, a little child could see a dog without having a concept of what a dog is supposed to be. In fact, you don't even need to be thinking about a dog to see it. I could see a dog while looking out my window as I ponder the topic of this chapter. Even though I wouldn't be thinking about the dog, I could still see it and, later, recall from memory the dog's color. In simple seeing, a person sees merely by means of the soul's faculty of sight.

Second, there is *seeing as*. Here I see an object as being something or other. I may see the dog as a dog. I may even see the dog as a cat if the lighting is poor and I have been led to believe that only cats, but no dogs, live in the area. I can see the dog as my neighbor's favorite pet. An act of seeing as involves classifying the object of sight as an example of a mental concept, and concepts are located in the mind. Thus, an act of seeing as requires both the faculties of sight and mind working together. When I see a dog as a dog, I must have some concept of what it is to be a dog and apply this concept to the object I am seeing. I could not see a dog as a dog the first time I saw one since I wouldn't have the relevant concept yet.[10] Likewise, to see a dog as my neighbor's favorite pet, I need the concepts of a neighbor, a pet, and being a favorite.

Third, there is *seeing that*. Here one judges with the mind that some perceptual belief is true. If I see that the dog is my neighbor's favorite pet, I judge that this belief is true of the object I am seeing. If I merely see the dog as my neighbor's favorite pet, I don't really have to think this is true. I may just be playing with different concepts in my mind. I may be thinking, *What would it be like to see this dog as my neighbor's favorite pet?* even though I don't think it really is.

**2. How a developed mind helps us see.** Simple seeing only involves the faculty of sight. But seeing as and seeing that involve the mind. This is why the more one knows, the more one can see. A doctor and I can look at the same skin problem (a case of simple seeing), but he observes more than I do. Why? Because his mind is filled with medical concepts and beliefs I do not have, which enable him to notice things I fail to observe. He can see the sore as a basal cell or as a squamous cell carcinoma—that is, he can look at the skin area in both ways to be in a position to look for the right things, so that he can identify it, or "see it as," a basal cell. I cannot do this because my mind lacks the relevant intellectual categories the doctor possesses. I can stare at the same sore all day long and not see what he sees.

Consider another example. The evening news covered a march on Washington in favor of children's rights. A congresswoman made the following argument: "Government should honor children's rights. Therefore, just as the government should vouchsafe a child's right not to be molested, so it should do so for a child's right to government-sponsored day care."

Now, what is wrong with this argument as it stands? Do you see what I see in this piece of reasoning? It may help your seeing if I place a mental distinction in your mind: the distinction between negative and positive rights. A negative right is a right to be protected from some sort of harm. Negative rights place a duty on the government to keep others from doing something to me. A positive right is a right to have something provided for me. Positive rights place a duty on the government to force others (for instance by taxation) to do something for me. For example, if health care is a negative right, the government must see to it that I can get whatever health care I can afford by my own labor unhindered by unfair limitations based on race, creed, or gender. But if health care is a positive right, the government has a duty to raise the taxes sufficient to provide me with health care.

In the congresswoman's argument about children's rights, she fails to make this distinction. Moreover, many people believe that New Testament teaching on the state implies that it is responsible for protecting negative rights, not for providing positive ones. The issue here is not that these people (conservatives) are correct in this regard (though I think they are). The issue is that, for a long time, the distinction between negative and positive rights has been recognized, and many informed political philosophers have raised arguments against positive rights. This means that a person cannot simply assert that because the government should guard a child's negative right to be protected against abuse, it is also the government's duty to provide day care for children.

A person could read the congresswoman's statement several times and not see this issue if he or she did not have the intellectual concepts and beliefs already in mind. This example illustrates the way knowledge helps one see things unavailable to one who has not developed his or her intellect in the relevant area of study.

We often read the Bible, hear the news, listen to a sermon, or talk to friends, yet we don't get much out of it. One central reason for this may be our lack of knowledge and intellectual growth. The more you know, the more you see and hear because your mind brings more to the task of "seeing as" or "seeing that." In fact, the more you know about extrabiblical matters, the more you will see in the Bible. Why? Because you will see distinctions in the Bible or connections between Scripture and an issue in another area of life that would not be possible without the concepts and categories placed in the mind's structure by gaining the relevant knowledge in those extrabiblical areas of thought. Thus, general intellectual development can enrich life and contribute to Bible study and spiritual formation.

There is a closely related reason why intellectual development can enhance spiritual development: The mind forms habits and falls into ruts. One day at a chapel meeting, a missions professor showed a film clip of a foreign culture unfamiliar to most of us. He asked us to write down everything we noticed. He then showed the clip a second time and asked us to repeat the exercise. Everyone in the chapel meeting compared his or her first and second lists and, in every case, they were virtually identical! The professor's lesson: our minds get into ruts in which we tend to look for things we have already seen in order to validate our earlier perceptions. We seldom look at things from entirely fresh perspectives!

If we're honest with ourselves, we have to admit that we get into ruts in our thinking and develop habits of thought that can grow stale after a while. This is where renewing the mind comes in. A life of study can give us a constant source of new categories and beliefs that will lead to fresh new insights and stave off intellectual boredom. Many people become bored with the Bible precisely because their overall intellectual growth is stagnant. They cannot get new insights from Scripture because they bring the same old categories to Bible study and look to validate their old habits of thought.

*3. How the mind interacts with other parts of the person.* Space forbids me to develop in depth the mind's role in shaping our willing, feeling, and desiring. But it should be easy to apply our discussion of the mind's role in seeing to these other areas of human functioning. I can't choose to do something if I don't know what it is or how it works. I can't desire something if I don't believe it is good, valuable, and desirable. I can't feel tender toward someone if my thoughts and beliefs about that person run in the opposite direction.

It is true that the other faculties of the soul affect the mind too. And an overall strategy for personal growth should work on developing and integrating every facet of human personality under Christ's lordship. Still, I think the mind stands out for special emphasis because it is so neglected today by many Christians. The contemporary Christian mind is starved, and as a result we have small, impoverished souls.

## The Mind, Truth, and Reality

There is another reason why the mind warrants special emphasis. Of all the soul's faculties, the mind is the one that ponders, contains, and judges truth and falsity. The mind places me in contact with the external world, and when functioning properly it conforms itself to the nature of the object of thought itself. As Richard Foster puts it:

> The ingrained habits of thought that are formed will conform to
> the order of the thing being studied. What we study determines

what kind of habits are to be formed. That is why Paul urged us to center on things that are true, honorable, just, pure, lovely and gracious.[11]

To understand this, let us consider two features of the mind: intentionality and internal structure.

*1. The intentionality of the mind.* Intentionality refers to the "of-ness" or "about-ness" of our mental states. We have a thought of God, a hope for a new car, a belief about the media. The mind points *beyond* itself to the objects we use our minds to contemplate. Because of intentionality, thought puts us in contact with the external world. For example, if I am in Los Angeles, I can be in direct contact with London by thinking about it. My mind is directed on London, and it makes contact with this object of thought. After all, I am not thinking about the word "London" (unless someone asks me to spell it) or something else; I am thinking about London itself.

*2. The internal structure of the mind.* Second, when we come to understand something, the mind develops a conceptualization of the thing so understood. If I come to understand the workings of a car, my mind will possess a conceptualization of those workings. If my understanding is accurate, the conceptualization in my mind will conform to the car itself. If my mind develops a conceptualization of morality, then there will be an order in my mind that locates the role of virtue and character in the overall moral life. If accurate, this conception of the role of virtue will conform to the nature of true morality that actually exists outside my mind.

If my conceptualizations are false, I will fail to grasp the object as it really is. But if my mind conforms to the nature of the object itself, I will not only grasp it truly but also gain a certain power that comes from a correct understanding of reality. Just as electricity was real but its power unavailable to us until Ben Franklin's discovery opened our minds to grasp the true nature of electricity, so the power of the spiritual life is real but unavailable to us if we don't understand the true nature of prayer, fasting, and so forth. This is why truth is so powerful. *It allows us to cooperate with reality, whether spiritual or physical, and tap into its power.* As we learn to think correctly about God, specific scriptural teachings, the soul, or other important aspects of a Christian worldview, we are placed in touch with God and those realities. And we thereby gain access to the power available to us to live in the kingdom of God.

## SUMMARY

It may be a good idea at this point to stop and ask yourself how you are feeling and thinking about all of this. In chapter 1 we saw that modern Christianity has become anti-intellectual, resulting in a softened impact for Christ, and has contributed to the secularization of American culture. In chapter 2 we wove together several strands of evidence that assure us of the biblical basis for the importance of the intellectual life and the cultivation of the mind. And in this chapter we have seen just how the mind works in affecting the transformation of our lives in the spiritual sojourn so important to all disciples of Jesus.

However, several years of teaching have led me to believe that you may still feel a certain sense of resistance to the idea that Christians should be concerned with developing intellectual lives. For many, this idea feels risky and can create a sense of a loss of control about where such a quest might lead them at the end of the day. For others, there is a sense of guilt or inadequacy about this whole topic. In the next chapter, I will identify and address certain enemies of the Christian mind, certain foes that hinder us in our spiritual journey.

# PART TWO

# HOW TO DEVELOP A MATURE CHRISTIAN MIND

# CHAPTER FOUR

# HARASSING THE HOBGOBLINS OF THE CHRISTIAN MIND

Have you ever inadvertently looked at the sun and then closed your eyes? What did you see? Most likely two spots. Have you ever tried to examine those spots? I did once, and was immediately presented with a difficulty. When I closed my eyes and tried to focus my attention on the spots, they would move and stay at a place in my visual field just ahead of the center of my focus. After a minute of chasing the spots around in my consciousness, I finally figured out what to do. I looked past the spots and focused my attention on a point in the background. When I did this, the spots stabilized and came into focus in the foreground of my awareness!

According to Jesus of Nazareth, our lives are very much like these spots. If we spend all of our time trying to look directly at ourselves, our lives dart around, become unstable, and get drastically out of focus. However, if we deny ourselves daily for Christ's sake (Matthew 16:24-27) — that is, if we gaze past ourselves and stare at Him with dedication and affection — as a byproduct we come into focus and stabilize in the foreground. This sort of self-denial actually requires a strong, integrated self. An immature, fragmented, narcissistic person cannot bring himself or herself to live with this sort of focus and discipline.

The intellectual life requires the same sort of self-denial and dedication to be part of a larger life of spiritual power and productivity for the kingdom of God. For Christians, the intellectual life of cultivating the mind and valuing rationality makes sense and receives its proper motivation and balance when seen as part of an overall view of what life is all about. The purpose of life is to bring honor to God, to know, love, and obey Him, to become like Him, and to live for His purposes in this world as I prepare to live in the next one. A life that is intentionally lived for this purpose will be characterized by certain attitudes and actions. For one thing, if I am to progress in this sort of life, I must regularly live for a larger whole. I must live for the kingdom of God and be involved aggressively in the war between that kingdom and the kingdom of darkness.

Further, while self-interest and personal joy are important components of Christian motivation, they are not adequate in and of themselves to carry the weight of a skillful Christian life. I must also seek to live for others. Among other things, this means that I need to discover my vocation, my overall calling in life, composed of my talents, spiritual gifts, historical circumstances, and so forth. And I should passionately seek to occupy my vocational place for the good of believers and unbelievers alike. This would be my understanding of the good life. Make no mistake about it. Such a life is not easy. It involves discipline, hard work, suffering, patience, and endurance in forming habits conducive to and characteristic of this kind of life. It requires taking a long-haul view of life and learning to defer gratification if required of me in my sojourn. And I must develop intellectual and moral virtues and habits before I can become fully skilled at living this way.

Unfortunately, the intellectual life, the life of intentional, habitual cultivation of my mind under Christ's lordship, can be valued and entered into only as a part of the overall approach to life just described, and this approach runs contrary to the conditions that define our modern lifestyles. Many people today, including many Christians, simply do not read or think deeply at all. And when believers do read, they tend to browse self-help books or other literature that is not intellectually engaging. I once wrote a piece for what is most likely the top

Christian periodical of the last thirty years, and I was warned to keep my prose to about an eighth-grade level. How far we have come since the time of Joseph Butler (1692–1752) when, as one historian put it, the church could still out-think her critics. Butler was an Anglican minister at Rolls Chapel in England. His fifteen-part sermon series on ethics is regarded as one of the finest pieces of moral reasoning in the history of philosophy and has, in the words of philosopher Stephen L. Darwall, "influenced moral philosophy ever since."[1]

The mind is like a muscle. If it is not exercised regularly and strenuously, it loses some of its capacities and strength. We modern evangelicals often feel small and without influence in the public square. We must recapture our intellectual heritage if we are to present to our brothers and sisters, our children, and a post-Christian culture a version of Christianity rich and deep enough to challenge the dehumanizing structures and habits of thought of a society gone mad. To do this, we must change our reading habits; indeed, we must alter our entire approach to the life of the mind as part of Christian discipleship.

This chapter offers help doing this in two ways. First, we will look at the modern emergence of the empty self and see how it has shaped our intellectual habits or lack thereof. Second, we will identify some specific hobgoblins — mischievous little enemies — of the life of the mind and offer advice for defeating them.

## THE EMPTY SELF AS A HOBGOBLIN TO THE LIFE OF THE MIND

### Seven Traits of the Empty Self

In modern American culture, what psychologists call the empty self has emerged in epidemic proportion. The empty self is constituted by a set of values, motives, and habits of thought, feeling, and behavior that perverts and eliminates the life of the mind and makes maturation in the way of Christ extremely difficult. There are several traits of the empty self that undermine intellectual growth and spiritual development.

**1. The empty self is inordinately individualistic.** Years ago, I was sitting in an elementary school gym with other parents at a DARE graduation (a public school program designed to help children say no to drugs) for my daughter's sixth-grade class. Five sixth graders were about to read brief papers expressing their reasons for saying no to drugs. I leaned over to the couple sitting next to me and made a prediction: Each paper, I said, would be a variation of the same reason for refusing to take drugs: *self-interest.* Sure enough, student after student said he or she would refuse drugs because of a desire to stay healthy, become a doctor or athlete, or do well in school. Conspicuous by its absence was one single reference to virtue or duty to community.

Not one student anathematized drug use because of the shame it would bring to family, community, or God. Individualistic reasons were the only ones given, a fact to be expected in a generation whose moral education is exhausted by values clarification. By contrast, when a Japanese ice skater fell during an Olympic performance a few years ago, her main concern was not the endorsement opportunities she had lost. She feared that shame had been brought onto her family and people. Community loomed large in the way she understood her own sense of self.

A healthy form of individualism is a good thing. Sadly, we have all known people who fail to draw appropriate boundaries and do not separate and individuate from others in a healthy way. Such people do not think or feel for themselves, they are easy to manipulate, and their well-being is far too dependent on what others think of them. A person with a healthy individualism learns to avoid these problems in order to mutually depend upon and relate to members of the body of Christ. This sort of individualism produces strong selves who have the power to practice self-denial to enrich the broader groups (for example, family, church) of which they are a part. But the empty self-populating American culture is a self-contained individual who defines his or her own life goals, values, and interests as though he or she were a human atom, isolated from others with little need or responsibility to live for the concerns of the broader community.[2] Self-contained individuals do their own thing and seek to create meaning by looking within their own selves. But as psychologist Martin Seligman warns, "the self is a very poor site for finding meaning."[3]

**2. *The empty self is infantile.*** It is widely recognized that adolescent personality traits are staying with people longer today than in earlier generations, sometimes manifesting themselves into the early thirties. Created by a culture filled with pop psychology, schools and media that usurp parental authority, and television ads that seem to treat everyone like a teenager, the infantile part of the empty self needs instant gratification, comfort, and soothing. The infantile person is controlled by infantile cravings and constantly seeks to be filled up with and made whole by food, entertainment, and consumer goods. Such a person is preoccupied with sex, physical appearance, and body image and tends to live by feelings and experiences. For the infantile personality type, pain, endurance, hard work, and delayed gratification are anathema. Pleasure is all that matters, and it had better be immediate. Boredom is the greatest evil, amusement the greatest good.

**3. *The empty self is narcissistic.*** Narcissism is an inordinate and exclusive sense of self-infatuation in which the individual is preoccupied with his or her own self-interest and personal fulfillment.[4] Narcissists manipulate relationships with others, including God, to validate their own self-esteem and cannot sustain deep attachments or make personal commitments to something larger than their own ego. Narcissists are superficial and aloof and prefer to "play it cool" and "keep their options open." Self-denial is out of the question.

The Christian narcissist brings a Copernican revolution to the Christian faith. Historically, the Copernican revolution dethroned the earth from the center of the universe and put the sun in its place. Spiritually, the narcissist dethrones God and His purposes in history from the center of the religious life and replaces them with his or her own personal fulfillment.

The narcissist evaluates the local church, the right books to read, and the other religious practices worthy of his or her time on the basis of how they will further his or her own agenda. God becomes another tool in a narcissistic bag of tricks, along with the car, workouts at the fitness center, and so on — things that exist as mere instruments to facilitate a life defined largely independent of a biblical worldview.

Narcissists see education solely as a means to enhance their own careers. The humanities and general education that historically were part of a university curriculum to help develop people with the intellectual and moral *virtues* necessary for a life directed at the common good, just don't fit into the narcissist's plans. As Christopher Lasch notes, "[Narcissistic] students object to the introduction of requirements in general education because the work demands too much of them and seldom leads to lucrative employment."[5]

**4. The empty self is passive.** The couch potato is the role model for the empty self, and without question, modern Americans are becoming increasingly passive in their approach to life. We let other people do our living and thinking for us: the pastor studies the Bible for us, the news media does our political thinking for us, and we let our favorite sports team exercise, struggle, and win for us. From watching television to listening to sermons, our primary agenda is to be amused and entertained. Holidays have become vacations. Historically, a "holiday" was a "holy day," an intrinsically valuable, special, active change of pace in which, through proactive play and recreation, you refresh your soul. A "vacation" is a "vacating" — even the language is passive — in order to let someone else amuse you. The passive individual is a self in search of pleasure and consumer goods provided by others. Such an individual increasingly becomes a shriveled self with less and less ability to be proactive and take control of life.

Many factors have contributed to the emergence of passivity as an aspect of the empty self. But in my view, television is the chief culprit, and its impact begins early in life. Elementary school children watch an average of twenty-five hours of television per week, and high schoolers spend six times as many hours watching television as they invest doing homework.[6] Studies indicate that such widespread television viewing induces mental passivity, retards motivation and the ability to stick to something, negatively affects reading skills (especially those needed for higher-level mental comprehension), weakens the ability to listen and stay focused, and encourages an overall passive withdrawal from life.[7] The widespread passivity of the empty self explains the proliferation of magazines like *People*, of television shows like *Entertainment Tonight*, and of an overidentification with sports teams and figures. Passive people do not have lives of their own, so they must live vicariously through the lives of others, and celebrities become the codependent enablers of a passive lifestyle. The very idea of a Christian celebrity is an oxymoron. But for the passive, empty self, it is a spiritual life-support system.

**5. *The empty self is sensate.*** As Christopher Lasch has observed, "Modern life is . . . thoroughly mediated by electronic images."[8] Lasch goes on to point out that today, we make decisions and even judge what is and is not real on the basis of sense images. If it's on TV, it's real. Advertisements sell us things based on images, not on thoughtful content about a product. Neil Postman complains that "on television, discourse is conducted largely through visual imagery, which is to say that television gives us a conversation in images, not words."[9]

The emergence of the sensate self has produced two disastrous results. For one thing, people no longer base their decisions on a careful use of abstract reasoning in assessing the pertinent issues, nor are they as capable of doing so compared to earlier generations when thought was communicated by writing and abstract ideas, not by images.

For another thing, people are coming to believe more and more that the sense-perceptible world is all there is. In 1941, Harvard sociologist Pitirim A. Sorokin wrote a book entitled *The Crisis of Our Age*.[10] In it, Sorokin claimed that cultures come in two major types: sensate and ideational. In a sensate culture people believe only in the reality of the physical universe capable of being experienced with the five senses. A sensate culture is secular, this-worldly, and empirical. By contrast, an ideational culture embraces the sensory world but also accepts the notion that an extra-empirical, immaterial reality can be known as well—a reality consisting in God, the soul, immaterial beings, values, purposes, and various abstract objects like numbers and propositions. Sorokin claimed that a sensate culture will eventually disintegrate because it lacks the intellectual resources necessary to sustain a public and private life conducive of corporate and individual human flourishing. And this is precisely what we see happening to modern American culture. The widespread emergence of the sensate self has caused us to be shallow, small-souled people.

*6. The empty self has lost the art of developing an interior life.* In a fascinating study, Roy Baumeister traces the changing views of the self and of success from medieval to modern times.[11] According to Baumeister, the self used to be defined in terms of internal traits of virtue and morality, and the successful person, the person of honor and reputation, was the person with deep character. In such a view, the cultivation of an interior life through intellectual reflection and spiritual formation was of critical importance. In the last few decades, however, the self has come to be defined in terms of external factors—the ability to project a pleasurable, powerful personality and the possession of consumer goods—and the quest for celebrity status, image, pleasure, and power has become the preoccupation of a self so defined. A careful development of an inner life is simply irrelevant in such a view of the good life.

*7. The empty self is hurried and busy.* Finally, the empty self is a *hurried, busy* self gorged with activities and noise. As Philip Cushman observes, "The empty self is filled up with consumer goods, calories, experiences, politicians, romantic partners, and empathetic therapists. . . . [The empty self] experiences a significant absence of community, tradition, and shared meaning, . . . a lack of personal conviction and worth, and it embodies the absences as a chronic, undifferentiated emotional hunger."[12]

Because the empty self has a deep emotional emptiness and hunger, and because it has devised inadequate strategies to fill that emptiness, a frenzied pace of life emerges to keep the pain and emptiness suppressed. One must jump from one activity to another and not be exposed to quiet for very long or the emptiness will become apparent. Such a life-style creates a deep sense of fatigue in which passivity takes over. And fatigued people either do not have the energy to read or, when they do, choose undemanding material. Shortly after noting that our capacity to think is on the decrease today, writer Robert Banks correctly observes that, frequently, the modern individual is too rushed and distracted to "look for something to 'improve his mind,' demand an effort from him[self], or give rise to reflection, awareness or sustained thought."[13] Distraction and noise are enemies of an intellectual and spiritual life; focus and quiet are its friends.

### Empty Selves Are a Danger to Society and the Church

A society filled with empty selves is a morally bankrupt, intellectually shallow society. To cite but one example: Many people approach the abortion debate not on the basis of a thoughtful analysis of the relevant arguments, but from an infantile craving to seek promiscuous sexual soothing of the empty self free from any responsibility or consequences. Moreover, a church with largely empty selves is an immature, dysfunctional church. It is clear that the empty self is contrary to the nature of the mature follower of Jesus Christ.

The empty self is also the enemy of the Christian mind and its cultivation. Try to think about what a church filled with empty selves would look like in a culture. What would be the theological understanding, the reading habits, the evangelistic courage, the articulate cultural penetration of such a church? Pretty inadequate, I'm afraid. If the interior life does not really matter all that much, why spend the time reading and trying to develop an interior, intellectual, spiritually mature life? If someone is basically passive, he or she will just not make the effort to read, preferring instead to be entertained. If a person is sensate in orientation, music, magazines filled with pictures, and visual media in general will be more important than mere words on a page or abstract thoughts. If one is hurried and distracted, one will have little patience for theoretical knowledge and too short of an attention span to stay with an idea while it is being carefully developed. Instead, there will be a rush to get to the bottom line, an overemphasis on practical application and how-tos, a *Reader's Digest* approach to sermon evaluation or reading selection.

And if someone is overly individualistic, infantile, and narcissistic, what will that person read, if he or she reads at all? Such a person will read Christian self-help books that are filled with self-serving content, many slogans, simplistic moralizing, a lot of stories and pictures, and inadequate diagnosis of issues that place no demand on the reader. Books about Christian celebrities will be selected to allow the reader to live vicariously through the celebrity. What will not be read are books that equip people to engage in "destroying speculations . . . raised up against the knowledge of God" (2 Corinthians 10:5, NASB), develop a well-reasoned, theological understanding of the Christian religion, and fill their role in the broader kingdom of God for the common good and the cause of Christ. Eventually a church without readers or with readers with the tastes just listed will become a marginalized, easily led group of Christians impotent to stand against the powerful forces of secularism that threaten to bury Christian ideas under a veneer of soulless pluralism and misguided scientism. In such a context, the church will be tempted to measure her success largely in terms of numbers—numbers achieved by cultural accommodation to empty selves. In this way, as Os Guinness has reminded us, the church will become her own grave digger; her means of short-term "success" will turn out to be the very thing that marginalizes her in the long run.[14]

## Casting Out the Empty Self

I'm afraid there are no quick solutions to the problem of the empty self, and we cannot simplify its impact on the Christian mind. Still, I want to list briefly suggestions that in one way or another focus on developing a set of habits that are conducive to the development of the Christian mind in order to replace the habits of the empty self that are inimical to the Christian life. The battle here will be won or lost in the area of habits.

*1. Admit the problem.* First, we must admit that this is a problem and we need to inform others about it. We do ourselves or our God no good if we hide from the fact that the empty self threatens all of us. Any movement that brings about lasting changes begins with consciousness raising. Start talking with your Christian friends about the value of the Christian mind. Mention the empty self in your Sunday school class, your home Bible study, and so on. Talk to your children about developing their intellectual abilities for the service of Christ and His people. Before a problem can be solved, it must be carefully defined and clearly acknowledged.

*2. Choose to be different.* Second, at some point we need to make a fundamental decision that we will be different no matter what the cost. We Christians simply must admit that we have allowed our culture to squeeze us into its mold. We must stand against the culture (including inappropriate tendencies in the evangelical subculture), resist the empty self, and eschew the intellectual flabbiness that goes along with it. Motivation is a key here. I am no expert on motivation, but I do have one piece of advice, derived from almost thirty years of ministry: Expose yourself to ideas with which you disagree and let yourself be motivated to excel intellectually by the exposure. Listen to talk shows, read the editorial page, and walk around a local university and look at bulletin boards or read the student newspaper. Get into discussions with people at work with whom you differ. The point is to spend time around those who do not simply reinforce your own ways of looking at things. There are two advantages to this. For one thing, we can learn from our critics. For another, such exposure can move us to realize just how serious the war of ideas really is and how inadequately prepared we are to engage in that contest.

*3. Change your routine.* For one week, note two things on a sheet of paper. First, observe your energy rhythms. When is your energy at a low point during the day and when is it vigorous? Second, note what you tend to do when you get home from work or just after you have finished eating dinner. Often, when our energy is low or when we get home from work or finish dinner, we go into a passive mode and turn on the television. I believe that an intellectual life is easier to develop if a person learns to limit television watching and spends more time getting physical exercise. I don't think I have to defend limiting television watching in this regard, but what about exercise? Your mind becomes more alert and you have more energy to be proactive and to read if you are in good shape.[15] I tell my graduate students that if they want to get the most out of the intellectual opportunities of graduate school, then they must learn to use low-energy times, or moments like after work or dinner, as occasions to engage in physical exercise. Try something. After dinner go for a walk instead of turning on the TV. When you get back, sit down for thirty minutes to an hour and read an intellectually challenging book. The important thing here is to get out of passive ruts, especially those passive couch-potato moments, and replace old habits with new ones that create energy to read, reflect, and be more proactive.

*4. Develop patience and endurance.* Fourth, learn how to suffer and develop patient endurance. A life of intellectual cultivation takes effort. And it can be painful. The mind is like a muscle: it needs to be stretched beyond itself. I often read books that are a little over my head so I can develop my intellectual strength. Also, it often takes time to work through an important topic with sufficient care and attention. One needs to take a long-term perspective toward reading and study. But such a perspective will require endurance in staying put in a chair, with pen in hand, long enough to read deeply and widely. This requires a spirit of quietness and an absence of distraction. If you are fidgety and have to get up every fifteen minutes, you must get control of yourself. And gaining such control will require self-denial, suffering, and endurance. The intellectual life is both a means to and a result of a life of discipline, self-control, and endurance.

The best way to develop these traits is to practice the spiritual disciplines, especially solitude and fasting. Through solitude, I am learning to be quiet, alone, and focused. Through fasting, I am learning to say no to immediate gratification and bodily distraction and control myself. The spiritual disciplines can facilitate endurance, patience, discipline, and self-control—virtues that constitute the soil in which the cultivation of the Christian mind takes place. Richard Foster's *Celebration of Discipline* and Dallas Willard's *The Spirit of the Disciplines* are excellent guides to these spiritual disciplines.

**5. Develop a good vocabulary.** Fifth, keep a dictionary handy and get in the habit of looking up words that you don't understand. The development of a good vocabulary is an important tool in the cultivation of the Christian mind. The ubiquitous and egregious (look them up!) avoidance of the dictionary today is no help to the person who wishes to love God with his or her mind.

**6. Set some intellectual goals.** Finally, it is important for you to set some study goals on a yearly basis. I suggest you team up with another person in your church who has similar study interests and commit yourselves to a mutually accountable reading program. For twenty-six years now, I have met every Friday morning for breakfast with a study partner. My friend and I read books in philosophy, psychology, contemporary culture, spiritual formation, and so on. We meet to discuss our reading. Also, we each subscribe to important Christian periodicals (for example, *Christianity Today*) and regularly browse in secular and Christian bookstores. We come together and share our discoveries each week, and our times together are rich! Find a plan that works for you and just do it!

## TWO THIEVES OF THE CHRISTIAN MIND

The empty self is a general foe of the Christian mind. But two specific thieves rob many people of the fruitfulness and flourishing that is part of a developing Christian intellectual life. In wrapping up this chapter, I shall discuss each thief in turn.

## *Thief 1: The Odd Bedfellows of Inferiority and Pride*

**1. Inviting these bedfellows to be guests.** Many times adult learners have a deep sense of insecurity about their own mental abilities. Defensiveness and a false sense of pride can arise to protect one from feeling embarrassed about not knowing something. Intellectual embarrassment is one of the worst forms of humiliation—no one wants to come off as stupid or uninformed.

I think our adult Sunday school classes have unintentionally contributed to this false sense of pride. I have spoken in hundreds of churches and have regularly observed Sunday school classes that divide into small groups to reflect on a passage or discuss an idea. Later, when the groups recombine to share their observations with the entire class, group feedback is almost always affirming no matter how inaccurate or poorly reasoned a point is. Over the years, this creates a feeling of safety in the class but at the price of generating both a false sense of pride and the mistaken notion that all opinions are equal, whether spontaneous and quickly conceived or the result of detailed study prior to class time. It also keeps adults from learning how to receive criticism for their ideas in the interest of truth and stifles growth in the ability to respond nondefensively.

If we don't work on this in the safety of the company of our own brothers and sisters, we will come off as small, reactionary, and inarticulate in the public square. We need to give one another permission to express inadequately thought-out points to each other and create the expectation that we can learn to argue with one another, critique and defend ideas, or leave class with more work to do on a subject. All of this is in the interest of learning to reason carefully to get to the truth of what we study together.

This may be a bit threatening at first, but over the long haul it will produce a church filled with people who are more secure about what they believe and why. The very forms that define our periods of study together often institutionalize false pride and a lack of intellectual growth. There is absolutely nothing wrong with admitting you don't know something or that you're currently inadequately equipped to think a topic through. What is unacceptable, however, is running from this fact and thereby giving up on intellectual and spiritual growth in the interest of avoiding embarrassment or possible rejection. We all need help in this area, and we should care enough about truth and reason to give that help. Even if we agree with one another's conclusions, we need to dedicate ourselves for Christ's sake to refusing to allow each other to reach those conclusions with poor argumentation and sloppy treatment of data.

Another form of inferiority comes from the simple fact that we are evangelicals. For some time now, our culture has told us that conservative Christians are intellectually inferior, that the Christian faith is irrational, and so forth. And we constantly watch our views caricatured as the news media, hostile university professors, and others regularly build straw men out of Christian positions and proceed to destroy those straw men. When a community is repeatedly told that it is ignorant, it will come to believe that message whether or not it is true.

*2. Asking them to leave.* What should we do about this problem? I think we need to work harder at holding forth and celebrating our past and contemporary Christian thinkers. We need to know who they are. Do you know who the top Christian intellectuals are today in various fields? Are these people and their work placed before our children as examples to be emulated? We do this for Christian sports heroes, missionaries, and public speakers, so why not do it for our intellectuals?

The effect of identifying and celebrating our Christian intellectuals before one another cannot be overestimated. Social historian John G. Gager has pointed out that even though the early church was a minority movement that faced intellectual and cultural ridicule and marginalization, it maintained internal cohesion and a courageous witness thanks in no small measure to the powerful role in the broader Christian community of Christian intellectuals and apologists.[16] The early church knew who her intellectuals and apologists were, and this gave them confidence and a feeling of strength.

In the same way, we must identify, celebrate, utilize, and make role models out of our Christian thinkers. And we need to celebrate the absolutely unequaled history of the intellectual life in the Christian church. If an alternative community of atheists, Buddhists, or anything else can rival the rich cultural and intellectual leadership in church history, let someone come forth and demonstrate it. The intellectual life is our heritage as Christians, and it is time to remind ourselves of this.

## Thief 2: Keeping a Sense of Control

**1. The fear of losing control.** I once told my children that if they ever got to the point where they thought it was unreasonable to believe that Christianity was true, then they should abandon the faith. Does that sound risky? It is, but what is the alternative? Should we tell our children to set their minds aside totally and accept the Christian faith without using their intelligence? It can be risky to encourage people to develop their minds and allow reason to help them decide what they believe and why. No one can predict where such an approach will lead in a specific individual's life. It's easy to lose control of the outcome.[17] If your church is Reformed, charismatic, or whatever, and if your church actually equips people to think widely and deeply about their own theological beliefs, there is no guarantee that they will all come down where the church leaders are on a specific topic. For some, this can create an uncomfortable heterogeneity; it forces us to work harder at drawing lines between what sort of theological diversity a church will or will not tolerate within its membership.

**2. Commitment to truth and reason.** The fears just mentioned are easy to understand. However, we cannot let our fears dictate to us our approach to Christian growth and ministry. We need to keep two things firmly planted in the center of our minds. First, we simply must reaffirm our commitment to truth and right reason and be confident that our Christian beliefs both warrant that commitment and will flourish in light of it. As Roger Trigg has noted, "Any commitment, it seems, depends on two distinct elements. It presupposes certain beliefs [to be true] and it also involves a personal dedication to the actions implied by them."[18] We are committed to Christianity in general, or some doctrinal position in particular, because we take that commitment to express what is true. And we are committed to the importance of our God-given faculty of mind to aid us in assessing what is true.

**3. Consequences of abandoning a commitment to truth and reason.** We need to remember the consequences of abandoning a fundamental commitment to truth and reason. A people that does not care about these will be easily led to behave in certain ways by rhetoric, image, narcissistic self-infatuation, and so on. This is extremely dangerous. Further, if our allegiance to Christianity is not based on the conviction that it is true and reasonable, then we are treating the faith as a mere means to some self-serving pragmatic end, and that demeans the faith. For example, if we are more concerned with practical application from the Bible than with having good reasons for thinking we have correctly interpreted it, then our bottom line will be that the Bible exists as a tool to make us a success, and we do not exist to place ourselves under what it really says.

In medicine, we all know what a placebo is. It is an innocuous substance that doesn't really do anything to help an illness. But the patient's false belief that it works brings some mental relief. Unfortunately, a placebo works due to the naive, misinformed, false beliefs on the part of the patient. Sadly, the placebo effect is not limited to medicine. Many people have worldview placebos—false, naive, misinformed beliefs that allow them to live in a safe fantasy world of their own mental creation. To see why this is sad, consider the fictitious story of Wonmug.

Wonmug was a hopelessly dumb physics student attending a large western university. He failed all of his first-semester classes, his math skills were around a fifth-grade level, and he had no aptitude for science. However, one day all the physics students and professors at his college decided to spoof Wonmug by making him erroneously think he was the best physics student at the university. When he asked a question in class, students and professors alike would marvel out loud at the profundity of the inquiry. Graders gave him perfect scores on all his assignments when in reality he deserved an F. Eventually, Wonmug graduated and went on for his PhD. The professors at his university sent a letter to all the physicists in the world and included them in the spoof. Wonmug received his degree, took a prestigious chair of physics, regularly went to Europe to deliver papers at major science conferences, and was often featured in *Time* and *Newsweek*. Wonmug's life was pregnant with feelings of respect, accomplishment, expertise, and happiness. Unfortunately, he still knew absolutely no physics. Do you envy Wonmug? Would you wish such a life for your children? Of course not. Why? Because his sense of well-being was built on a false, misinformed worldview placebo.

Often, life is a struggle. We grow sick, lose our jobs, experience fragmented relationships with others, and eventually die. We want to know if there is anything real upon which to base our lives. Is there really a God and what is He actually like? What does God believe about the things that matter most? Is there any purpose to life and, if so, what is it? Why was I thrust into this world? Are values objective and real, or arbitrary and invented? Is there life after death? In what ways can I really count on God, and are there any true, effective ways to get close to Him? When we ask these questions, we don't just want answers that help us merely because we believe them. We want to be comforted because our answers to these questions are really true. For the wise person of virtue, a life well lived is based on the truth, not on a placebo.

But if truth really matters after all, then it follows that rationality also is crucial to a life well lived. Why? Because if we want a life built on truth, we want to be sure that our worldview consists of the highest percentage of true beliefs and the lowest percentage of false ones. The only way available to us for making sure this is the case with our own belief system is through the careful use of our faculty of reason. In the ordinary decisions of daily life, we try to base our beliefs and actions on the best evidence we can get. From sitting on a jury to buying a new house, we try to base our decisions on a careful assessment of all the relevant evidence we can get. Who would respect someone who voted in a jury trial or decided which house to buy with no regard to the evidence relevant to these decisions? If someone used blind faith and bought the first house he or she saw with a For Sale sign in front of it, but made no effort to get information about the house and neighborhood, we would consider that person foolish. Why? Because when we use our reason and base decisions on the best assessment of the evidence we can make, we increase our chances that our decisions are based on true beliefs.

Now if this is the case for day-to-day issues, why should we suddenly abandon the importance of reason and evidence when it comes to religion? We should not. Any religious belief worthy of the name should be accepted because we take the belief to be true and do so by the best exercise of our mental faculties we can muster. In the long run, it is better to risk losing control, face our doubts, be patient, and do the best job we can of using our minds to get at the truth. Not only is the Christian faith secure enough to withstand such an approach, but the faith actually encourages it.

## SUMMARY

If we are going to make progress in our Christian lives, then we must defeat the empty self and take back what insecurity and fear of losing control have taken from us. This is the first step toward making progress in cultivating the Christian mind as part of an overall spiritual journey pleasing to God and good for others and ourselves. But just exactly how does one develop a more careful intellect? How can a person learn to think better and be more assured that his or her beliefs are, in fact, true? To these questions we now turn.

# CHAPTER FIVE

# CLEARING THE COBWEBS FROM OUR MENTAL ATTICS

I attended the University of Missouri and received a BS in chemistry in 1970. The vast majority of my course work consisted of math, physics, and chemistry. In a typical science course, we would cover around three hundred pages of textbook per semester. I read very little prose and spent most of my time solving mathematical problems associated with my chemistry, physics, and math textbooks. I roomed with a literature major my freshman year, and it was not uncommon for him to have 1,500 pages of assigned reading in one course. Intellectually speaking, our college experience was very different until my conversion to Christ in the fall of my junior year.

As a new convert, I entered a world entirely new to me, a world filled with philosophical, theological, biblical, ethical, political, and historical ideas. As my tender, newly regenerated soul began to grow close to Christ, I began to care deeply about ideas in those areas, so I started reading anything I could get my hands on. At first, the reading was hard for me because I was unprepared for it. My scientific training had been valuable in many ways, but reading a book on theology is very different from solving problems in organic chemistry. I simply was not in the habit of reading demanding prose in the humanities about broad ethical, theological, or philosophical themes. But I persevered, and in the process I cleared away some of the cobwebs that covered vast regions of my mental attic.

Nothing that is worth doing is pleasurable or easy in the early stages of learning how to do it. But through regular practice, patient endurance, and proper mentoring, skills emerge and habits are formed that enable a person to be good at the activity in focus. This is clearly the case in learning to play golf, hit a baseball, or read in completely new areas of study. It is no less true of becoming a deep, careful thinker in general. If we are to love God adequately with the mind, then the mind must be exercised regularly, trained to acquire certain habits of thought, and filled with an increasingly rich set of distinctions and categories. There is no simple way to do this, and it would be presumptuous to attempt to describe fully how to develop a mature mind in one short chapter. Still, there are certain aspects of intellectual cultivation that we can discuss briefly yet profitably. My intent here is to help you get started. In this chapter, we will probe two of these aspects: forming habits of the mind and principles of reasoning.

## FORMING HABITS OF THE MIND
### *The Formation of Virtue*

A mature person has a tightly integrated, well-ordered soul. A carefully developed mind is a crucial part of a well-ordered soul. A mind that is learning to function well is both part of and made possible by an overall life that is skillfully lived. You cannot learn to use your mind well for Christ's sake by just reading a logic book or taking more adult education courses. You must order your general lifestyle in such a way that a maturing intellect emerges as part of that lifestyle. If you want to develop a Christian mind, you must intend to order your overall form of life to make this possible. You cannot just read a book or two and add this to a lifestyle otherwise indifferent to the intellect.

Moreover, learning to be a careful Christian thinker results in an entire way of being present in the world. To see what I mean by this, recall from chapter 3 that what a person spends time learning will affect the way that person sees, hears, thinks, and behaves. A trained lawyer actually hears things on the evening news, sees things in the newspaper, and approaches conversations with others in ways that would be unavailable to her if she had gone into psychology or business. A person with a well-developed lawyer-type mind will have a distinctive way of being present in the world. This is also true of a person who is cultivating a careful Christian mind. That person will be present to the world in a distinctively Christian intellectual way. He will notice certain things others miss, read things (for example, theology, church history) others eschew, and so forth. To develop a Christian mind skillfully, you must want to *be* a certain sort of person badly enough that you are willing to pay the price of ordering your lifestyle appropriately. Of course, some Christians are called to a vocation of being a Christian intellectual in one way or another—a Christian philosopher or New Testament scholar, for example. This requires a more intense, focused ordering of one's life than is needed for those without this calling. But every believer, regardless of vocational calling, needs to cultivate a Christian mind.

## Virtues and the Good Life

A life so ordered to facilitate intellectual growth is characterized by a certain set of virtues that makes such growth possible. A virtue is a skill, a habit, an ingrained disposition to act, think, or feel in certain ways. Virtues are those good parts of one's character that make a person excellent at life in general. As with any skill (for example, learning to swing a golf club), a virtue becomes ingrained in my personality, and thus a part of my very nature, through repetition, practice, and training. If I want to develop the virtue of compassion, I must regularly practice acts of mercy, self-sacrifice, and kindness. Knowing what these virtues are will give you something specific at which to aim in your efforts to cultivate your mind.

Certain virtues are especially relevant to the development of an intellectual life.[1] Moreover, these virtues are not isolated from each other. They are deeply interrelated. Growth in one virtue can aid maturity in another skill and vice versa. If you want a maturing Christian mind, you'll need to cultivate these virtues through regular practice. Five groups of virtues are especially important for cultivating a Christian mind. Let's take a look at each of these groups.

*1. The first group contains* **truth seeking, honesty,** *and* **wisdom.**
The Christian mind is committed to seeking and finding the truth even
if that truth is not what one wanted to hear. The Christian seeks to
know and do the truth. In fact, in a certain sense the believer's commitment to the truth is even more basic than his or her dedication to the
Christian faith in general or some doctrinal position in particular: If one
came to believe that Christianity or some doctrinal belief were false,
then one ought to give up the belief in question. By way of application,
we should learn to listen to what our critics say about us even if we don't
like the way they express their views. A wife or husband should try to get
at the truth of a spouse's criticisms even if it was expressed angrily and
inappropriately. Practice this in all areas of your life to cultivate the habit
of wanting the truth.

Honesty is closely related to truth. The Christian mind is honest
about what it does and does not believe. The thinking Christian tries to
be honest to himself or herself and to others. An important part of
honesty is proportionality. Proportionality is the measure of the degree
to which one ought to accept a belief or the degree to which a specific
argument actually supports that belief. We ought to proportion our
degree of belief to the degree for which we have grounds for accepting it.
Many times we think that believing something with less than complete
certainty means we really do not believe it. But this is not true. If you
believe something, you must be at least slightly more certain that it is
true than you are that it is false—you must be more than fifty-fifty
regarding the belief. And your certainty about the belief can grow.

This growth ought to be based on and proportional to the rational
considerations relevant to the belief. It is unproductive to try to believe
something beyond your grounds for believing it and dishonest to act as
if you believe something more strongly than you do. Overbelief is not a
virtue. For example, I am far from certain on many Christian beliefs
I hold. I lean toward the view that the days of Genesis are vast periods
of time and not literal twenty-four-hour periods. But about two days of
the week I flip-flop and accept the literal view. Based on my study,

I cannot convince myself either way, and I'm about sixty-forty in favor of the old-earth position. Other beliefs of mine have grown in certainty over the years—that God really exists, for example. We should be honest with ourselves about the strength of our various beliefs and work on strengthening them by considering the issues relevant to their acceptance.

We should also be honest about what arguments are and are not good in supporting our beliefs. Recently, I heard a guest minister preach a sermon about condom distribution in the public schools. He began by acknowledging that he was against this practice and went on to lecture on the various arguments for and against it. At one point he criticized as inadequate an argument used by many Christians against condom distribution. He was not promoting condom distribution, he was demoting a bad argument against it. What happened after the service was very sad. A number of people criticized him behind his back because, in their view, he had come down in favor of condom distribution. But this was clearly wrong. He had simply criticized one argument raised against condom distribution. His point was this: God is not honored when His people use bad arguments for what may actually be correct conclusions. Proportionality involves distinguishing a conclusion from arguments used to reach it and recognizing that rejecting certain arguments is not the same as rejecting a conclusion. Because of minds not trained to be sensitive to proportionality, people in the congregation could not hear what the minister said and missed a great chance to learn something.

Wisdom is also related to truth seeking. Wisdom is the wise use and application of knowledge. It involves knowing how to use good means to accomplish worthy ends in a skillful manner. The New Testament clearly teaches that the more one is willing to obey and apply the truth, the more one will be in a position to gain knowledge about more truth. For the Christian, seeking the truth is no mere abstract activity unrelated to life. The more we practice living what we already know, the better we will be at learning more. Some Christians misunderstand the nature of wisdom, preferring practical wisdom and disdaining theoretical knowledge. However, since wisdom is the application of knowledge, you cannot be practically wise without being theoretically informed. Truth seeking, honesty and proportionality, and wisdom are important virtues to cultivate if a growing Christian mind is to become a reality.

**2. A second group of virtues contains faith (trust) and hope.** One must have peace and serenity of mind in order to develop a life of understanding, reflection, and meditation. An anxious, depressed, distracted soul is not conducive to intellectual growth. We Christians trust and hope that truth is good and worth having because we are confident in the God of truth. In my opinion, this is one reason why intellectual growth and cultural flourishing are often a result of the Christian penetration of a society. Trust and hope in God help build confidence that truth is a valuable thing to have because it is ultimately good. A confident mind is a mind free to follow the truth wherever it leads, without the distracting fear and anxiety that come from the attitude that maybe we're better off not knowing the truth. This is one reason why Christians need not fear the honest examination of their faith.

A lack of faith and hope creates a distracted mind incapable of intellectual growth and devotion to God. Noise and busyness can rob one of serenity of mind as well. If you truly desire to develop a Christian mind, then you must squarely face this fact: The mind cannot grow without reflection and meditation on what has been studied, and reflection and meditation require periods of quiet and solitude on the one hand and simplicity of life on the other. You must order your life so as to remove as far as possible, given your other commitments, unnecessary modern gadgets and distractions to maintain focus and quiet in your life. Unplug or turn off the phone regularly. Don't just rely on voice mail, because even a ringing phone will rouse your curiosity about the identity of the caller and distract you. Don't spend all your time in front of a computer or the television. If you can afford it, pay to have your taxes done or your yard mowed. Do what you can to free yourself from unnecessary distractions. As an application, you may want to draw up a list of ways you can simplify your life and create more time for quiet reflection.

**3.** *The third group of virtues relevant to the intellectual life includes* **humility** *and the associated traits of* **open-mindedness, self-criticality,** *and* **nondefensiveness.** We must be willing to seek the truth in a spirit of humility with an admission of our own finitude, we must be willing to learn from our critics, and we need to learn to argue against our own positions in order to strengthen our understanding of them. I once heard a Christian college professor tell a group of parents that the purpose of a Christian college is to challenge the students' faith. I piped up in disagreement and argued that the purpose (among other things) was to strengthen and develop their faith, and one way to do this was to face questions honestly. The purpose of intellectual humility, open-mindedness, and so forth is not to create a skeptical mind that never lands on a position about anything, preferring to remain suspended in midair. Rather, the purpose is for you to do anything you can to remove your unhelpful biases and get at the truth in a reasoned way. A proper development of this group of virtues can aid in that quest.

Here is something to practice. When your view is criticized or even ridiculed on television, on a radio talk show, or in a newspaper editorial, don't just react angrily. Take a moment to jot down on paper the person's main thesis and how that thesis was supported. Then do two things. First, assume the person is expressing at least some good points and try to identify them. This assumption may be false, but the search for common ground with intellectual opponents is a good habit. In the process of identifying these good points, try to argue against your own view. Second, try to state on paper exactly how you would argue against the view being expressed in an intellectually precise yet emotionally calm way. This exercise may take a few minutes, but if repeated regularly it will aid you in developing this third group of virtues.

**4.** *The Christian mind requires the virtues of* **ardor, vigilance,** *and* **fortitude.** The Christian thinker should be a passionate person filled with ardor or zeal—zeal for God and truth. This zeal expresses itself in a passion to know and do the truth and to live a religiously reasonable form of life. It also helps make possible the vigilance necessary to stick to a life of study when it is not convenient or not particularly valued by those around you. Often a topic of study requires the patient development of a long, complicated chain of arguments before the issue can be understood, and vigilance is needed to see it to completion. An impatient generation looking for instant solutions and quick answers will be a generation of shallow slogans.

Fortitude or courage is also needed, and this comes from confidence in God's providential care of His children, including His availability to comfort them even in the face of martyrdom. The Christian mind requires the courage to face the truth and to stand up for it even when doing so is not popular. Bravery does not imply the absence of fear, but the ability to rise above and not be controlled by it. The person with an articulate, well-reasoned Christian worldview will be attacked if he or she defends unpopular Christian positions in the public square. Fortitude will be needed to enable one to continue to hunger for, cling to, and propagate the truth in such circumstances. Joseph Pieper astutely observes that fortitude contains two elements: endurance and attack.[2] The courageous person, especially one with intellectual courage, must learn to endure suffering and hardship in the interests of the truth and to continue attacking harmful falsehoods even if that is risky and painful.

A person must have motivation to develop zeal, vigilance, and courage. One of the best ways to gain this motivation is to put yourself in a slightly threatening yet not overwhelming situation in which you must defend your views. Regularly, when I teach an adult education class in a church, I require class members to develop a ten-question survey and interview five different people they do not know to be Christians—at a mall, at work, or somewhere else. Inevitably, two things happen. First, the class members gain firsthand exposure to the menagerie of ideas held by those in their own community. Second, they realize how ill-prepared they are to articulate and defend their own beliefs. Such exposure creates an initial hunger to grow in diligence as a learner and to be more courageous about what one believes.

   *5. The final virtue is* **fidelity to God *and* dedication to His cause in the world as one's chief end.** The Christian intellectual is here to serve a Name, not to make one. Unfortunately, I have seen too many Christian thinkers who have a certain texture or posture in life that gives the impression that they are far more concerned with assuring their academic colleagues that they are not ignorant fundamentalists than they are with pleasing God and serving His people. Such thinkers often give up too much intellectual real estate far too readily to secular or other perspectives inimical to the Christian faith. This is why many average Christian folk are suspicious of the mind today. All too often, they have seen intellectual growth in Christian academics lead to a cynical posture unfaithful to the spirit of the Christian way. I have always been suspicious of Christian intellectuals whose primary agenda seems to be to remove embarrassment about being an evangelical and to assure their colleagues that they are really acceptable, rational people in spite of their evangelicalism. While we need to be sensitive to our unbelieving friends and colleagues, we should care far less about what the world thinks than about what God thinks of our intellectual life. Fidelity to God and His cause is the core commitment of a growing Christian mind. Such a commitment engenders faithfulness to God and His people and inhibits the puffiness that can accompany intellectual growth.

## Study as a Spiritual Discipline

Dallas Willard defines a spiritual discipline as "an activity undertaken to bring us into more effective cooperation with Christ and His Kingdom."[3] In any human endeavor, repetitive exercise and practice bring skill and excellence. Sometimes a particular activity is good because it accomplishes a specific result. Swinging a baseball bat is good if it produces a base hit. However, that same activity can also be done, not for the result alone, but for the training it offers. A person can repeatedly swing a bat in a batting cage for the purpose of training, and not to increase his output of base hits. And other good results can follow from such training besides the one usually or normally intended; for example, regular trips to a batting cage can get a person in good overall condition besides helping him get base hits.

The same thing is true of study. We often correctly approach study specifically for some direct end—preparing a lesson or learning a topic covered in a book. But study should also be approached as a set of training activities, as spiritual and intellectual exercises. Study is a discipline that strengthens the mind and enriches the soul. Sometimes I study a book for the sheer value of engaging my intellect in a stretching, strenuous activity. At other times, I read to help myself cultivate the intellectual virtues listed above. Seen as a discipline, study becomes a means of building my character, ingraining habits of thought and reflection, and reinforcing in my own soul the value of the life of the mind. We study, then, not simply to gain knowledge about the topic of study, but as a broader spiritual discipline. By way of application, it is important to read books from time to time as a form of spiritual discipline and intellectual exercise, even if the topic of the book does not address one of your immediate, felt needs. If all you do is read simple books or those that overemphasize stories or practical application, you'll never learn to think for yourself as a mature Christian, nor will you develop a trained mind.

### The Importance of English Grammar and Syntax

Jane Healy observes that "the way people use language is braided together tightly with the way they think."[4] Healy is right. While we do not need to think in language (a child can think prior to language acquisition, and, in fact, since language is a vehicle for thought, language presupposes thought and not vice versa), nevertheless, language development is critical for cultivating a careful, precise, attentive mind.[5] Most people today do not use good grammar or syntax in sentence construction. Interestingly, the demise of grammar and syntax reflects a change in the main way language is currently used.

Today, we primarily use language to express emotions, create experiences, or get someone to do something, like buy a product. Careful thought is not always relevant to these modern appropriations of language. How many television commercials actually persuade us to buy something on the basis of an articulate defense of a product! The devaluation of grammar correlates closely with a devaluation of the mind, truth, and thought. When a main purpose of language is the careful, precise expression of thought, grammar and syntax become critical because they make such expression of thought possible.

If we Christians are to develop our minds, we must take greater care to improve our syntax and grammar, and we must expect this from each other. From years of experience grading student papers, I can tell you that if a student's grammar is poor, he or she has a difficult time developing a coherent line of thought clearly and carefully. Let's give ourselves permission to correct one another's grammar with a gentle, nonarrogant spirit in our fellowship meetings. Isn't a developed intellectual love for God worth the price of an initial embarrassment at such correction? After all, the alternative is to continue to allow one another to speak incorrectly and fail to realize the intellectual benefits that come from the correct use of language.

Having seen the importance of a Christian mind, and having (hopefully) been persuaded of the importance of good thinking, ordered language, and good grammar, you may be asking, "Okay, what is well-reasoned thinking?" Let's look now at the principles that govern reasoning and why they are important to the mind.

## PRINCIPLES OF REASONING
### Why Logic?
Besides cultivating virtue, taking study as a spiritual discipline, and being more disciplined about your grammar and syntax, you should be acquainted with certain logical tools that constitute the very nature of thought. Even young children use these tools without knowing the names for them. In this section, I want to examine briefly some of the

more important principles of argument. If you really want to develop your intellectual skills, you should memorize these and practice using them and recognizing their presence in things you hear or read. For a more thorough discussion of principles of reasoning and argument, consult any standard introductory logic text.[6]

We Christians must never forget that our God is a God of truth, reason, and logic. He speaks wisdom to His children, invites them to reason and argue with Him logically, and demands that they present in logical fashion the reason why they believe. The image of God within us includes the faculty of abstract reasoning and logical thought. In Romans, the apostle Paul presents in a careful, logical fashion a host of Old Testament texts about the nature of sin, judgment, and justification. In public debate, Jesus Himself regularly used careful logic to refute opponents' arguments and present them with a carefully reasoned alternative. When John Wesley told a group of ministers to become proficient in logic as a part of their calling, he was expressing a deep understanding of the Christian faith as that faith is depicted in the Bible and throughout church history.

In logic, an *argument* is defined as a group of statements containing premises and a conclusion in which the former are claimed as support for the latter. Using an argument is not the same as being argumentative. In using an argument, one simply supports a conclusion with premises. Being *argumentative* is a defensive personality defect. Christians are required by God to argue, *not* to be argumentative (1 Peter 3:15).

Arguments are either *deductive* or *inductive*. In a valid deductive argument, if the premises are true, then the conclusion *must* be true. For example, "(1) All dogs are ducks, (2) All ducks are cats, (3) Therefore, all dogs are cats" is a valid deductive argument. In spite of the fact that premises 1 and 2 are false, *if* they were true, the conclusion would have to be true.

In an inductive argument, the premises do not guarantee but merely provide support or grounds for the truth of the conclusion. An inductive argument with true premises does not guarantee but only *makes probable* the truth of its conclusion. It would be possible to have a good inductive argument with true premises and a false conclusion. For example, "(1) Ninety-five percent of people who receive the antibiotic get well, (2) We are about to give John the antibiotic, (3) Therefore, John is about to get well" is a good inductive argument. Premises 1 and 2 do in fact provide good support for the conclusion, even though the premises could be true and the conclusion false.

Deductive arguments can be either *valid* or *invalid*. As we have seen, if a deductive argument is valid, its conclusion must be true if its premises are true. An invalid deductive argument is one in which the premises could be true but the conclusion false. For example, "(1) All dogs are mammals, (2) All cats are mammals, (3) Therefore, all dogs are cats" is invalid because it contains true premises and a false conclusion. A *sound* argument is a deductive argument with true premises (and therefore, a true conclusion), and this is what we want to employ as best we can. A *syllogism* is a deductive argument that consists of exactly two premises and one conclusion.

The argument above about dogs and cats is a syllogism (an invalid one). Since these terms may be new to you, we'll follow this general introduction with a discussion of important principles of reasoning, followed by a list of certain fallacies of reasoning that occur regularly.

## A Brief Lesson in Logic
### *Principles of Reasoning and Argument*

A number of principles of reasoning and argument are crucial yet easy to grasp and, in fact, can be taught profitably to children.

*1. Three important syllogisms.* There are several different types of syllogisms, but these three are easy to spot and occur all the time in our thinking and arguing. Let P and Q in the following stand for any two sentences. (*Modus ponens* is a Latin term meaning "in the mood of affirming"; *modus tollens* means "in the mood of denying.")

| Modus Ponens | Modus Tollens | Disjunctive |
|---|---|---|
| (MP) | (MT) | Syllogism (DS) |
| 1. If P then Q. | 1. If P then Q. | 1. Either P or Q. |
| 2. P. | 2. Not Q. | 2. Not P. |
| 3. Therefore, Q. | 3. Therefore, not P. | 3. Therefore, Q. |

Take a look at MP and MT. Note that premise 1 is the same in both syllogisms: "If P then Q." In an "if-then" sentence like this, P is called the antecedent and Q the consequent. Here is an example of MP (*modus ponens*):

1. If you believe in Jesus Christ, then you are saved.
2. You believe in Jesus Christ.
3. Therefore, you are saved.

You will observe that premise 2 ("You believe in Jesus Christ") is actually an affirmation of the antecedent of premise 1 (the antecedent is what comes after "if" in premise 1). MP is a valid deductive argument form: If the premises are true, then the conclusion must be true. However, there is sometimes invalid reasoning associated with MP called *the fallacy of affirming the consequent*:

1. If P then Q.
2. Q.
3. Therefore, P.

Note that premise 2 makes the mistake of affirming the consequent of premise 1 instead of the antecedent; that is, it asserts Q instead of P. This is a fallacy because such an argument could have true premises and a false conclusion, as follows: (1) If it is raining outside (P), then it is wet (Q), (2) It is wet (Q), (3) Therefore, it is raining (P). But it may be wet due to a sprinkler system and not because it is raining.

Here is an example of MT (*modus tollens*):

1. If atheistic evolution is true, then organisms are simply physical systems.
2. It is not true that organisms are simply physical systems (for example, they may have souls).
3. Therefore, it is not the case that atheistic evolution is true (it is false).

Note that premise 2 correctly consists in a denial of the consequent of premise 1. As with MP, there is sometimes invalid reasoning associated with MT called *the fallacy of denying the antecedent*:

1. If P then Q.
2. Not P.
3. Therefore, not Q.

For example:

1. If Jones took the car, then he went to the store.
2. It is not true that Jones took the car.
3. Therefore, it is not true that Jones went to the store.

Here, 1 and 2 could be true, but 3 is false. Maybe Jones went to the store in a taxi.

Finally, here is an example of a disjunctive syllogism:

1. Either Jones left the house or he is at home.
2. It is not true that Jones left the house.
3. Therefore, he is at home.

In premise 1, we are presented with an option: either Jones left his house or he is at home. One of these is true because the dilemma is an exhaustive one and there are no third options. One of these alternatives must be true. So, if it isn't true that Jones left the house, he has to be at home.

Medieval theologians noted that even dogs appear to behave as if they understand disjunctive syllogisms. They observed that when a dog chased a rabbit down a road that suddenly forked, either the rabbit went left or it went right. If the dog sniffed the left fork with no success (it discovered that the rabbit had not taken the left fork), *it would not sniff the right fork.* Rather, *it would immediately run down the right fork,* apparently because it already knew that's where the rabbit went.

In Deuteronomy 30:15,17-19, Moses presents a disjunctive syllogism. See if you can find the two premises and the conclusion:

> See, I have set before you today life and prosperity, and death and
> adversity. . . . But if your heart turns away and you will not obey, . . .
> I declare to you today that you shall surely perish. . . . So choose life
> in order that you may live. (NASB)

**2. Necessary and sufficient conditions and counterexamples.** While we are on the subject of "if-then" statements, it is absolutely crucial to learn to distinguish the difference between necessary and sufficient conditions. A *necessary condition* is one that must prevail before a second condition can occur. If P is a necessary condition for Q, then if Q is true, P must be true, but P alone may not guarantee the truth of Q. (Example: reread the sentence above, asserting the following conditions: P = Doug Geivett is alive; Q = Doug Geivett is married.) To refute a claim that P is necessary for Q, simply give a counterexample in which Q is true and P is false (in which case P could not be necessary for Q). For example, if someone claims that a necessary condition for practicing science is that you are studying something that can be directly observed, then we can refute this claim by citing examples of scientific practice that do not involve studying something that can be directly observed (the death of the dinosaurs, electrons). In English, a necessary condition is often introduced by the words "only if," "entails that," "implies that."

A *sufficient condition* is one that is adequate for another condition to succeed. If P is a sufficient condition for Q, then if P is true, Q must be true, but there may be other ways for Q to be true besides the truth of P. (Example: P = Doug Geivett is married to Diane; Q = Doug Geivett is married.) To refute a claim that P is a sufficient condition for Q, simply give a counterexample in which P is true and Q is false (in which case P could not be sufficient for Q). For example, if someone claims that a sufficient condition for practicing science is that you are studying something that can be directly observed, then we can refute this claim by citing examples of nonscientific practice that do involve studying something that can be directly observed (for example, doing a word study in literature where you directly observe an author's uses of a term). In English, a sufficient condition is often introduced by the words "if," "in case," "provided that," "given that." In an "if-then" statement, the antecedent is the sufficient condition and the consequent is the necessary condition. Sometimes in logic, "if-then" is symbolized by the sign ⊃. A useful device for remembering which is the necessary and which is the sufficient condition in an "if-then" statement is to remember "SUN," because such a statement in logic looks like this: S⊃N.

Let's test your understanding. Of the following pairs, which is the necessary and which is the sufficient condition (answers are in the note)? Pair 1: P = The apple is red; Q = The apple is colored. Pair 2: P = The box is shaped; Q = The box is square. Pair 3: P = Jones is a human; Q = Jones is a person.[7]

**3. The law of identity.** Sometimes people make reductionist claims that one thing is nothing but (is identical to) something else — for example, that the soul is nothing but the brain, that sex is nothing but a certain bodily activity, that religious experience is nothing but a psychological phenomenon. The law of identity helps us evaluate such claims. Bishop Joseph Butler (1692–1752) once remarked that everything is itself and not something else. This simple truth has profound implications. Suppose you want to know whether J. P. Moreland is Eileen Spiek's youngest son. If J. P. Moreland is identical to Eileen Spiek's youngest son, then in reality, there is only one thing we are talking about: J. P. Moreland, who is Eileen Spiek's youngest son. Furthermore, J. P. Moreland is identical to himself; he is not different from himself. Now if J. P. Moreland is not identical to Eileen Spiek's youngest son, then in reality we are talking about two things, not one.

This illustration can be generalized into a truth about the nature of identity: For any $x$ and $y$, if $x$ and $y$ are identical (they are really the same thing, there is only one thing you are talking about, not two), then any truth that applies to $x$ will apply to $y$ and vice versa. This suggests a test for identity: if you could find one thing true of $x$ not true of $y$, or vice versa, then $x$ cannot be identical to (be the same thing as) $y$. If there is something true of a state of my brain (for example, it has electrical activity, weight, is composed of chemicals) that is not true of a state of my mind, say a thought (thoughts don't have weights and aren't built out of chemical or electrical components), then the state of my brain is not the same thing as the state of my mind.

**4. Self-refutation.** Whenever you are listening to someone argue for a position on something, always pay attention to whether or not the person is asserting something that is self-refuting. What is self-refutation? A statement is about a subject matter. "All electrons have negative charge" is about the subject matter called electrons. Some statements refer to themselves, that is, they include themselves in their own field of reference. "All English sentences are short" refers to all English sentences whatsoever, including that very sentence itself. Sometimes a statement refers to itself and fails to satisfy its own criteria of rational acceptability or truthfulness. "No English sentence is longer than three words," "I do not exist," and "There are no truths" are self-refuting. They refer to themselves and they falsify themselves. Self-refuting statements are necessarily false; that is, they cannot possibly be true.

Here are some common self-refuting assertions:

- "I believe that no one can believe something that cannot be tested by the five senses or by science." (The belief itself cannot be so tested.)
- "All morality is relative to private taste, so you morally ought to be more tolerant of others." (How can I have an objectively true moral duty to be tolerant if all duties are merely relative to private tastes?)
- "All attitudes and behaviors are caused by our genes, so we are not responsible for them and people ought to stop passing judgment on others, for example, on homosexuals." (If all behavior is beyond judgmental evaluation because it is determined by things — genes — over which I have no control, then this should apply to homophobia, child molestation, and everything else, and not merely to someone's favorite hobbyhorse like homosexual freedoms.)

What would you say about this statement: "There are no moral absolutes"? Is it self-refuting?[8]

## Important Informal Fallacies

In addition to good principles of reasoning and argument, everyone should learn to spot certain informal fallacies of reasoning in his or her own communication as well as others'. Here are some of the most important informal fallacies.[9]

*1. Appeal to pity.* In an appeal to pity, the premises of an argument are logically irrelevant to the conclusion, but they are psychologically moving in such a way that the conclusion may seem to follow. In an appeal to pity, the arguer attempts to evoke pity from the reader or listener in support of a conclusion. For example, "If abortion is forbidden, then the rich will still be able to secure safe abortions, but the poor will either have back-alley abortions or keep producing children to draw more welfare."[10] Here an appeal is made to our sense of pity for the poor, heightened by our sense of disgust with the rich in contrast to the poor, and the conclusion reached is that abortion should be morally permissible. But the question of the moral permissibility of abortion is an issue of the moral status of the fetus, not a question of how we feel about the rich or poor in this context. Consider a parallel counterargument: "If handguns are not kept legal, then the poor either will have to use black-market, illegal guns that could misfire and be a danger to the shooter, or else stop stealing and remain poor while the rich will still be able to secure good handguns." The fact that this argument is such a poor one shows the folly of using an appeal to pity.

*2. Appeal to the people.* In this fallacy, one argues that if you want to be accepted, included in the group, loved, or respected, then you should accept conclusion X as true. Here the arguer incites group emotions or the enthusiasm of the crowd, appeals to people's vanity or snobbery, or challenges people to jump on the bandwagon to support a conclusion. For example, "Everyone who is really with it and modern in orientation recognizes that condoms ought to be distributed in the schools, so you should get with it and accept the same verdict." Or, "Modern, cultured people are not so narrow to think that one religion is the absolute truth, so you Christians should stop claiming that Christ is the only way to God." This type of argument is wielded widely among teenagers, and unfortunately, sermons sometimes employ this form of fallacious reasoning to "establish" what in fact may be a true conclusion. Remember, a fallacious argument may or may not have a true conclusion. Either way, such an argument fails to establish that conclusion properly.

*3.* **Ad hominem** *argument.* In this fallacy, one argues against an opponent's position by attacking the other arguer and not the argument. For example, "Your argument against affirmative action could not possibly be a good one because you are a white male." Here is another one: "Newt Gingrich has argued for lowering taxes. What a joke! Gingrich is just a rich Republican who could never understand what it means to have compassion on those less fortunate than he." Again: "Why don't pro-lifers adopt babies if they're so concerned about abortion. Their position is nothing but hypocrisy! And men have no right to speak about abortion since they can't get pregnant." Sometimes it can be relevant to attack a person if the person's character or credibility is relevant to the truth of his or her claims, for example, in evaluating the testimony of a witness in court. In such a case, no *ad hominem* fallacy is committed.

**4. Genetic fallacy.** This fallacy occurs when someone confuses the origin of an idea with the reasons for believing the idea and faults the idea because of where it came from (for example, because of who said it or how the idea first came to be believed) and not because of the adequacy of the grounds for the idea. For example, "The idea of God originated out of fear of the dark and a terror of death, so it is not reasonable to believe in God." This is not how the idea of God originated, but even if it were, that fact would be utterly irrelevant in judging whether or not one ought to believe in God. Again: "You are a Christian and not a Buddhist because you were raised in a Christian country and your parents taught you to be a Christian. Therefore, there is no good reason to prefer Christianity to Buddhism." The fallacy of this argument should be apparent. When we answer the question, "*Why* do you believe in *x*?" we need to keep separate a psychological or originating "why" from a rational "why." A psychological or originating "why" is a request to give the motive for a belief or to state how you came to have the belief in question ("my parents taught it to me"). As interesting as these issues are, they must be kept distinct from the request to cite the reasons you have for thinking that some belief is true. Motives are one thing, rational grounds and evidence are another.

**5. Straw man.** This fallacy is committed when an arguer distorts an opponent's position for the purpose of making it more easy to destroy, refutes the distorted position, and concludes that his opponent's actual view is thereby demolished. For example, "All creationists think that the world began in 4004 BC, that Noah's ark contained every single pair of species we see today, and that no evolutionary change has occurred, period. Moreover, the only reason creationists appeal to miracles is to cover their ignorance of scientific causes. They believe in a god-of-the-gaps. These ideas cannot withstand rational scrutiny, so creationism ought to be rejected." This argument draws the conclusion that creationism in any form ought to be rejected by refuting claims that virtually no creationist would accept. Here is another example: "Everything needs a cause, God is a thing; therefore, God needs a cause." This argument is a straw man because it ignores the nature or identity of God.

**6. Red herring.** This fallacy gets its name from a procedure for training dogs to follow a scent. A red herring would be dragged across the trail with the intent of leading the dog astray with its potent scent. Well-trained dogs do not follow red herrings but stick to the original scent. In logic, a red herring fallacy takes place when someone diverts the reader's or listener's attention by changing the subject to some different and irrelevant issue. The arguer finishes by either drawing a conclusion about this different issue or by simply presuming that a conclusion has been established.

Here is a common red herring: "Pro-choice is something all Americans should accept. Unfortunately, the religious right wants to invade our bedrooms and force their narrow-minded, mean-spirited views on others. Loosen up, religious right! You should learn to be more compassionate for those less fortunate than you!" The argument begins with a conclusion to be established, namely, that all Americans should be pro-choice. But the argument quickly gets off track and follows a red herring—it turns into an argument about the personality traits of those in the religious right and draws a conclusion about the people so characterized. What happened to the original issue? Along the way, the argument got off track and followed a red herring.

**7. Begging the question.** There are different versions of begging the question, but a major form of this fallacy occurs when a disputant uses his conclusion as one of the premises employed to establish that conclusion. The conclusion is simply asserted as one of the premises in the argument used to justify that conclusion. Often, this fallacy is concealed by stating the proposition in question one way when it is a premise and another way when it is the conclusion. For example: "Capital punishment is *wrong* because it is an example of doing something we have *no business doing*, namely, taking a person's life." Here the conclusion "Capital punishment is wrong" includes the term *wrong*. The premise used to argue for this conclusion is actually just a different way of stating the conclusion itself. This is masked, however, because the proposition uses "no business doing" when it is stated as a premise. It should be clear, however, that "no business doing" is just another way of saying "wrong."

Here is another example: "I know the Bible is completely true and trustworthy because it is the Word of God and as the Word of God the Bible teaches the complete truthfulness of everything it asserts." The conclusion (that the Bible is completely true and trustworthy) is correct, but the argument used to establish that conclusion begs the question. Can you think of a better argument for the conclusion that does not beg the question?[11]

## SUMMARY

Much more could be said about the topics of this chapter than space has allowed. For example, there are more informal fallacies than I have listed above. But this chapter provides you with enough material to allow you to form some concrete goals and practices in developing a better Christian mind.

In part 1, we looked at why we modern evangelicals have lost the emphasis on the intellectual life characteristic of our ancestors and affirmed in the Bible. We also saw from Holy Scripture and from the way the mind works that developing a careful Christian mind is not an option for someone serious about Christian discipleship and mature human flourishing. In part 2, we looked at some suggestions for how one can actually go about developing a Christian mind. In part 3, we will turn to a different area of reflection. We will look at different aspects of a properly functioning Christian mind in the tasks of evangelism and building a case for Christianity.

# PART THREE

# WHAT A MATURE CHRISTIAN MIND LOOKS LIKE

# CHAPTER SIX

# EVANGELISM AND THE CHRISTIAN MIND

Syndicated columnist Thomas Sowell once wrote the following:

> Many studies have shown how ignorant our high school and even college graduates are of basic knowledge that was once taken for granted. What is even more alarming is how lacking they are in the ability to think systematically. Such elementary things as defining terms and going step-by-step from evidence to conclusions have given way to emotional rhetoric and automatic responses to buzz-words and visions. As someone who has taught at several colleges, I am all too painfully aware of the erosion of thinking over the years. But even after leaving the classroom, I have continued to encounter the same mindlessness everywhere. For example, an environmentalist to whom I presented certain facts responded by saying, "But they are raping the planet!" "What specifically does that mean?" I asked. He was as speechless as someone who had just played the ace of trumps and was then told that that was not enough to win.[1]

Sowell's point is a serious one that has dramatic implications for the way we Christians usually present the gospel to unbelievers. Because of the mindlessness of our culture, people do not persuade others of their views (religious or otherwise) on the basis of argument and reason, but rather, by expressing emotional rhetoric and politically correct buzzwords. Reason has given way to rhetoric, evidence to emotion, substance to slogan, the speech writer to the makeup man, and rational authority (the right to command compliance and to be believed) to social power (the ability to coerce compliance and outward conformance). The way we reach decisions today, the manner in which we dialogue about issues, and the political correctness we see all around us are dehumanizing expressions of the anti-intellectualism in modern society when it comes to broad worldview issues. Rhetoric without reason, persuasion without argument are manipulation. Might—it is wrongly believed—makes right.

When was the last time you saw or read in media coverage of the abortion controversy any attempt at all to clarify and state the crucial arguments offered by each side? Instead, a media already widely sympathetic with the pro-choice position continues to use rhetoric to "persuade" people to see abortion rights in favorable ways. One example of this is the constant use of the labels "pro-choice" and "anti-abortion." Apart from the inaccuracy of these labels, pro-life advocates are not against abortion per se, but are *for life*, a fact that would be evident if an abortion technique were developed that saved the life of the child and allowed it to be put up for adoption. This media practice amounts to nothing less than subliminal propaganda that is swallowed all too easily by a nation of empty selves.

No movement, political, religious, or otherwise, can survive with dignity or flourish in a culture if it allows the following to arise:

- A culture where its viewpoint is considered irrational by a significant number of people and is not adequately represented among the intellectual leaders who shape the plausibility structure of that culture.
- A culture in which the movement itself enlists others to join, not primarily in terms of the importance of the ideas and the truth that defines that movement, but in terms of the satisfaction of felt needs for those who sign up.
- An atmosphere wherein the movement does not mobilize a growing number of its soldiers to be articulate advocates and defenders of its ideology who can engage in debate in the public square.

It saddens me to say that Sowell's remarks, along with the observations just expressed, accurately describe many of the current approaches to evangelism employed by the evangelical community. I should know. One of my spiritual gifts is evangelism, and I have been involved in it for over forty years. I have trained thousands of people to communicate the gospel to others, and I have given evangelistic talks in most of the states in this country. I say this not to boast, but to assure you that I am no ivory tower academic (whatever that means). I am a practitioner. In the last quarter of a century I have seen a slow, steady erosion of apologetical reasoning and argument as part of the texture of our evangelism. Instead, evangelism is increasingly associated with the things Sowell bemoans: rhetoric, Christian buzzwords, and an overdone appeal to felt needs. In the very way we do evangelism, we have inadvertently let the world squeeze us into its mold.

One day I was in the Baltimore airport waiting to get on a plane to the Midwest. I overheard three women talking next to me. One woman was explaining to the others why she had left Catholicism and become a Baptist. Her "reasons" were that she liked the people, the music, and the feeling she got in the Baptist church, and she found the minister's sermons interesting and pleasurable to hear. Now, these are all wonderful, but they do not justify changing one's basic religious commitment. Conspicuous by its absence was one single reference to the woman's attempt to compare Catholic and Baptist theology to see which was more likely to be true. Reason played the same role in this woman's religious life that it did in the environmentalist's commitment in Sowell's article. If reason plays no practical role in such religious decisions as choosing a denomination or becoming a Christian in the first place, why should we expect it to inform subsequent decisions within the religious life?

Given the contemporary cultural climate, it is easier to get people to buy a product, join a movement, or accept a set of ideas if you use rhetoric, appeal to emotions and felt needs, and set aside a rational presentation of the topic at hand. But the short-term "successes" of such an approach can dull us to the long-term harm that will be done by taking this easy way out. As British sociologist and theologian Os Guinness has argued, the Devil will allow short-term success in evangelism and church growth if the means used to achieve it ultimately contribute to the marginalization of the church and her message.[2] In this case, the church becomes her own gravedigger. By eschewing the role of reason in evangelism and substituting in its place an overemphasis on a simple gospel appeal directed at felt needs, short-term gains are to be expected in a culture of empty selves. But who can deny that while our numbers have grown, *our impact has not been proportionate to our numbers?*

There is too much at stake for this situation to continue. What is needed is a rethinking of the very nature of evangelism, more specifically, of the role of reasoning and argument in the way we do evangelism. In what follows, I will describe the role of reason in evangelism.

## APOLOGETICS AND EVANGELISM
### Evangelism and Apologetics

Apologetics is the primary form through which the Christian mind expresses itself in the task of evangelism. *Apologetics* comes from the Greek word *apologeomai*, whose root meaning is "to defend something." *Apologetics* can be defined as "that New Testament ministry which seeks to provide rational grounds for believing Christianity in whole or in part and to respond to objections raised against Christianity in whole or in part." So understood, apologetics is a ministry designed to help unbelievers overcome intellectual obstacles to conversion and believers remove doubts that hinder spiritual growth.

In chapter 2, we saw that there is a biblical basis for the use of the mind in doing apologetics. First Peter 3:15 commands us to be ready to give a reasoned defense to someone who asks us for a credible reason why we believe what we do. Jude 3 admonishes us to "contend earnestly" for the faith (NASB). "Contend earnestly" carries with it the idea of engaging in a contest, a struggle, a conflict, or a debate by the pious in the heroic struggle for religious truth, justice, and virtue. The term clearly includes the idea of an intellectual struggle, an idea also expressed by Paul when he said spiritual warfare involves "destroying speculations and every lofty thing raised up against the knowledge of God, . . . taking every thought captive to the obedience of Christ" (2 Corinthians 10:5, NASB). Spiritual warfare is a struggle with persons, demonic and human, and the primary way persons influence other persons is through the ideas they get others to accept. Thus, intellectual tools and reasoning are an important part, though not the whole of spiritual warfare. The other primary components are spiritual preparedness, discernment, courage, and wisdom.

We see examples of apologetics everywhere in the Scriptures. In Acts, Paul argued, reasoned, presented evidence, and tried rationally to persuade others to become Christians (Acts 14:15-17; 17:2-4,16-31; 18:4; 19:8-9). He brought to center stage the truth and reasonableness of the gospel, *not* the fact that it addresses felt needs. Though both are important, there is a clear Pauline emphasis placed on the former. Jesus Christ Himself regularly engaged in logical debate and rational argument with false, destructive ideologies in His culture, and on several occasions He told people to believe in Him, not simply on the basis of His words, but because of the evidence of His miracles.

In this way, Jesus and Paul were continuing a style of persuasion peppered throughout the Old Testament prophets. Regularly, the prophets appealed to evidence to justify belief in the biblical God or in the divine authority of their inspired message: fulfilled prophecy, the historical fact of miracles, the inadequacy of finite pagan deities to be a cause of such a large, well-ordered universe compared to the God of the Bible, and so forth. They did not say, "God said it, that settles it, you should believe it!" They provided a rational defense for their claims.

It is sometimes said that Genesis does not try to "prove" the existence of God, it merely assumes it. But this is inaccurate. True, Genesis does not argue against atheism because atheism was not a major ideology among the pagan nations surrounding Moses and Israel. But those nations did believe in fickle, finite, immoral deities. In fact, a widespread pagan belief was the idea that each spring the gods copulated, their seed fell to the ground, and that was why crops sprouted and grew each year. Based on that belief, yearly pagan rituals included frenzied orgies to induce the gods to copulate and insure a new season of crops. Genesis takes this view to task and presents a testable claim: The God of Israel delegated to living things the intrinsic power to reproduce after their own kinds, an odd and foreign idea to the nations of the ancient Mideast. But this claim carried with it a test. If the pagans ceased their orgies, then no crops would grow if their views were correct and the gods needed inducement to copulate. But if the biblical view were correct, crops would continue to arise.

## The General Value of Apologetics

I am not suggesting that the only thing in Scripture relevant to evangelism is rational argument and apologetics. However, I am suggesting that *apologetics is an absolutely essential ingredient to biblical evangelism.* And it is easy to see why. An emphasis on reasoning in evangelism makes the truthfulness of the gospel the main issue, not the self-interested "fulfillment" of the listener. Felt needs are important, but if they are made the issue, Christianity will be seen as just another means of helping the convert overcome his problems, along with his therapist and workout routine. Let me repeat—there is a place for a simple gospel presentation and for addressing people's felt needs in our evangelistic strategy. But these should never be the tail that wags the dog, at least not if our evangelism is to express biblical teaching and common sense. If the truth of a message is important, apologetical reasoning will be a crucial part of evangelism because it places the emphasis where it should be—on the truth of the message.

None of this means you must have a PhD before you can share the faith with an unbeliever. In the Gospels, people touched by Jesus bore testimony to Him immediately without training. But these gospel examples are not there to teach us how to do evangelism—the book of Acts does that. They're there to show that all manner of people were coming to faith in Jesus and to provide testimony about who Jesus was. Clearly, a new Christian should witness for Christ as opportunity presents itself, irrespective of the amount of training acquired. But it does not follow that a maturing Christian, five, ten, or twenty years old in the Lord, should still be unskilled in reasoning on behalf of the gospel.

Will this approach to evangelism take work? You bet it will. We'll have to do a lot of reading, studying, and thinking. But if someone can spend several hours a day learning to swing a golf club, at least the same effort would not be inappropriate for someone who wants to be a more effective witness for Christ.

A life of study and intellectual growth enhances one's effectiveness in personal evangelism in many ways. Many times we want to communicate the gospel to friends, coworkers, or relatives. But this can create tension and a certain unnaturalness when we are with them, because we feel pressured to find some seam in the conversation from which we can artificially redirect the discussion to our testimony or something of the sort. If a person has a secular/sacred dichotomy in his life due to a lack of a carefully thought-out, integrated Christian worldview, then the gospel will have to be forced into an otherwise secular discussion. But if a person has developed a Christian mind, she can relax because she has an understanding of and a Christian view about a number of "secular" topics. In such a situation, it would be hard to have a normal conversation without Christianity coming up naturally and in a way relevant to the topic of discussion. Moreover, a well-developed mind can see connections between what a friend is saying and other issues of which the friend may not be aware. For example, a friend may be espousing moral relativism yet inconsistently hold that we all have an absolute duty to save the environment. If a person sees the connections, she can simply ask well-placed questions that naturally lead to a discussion of broader worldview issues, including God and our relationship to Him. In such a case, the pressure is off because a person has the intellectual categories necessary to make natural connections between Christianity and a host of regular conversation topics. There is no need to try to find a crack in the discussion to insert a gospel presentation utterly unrelated to the flow of conversation. What a joyful fruit of the intellectual life this is!

## Apologetics and Children

Two hundred years ago, the great spiritual master and Christian activist William Wilberforce (1759–1833) wrote a book about the nature of real Christianity and authentic spiritual growth. In a modern book about the spiritual life, especially the cultivation of spirituality in children, I doubt that the first issue addressed would be apologetics! But this is precisely what was at the forefront of Wilberforce's mind. His statement is so powerful, I will cite it in full:

> In an age in which infidelity abounds, do we observe them [parents] carefully instructing their children in the principles of faith which they profess? Or do they furnish their children with arguments for the defense of that faith? They would blush on their child's birth to think him inadequate in any branch of knowledge or any skill pertaining to his station in life. He cultivates these skills with becoming diligence. But he is left to collect his religion as he may. The study of Christianity has formed no part of his education. His attachment to it—where any attachment to it exists at all—is too often not the preference of sober reason and conviction. Instead his attachment to Christianity is merely the result of early and groundless possession. He was born in a Christian country, so of course he is a Christian. His father was a member of the Church of England, so that is why he is, too. When religion is handed down among us by hereditary succession, it is not surprising to find youth of sense and spirit beginning to question the truth of the system in which they were brought up. And it is not surprising to see them abandon a position which they are unable to defend. Knowing Christianity chiefly by its difficulties and the impossibilities falsely imputed to it, they fall perhaps into the company of unbelievers.[3]

Having witnessed hundreds of evangelical children hit the college campus, I can attest to the fact that we need to follow Wilberforce's advice and start early in teaching them the reasons for their faith. Make no mistake about it. Young children can ask profound intellectual questions about God and religion. And if we do not take them seriously and work to provide them with good answers, it will impact the vibrancy of their Christian commitment sooner or later.

I received a phone call from a woman in our neighborhood I'll call Beth. Beth has a son in high school who is a friend of my youngest teenage daughter, Allison. Beth became a Christian five years ago, and her son is a believer too. Unknown to me, a friend of Beth's had recommended she read an apologetic book I wrote years ago titled *Scaling the Secular City*. Yesterday, someone told Beth that Allison's father was the author of the book. She called me to ask some apologetical questions.

The conversation was quite interesting. She opened up on the phone about a frustration and a fear. The frustration was that she still had a large number of non-Christian friends and relatives who regularly asked her hard questions about her faith that she was not able to answer. She felt fear because the spiritual life of her son, like most teenagers, was something she could not take for granted, and her son regularly asked her questions about Christianity that she could not address. She feared not only for her son's spiritual growth but also that he would not respect her own dedication to Christ if she did not take hard questions seriously enough to find out answers. Her son had pointed out that because she had time to do a number of hobbies, watch television, and so on, if getting good answers to certain questions mattered to her, she would have gotten them by now. He concluded that her faith must not matter that much to her because she had not taken the time to wrestle with issues that might show that her faith was false. I encouraged her to continue growing and to be intentional about making progress in learning apologetical answers to various questions. My experience leads me to believe that Beth's situation is not unique.

Beth's call reminded me that it is important to develop our Christian minds by learning why we believe what we believe. This is an important aspect of our spiritual lives. As we grow in our apologetical knowledge and skills, our faith becomes more steady, powerful, and confident. We also grow in our courage and boldness as witnesses for Jesus Christ. And we learn to be attractive, nondefensive ambassadors for Christ who are prepared to give an answer to someone who asks us what we believe and why.

This chapter has demonstrated the importance of the transformation of our minds toward Christlikeness as it relates to evangelism. An important foundation for evangelism is the ability to answer questions, much like Beth's need just mentioned. In the next three chapters, we will examine the use of the mind in developing a rationally persuasive case for Christianity.

# CHAPTER SEVEN

# THE QUESTION OF GOD (PART I)

Christians believe two things: *(1) That God really exists, has a certain nature, and has a set of ideas about various things that He has disclosed to us. (2) That the things claimed in the first premise can be known to be true and need not be accepted by a blind, arbitrary act of privatized faith exercised by weak people who need such a crutch.* It should go without saying that within the span of a single volume, it would be impossible to adequately defend these claims. So I won't try. However, what I will do is talk my way through considerations that have been central and persuasive in my own journey in the hopes that you will find something of value for your own pilgrimage. And I will provide footnotes that can guide you into fuller, more sophisticated treatments of these themes in case you wish to pursue these matters further. Part of loving God with all of your mind is being able to defend your views about God, and the next three chapters will lay out one way of doing that.

## GETTING STARTED

So, how should you approach this topic of defending your faith? How does one search for God, anyway? Let me, first, tell you how not to do it. You don't want to look for something that works for you or helps you irrespective of whether or not it's true. To see why, recall the case in chapter 4 of a fictitious figure we called Wonmug.

Wonmug was a hopelessly dumb physics student attending a large Western university. He failed all of his first semester classes, his math skills were around a fifth-grade level, and he had no aptitude for science.

However, one day all the physics students and professors at his college decided to spoof Wonmug by making him erroneously think he was the best physics student at the university. When he asked a question in class, students and professors alike would marvel out loud at the profundity of the question. Graders gave him perfect scores on all his assignments, when in reality he deserved an F. Eventually, Wonmug graduated and went on for his PhD. The professors at his university sent a letter to all the physicists in the world and included them in the spoof. Wonmug received his degree, took a prestigious chair of physics, regularly went to Europe to deliver papers at major science conferences, and was often featured in *Time* and *Newsweek*. Wonmug's life was pregnant with feelings of respect, accomplishment, expertise, and happiness. Unfortunately, he still knew absolutely no physics. Everyone hated and disrespected Wonmug and mocked him behind his back. In short, he was a dunce.

Do you envy Wonmug? Would you wish such a life for your children? Of course not. Why? *Because his sense of well-being was built on a false, misinformed worldview placebo.* If you approach the question of God in this manner—with no regard for truth, guided only by what you will get out of it—you are trivializing your life and should be pitied just like Wonmug. And it would be naive to think that if you are an atheist, agnostic, or mildly irreligious person, you have somehow escaped the Wonmug problem. I would like you to consider the fact that if you satisfy one of these descriptors, you may well have chosen your view of God—perhaps unconsciously—precisely because your view "works" for you; it allows you to live the lifestyle you currently exhibit without threat of being wrong.

Now, if truth is going to be our concern, we immediately confront a problem. While some of the surface principles and moral rules of various religions may be similar, when it comes to their deeper aspects—what is real, what God, the self, the afterlife are like, what the purpose of life is—there are contradictions among them. Atheists and conservative Buddhists deny there is a God, popular Hinduism says there are millions of Gods, Islam says the greatest source of infidelity is to believe Jesus is God, yet that is precisely what Christians claim. These diverse viewpoints contradict each other and cannot all be correct.

To see this, consider an illustration I used while speaking at a fraternity house at the University of Massachusetts. Though I had never met them before, I asked three young men to describe my mother. Here's what resulted: she's 5'2" tall, has blond hair, and weighs 105 pounds; she's 5'4" tall, has brown hair, and weighs 125 pounds; she's 5'7" tall, has black hair, and weighs 140 pounds. I pointed out two things to the young men in attendance. First, *they couldn't all be right*. My mother could not simultaneously satisfy all three descriptions. Second, *sincerity is not enough*. For example, the first young man could sincerely believe he was correct and, in fact, persuade a million people he was correct, but if my mother did not satisfy his description, then he and all his followers were wrong.

A good way to think about the diversity of religions is in terms of a maze. The most famous maze in the world is located in the gardens of Hampton Court near London. The maze, consisting of eight-foot hedges, was planted in 1702. It covers a third of an acre and its winding paths are over a half mile long. When entering the maze you immediately face a dilemma—which path should I take? The goal is to reach the center of the maze, but which path will take you there? Some routes quickly lead to a dead end while others take you deep into the maze only to eventually fail. Some paths run parallel to each other for long periods of time only to have one hit a wall while the other continues. The challenge is to find the *one* path that leads you to the final destination—the center.

There are several reasons why this analogy is a good one. First, the maze analogy places a value on exploration and self-discovery. The only way to assess the effectiveness of a route is to consider where it takes you. Does the route lead you to a dead end or take you to the center? If you are to be a serious seeker of God, you need to carefully assess the different routes endorsed by competing religions. What deficiencies found in a route will cause you to abandon this route and look for another?

Second, viewing religions as a maze with multiple routes heading in different directions acknowledges the wildly contradictory views of the religions we've just considered. In a maze participants are confronted with choices that will send them in completely different directions. Heading into the maze, the participant accepts the challenge of finding the one path that will lead him or her to the center.

Third, as in any maze some routes will at times head in the same direction or run parallel to each other. The Muslim, Jewish, and Christian routes run parallel to each other in their belief that God is one (monotheistic). Hinduism and Buddhism run parallel to each other in their belief of the laws of karma and reincarnation. The maze analogy lets travelers acknowledge similarities as paths head in the same direction even though only one will ultimately arrive at the center.

I don't want to press the point further except to say one thing. Given such diversity of religious worldviews (including atheism or agnosticism), you are going to have to find a way to increase your chances of arriving at the truth of the matter. In the last forty years, I have watched literally thousands of people navigate this issue in the wrong way. And before I give you my take on the correct way to seek God, I owe it to you to warn you about this often-taken, mistaken pathway.

The approach I have in mind is a smorgasbord approach. Here one places all the various religions before him, picks and chooses a little from each, and formulates his or her own picture of God as a collage. It should be obvious why this approach virtually guarantees failure. When people seek God in this way, they always end up with a picture of God that looks strangely like the person who went looking for Him! If one is a liberal Democrat, a conservative Republican, or lives in Kansas City, then God will turn out to be a big Ted Kennedy in the sky, a Rush Limbaugh figure, or a Chiefs fan, respectively! No, *this approach is really nothing but a projection of one's own likes and dislikes onto reality in order to feel safe without having to change.*

Let me remind you that you don't want to make a mistake in the view of God you eventually embrace. Here's why. The other day our yardman mistakenly pulled a flower he mistook for a weed. It was no big deal. We bought a new flower, planted it as a replacement, and informed the yardman about the situation. Contrast this incident with someone who desperately needs brain surgery and, upon meeting a brain surgeon to schedule the operation, hears the surgeon say, "Of course I will do the operation for you. By the way, isn't the brain located right near the navel area?" If this ever happens to you, it would be time to find another doctor! Here's the lesson: *The more important the issue, the greater the damage done by holding to a false belief.* One's view of God is more like brain surgery than flowers and weeds. I labored in chapters 1 and 2 to convince you that the question of God is momentous.

So, where does that leave us? I suggest that the only approach to seeking God worthy of the decisive nature of the quest and adequate to be done with integrity is one in which you are guided by your mind. You must think hard, carefully, and as nondefensively as you can. You must look for and at the evidence, weigh it along with alternative explanations, and make the most reasonable decision you can. In short, this issue should lie at the foundation of your rational life plan.

## FACTS, EXPLANATIONS, AND PROOF

Is it possible to prove there is a God? In my view, this is the wrong question because the notion of "proof" sets such a high standard that it invites one to imagine a situation in which one's intellectual opponents have to get on their knees after you present your case to them and admit that they are completely wrong, with no possibility that your position could be mistaken. This sort of proof is so rare that it is almost impossible to think of an example that satisfies it. About all I can come up with is proof in logic and math. For example, one might say he can prove that $y = 8$, given that $x = 5$ and $y = 3x-7$. But even here, there will be dissenters. I had a professor in my doctoral program at the University of Southern California who did not believe the simple statements of arithmetic (for example, 1+1=2) were true. According to him they were useful fictions. I disagree with him, but my point is that "proof" in the sense described above is hard to come by.

Besides, we all know many things that fail to live up to the "proof" standard, for which we have more than adequate grounds and about which we may have doubts, unresolved questions, and be willing to admit that it is possible we are mistaken. I know I had coffee this morning, that 1+1=2, that kindness is a virtue, that my wife is a person, that I am feeling pain in my ankle, that the banana on the table is yellow, and a host of other things. Yet each of these claims has its critics. I can't "prove" any of them, but I know them nonetheless.

There's a better way to approach the question of the existence of God, and it is one that is successfully practiced in science, history, law, philosophy, and other areas. I shall call it "A Cumulative Case Inference to the Best Explanation." This intellectual strategy has two characteristics. First, at the name suggests, it involves an "*inference to the best explanation.*" This occurs when we identify a range of data to be explained, formulate a pool of possible explanations, and judge that one is the best among that pool. When this happens, the data provide evidence that the explanation is true. For example, if we observe lightning, static electricity, and so forth, then if we postulate that there are such things as electrons with certain characteristics (a certain charge and mass), we are entitled to believe in electrons if they provide the best explanation of the data. Similarly, if a range of data is surfaced in a jury trial, and the best explanation is that the defendant committed the crime in a certain way, then we are entitled to believe that this is so. In what follows, I will identify a range of factual data that find their best explanation by far, if there is a single, personal God.

Second, this intellectual strategy involves a *cumulative case*. This occurs when several independent strands of evidence support the same conclusion. In this case, it could easily happen that no single piece of evidence warrants accepting the conclusion, but, nevertheless, one still ought to believe the conclusion in light of the combined weight of all the evidence taken together. This regularly happens in a trial, in historical explanations, and in science. In what follows, I will offer a range of factual data that, taken together, provide sufficient grounds for believing in God. I believe some of these data are sufficient by themselves to warrant belief in God. But all I am asking of you is that you take the cumulative evidence into account as you reflect on the issues to follow.

## THE EXISTENCE OF THE UNIVERSE

In quiet moments, I suspect you have taken a walk at night, gazed up into the starry heavens, and felt a strong inclination to believe that all of this had to have a cause. My parents were blue-collar workers who never finished high school, but this line of thinking seemed so evident to them that it passed as common sense. And I think they were correct. Here is a way of putting this thought into an argument:[1]

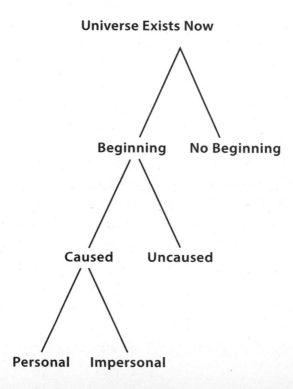

The defender of the argument tries to establish one horn of each dilemma and, thus, to argue for these three premises:

1. The universe had a beginning.
2. The beginning of the universe was caused.
3. The cause of the beginning of the universe was personal.

Let us look briefly at each premise, starting with 1.

### Premise 1: The universe had a beginning.

These days it is beyond reasonable doubt that the universe began to exist. By "universe" I just mean the world of objects that exist in space and time: space, time, and matter make up the universe. You may think of the universe in this way: Take any arbitrary volume of space and everything that exists within that volume. Now, add up all these volumes until you have taken into account all the space that exists and all the objects within the space. Finally, factor in the passage of time that has taken place since the beginning, and you have the universe.

The fact that the universe had a beginning has received overwhelming philosophical and scientific support in recent years. One important philosophical argument for premise (1) involves the impossibility of crossing or traversing an actual infinite number of events one at a time. It is impossible to cross an actual infinite. For example, if a person started counting 1, 2, 3, . . . then he or she could count forever and never reach a time when an actual infinite amount of numbers had been counted. This is due to the nature of infinity — it is infinitely larger than *any* finite number. The series of numbers counted could increase forever without limit but it would always be finite. *Trying to count to infinity is like attempting to jump out of a pit with infinitely tall walls — walls that literally go forever without top edges to them.* No matter how far one counted, no meaningful progress would be made because there would always be an infinite number of items left to count.

Now, suppose we represent the events in the history of the universe as follows:

The present moment is marked "zero" and each moment in the past (for example, yesterday, 1500 BC) are points on the line. If the universe never had a beginning, then there is no end on the left side of the line. Rather, it extends infinitely far into the past. If the universe had no beginning, then the number of events crossed to reach the present moment would be actually infinite. It would be like counting to zero from negative infinity. But since one cannot cross an actual infinite (regardless of whether you count to positive infinity from zero or to zero from negative infinity), then the present moment could never have arrived if the universe had no beginning. This means that since the present is real, it was only preceded by a finite past and there was a beginning or first event!

One important objection has been raised against this argument.[2] According to some critics, the argument assumes what it is trying to prove, namely a beginning. They claim that the argument pictures a beginningless universe as a universe with a beginning time, T, infinitely far away, from which the present moment must be reached. But, they claim, a beginningless universe has *no* beginning, not one infinitely far away. These critics go on to assert that if one begins with the present and runs through the past one event at a time (for example, yesterday, day before yesterday, etc.), then one will never come to an event from which the present is unreachable.

Unfortunately, this criticism represents a gross misunderstanding of the argument. It does not assume a beginning time infinitely far from the present. It is precisely the lack of such a beginning that causes most of the problems. If there were no beginning, then coming to the present moment would require crossing an actual infinite number of events—analogous to counting to zero from negative infinity—and such a cross is impossible, as was pointed out above.

Further, coming to the present moment by crossing an infinite past would be a journey that could not even get started. Counting to positive infinity from zero can at least begin, even if it cannot be completed. Counting to zero from negative infinity cannot be completed or started. *Such a task is like trying to jump out of an infinitely tall bottomless pit!* The whole idea of getting a foothold in the series in order to make progress is unintelligible. Take any specifiable event in the past. In order to reach that event, one would already have to traverse an actual infinite, and the problem is perfectly iterative—it applies to each point in the past.

Critics of the argument go wrong in picturing a beginningless universe as an indefinite, unspecified past, not an infinite one. They invite us to start at the present, work through the past mentally by form- ing a growing series of events as one works backward, and try to specify a point you could reach that is unreachable from the present! But that is not the correct picture. If we count backward a day at a time, the prob- lem will not be in trying to reach the present from the day we have counted (say we count back 50 million years, stop momentarily, and ask if the present is reachable from that moment). The problem will reside in the fact that for each point (for example, the moment that was real- ized 50 million years ago) we count, that point is no better off than the present moment—it could not have happened either if the universe was beginningless, because it would require crossing an actual infinite to reach it, just as the present moment requires.

There is, then, a good philosophical argument for the fact that the universe had a beginning (premise 1). But premise 1 can be given scien- tific support from at least two sources: *the big bang theory* and *the second law of thermodynamics*. Regarding *the big bang theory*, it is currently the most reasonable and widely respected view, and it confirms the fact that the space-time physical universe had a beginning. Scientists have discov- ered evidence that the galaxies are accelerating away from each other. You can picture this by imagining a balloon with dots drawn on it. Each dot represents a single galaxy. Now, as the balloon is blown up, its surface expands and stretches and the dots travel away from each other. This is exactly what is going on in our universe. Now, if one reverses time and extrapolates backward, you reach a point at which time, space, and matter spring into existence at an initial creation event. A few years ago, my wife and I entered a room about the cosmos at a science museum in Denver. One exhibit stated firmly and without qualification that the big bang theory implies an absolute beginning to our universe. So this implication should not be controversial.

Regarding *the second law of thermodynamics* and its applicability to the question of a beginning of the universe, an argument can be developed along the following lines: The second law states that the universe is irreversibly running out of its useful energy (called "entropy," that is, the amount of disorder in the universe or, alternatively, energy available to do work in the universe), and since it hasn't reached an equilibrium state yet, it must have had a finite past. Why? If the universe had already existed throughout an actually infinite past, then it would have reached an equilibrium state an infinite number of days ago, but it obviously has not done so.

Think of it this way. Suppose you woke up in a room so tightly sealed that there was nothing whatsoever, including matter or energy, that could enter or escape the room. Now, suppose you found a warm cup of coffee and a burning candle. You would know that the room was not beginningless, that is, that it had not been built and sealed an infinite number of years ago. If fact, you would know that the room could not have been built and sealed more than, say, an hour ago. Why? Because had it been longer, all the warm, burning objects would have run out of energy and the entire room would be a uniform temperature (equilibrium).

A few years ago, *Time* magazine featured a story about how the universe will end.[3] The bottom line is that a day will come when the universe's temperature will be at absolute zero (-273° Centigrade), there will be no local pockets of heat or light (for example, the sun), and the objects in the universe will be motionless and disintegrated into infinitesimally small, motionless fragments. Since this has not happened yet, the universe could not be infinitely old, or else this state would have already been reached an infinite number of days ago.

### Premise 2: The kalam cosmological argument (the beginning of the universe was caused).

The principle that every event has a cause is quite reasonable. While we may not always know the cause for some event, it seems reasonable to always believe that a given event has a cause. In favor of this principle is, arguably, our entire, uniform experience. We simply find the world to be such that events don't pop into existence without causes.

Some argue that certain quantum events (for example, the exact time a specific atom of uranium decays into lead; the exact location where an electron hits a wall after being shot from an electron gun through a tiny slit) do not have causes. But in light of the reasonableness of the causal principle, it seems best to say that we do not know what the causes are for some of these events, rather than conclude that there are no causes. Both of these positions — there are causes for quantum events currently unknown to us versus there are no causes for quantum events — are equally compatible with observations (try to think of an observation consistent with one view and not with the other), and the former harmonizes with and preserves a principle for which there is tremendous, empirical evidence.

But even if we grant that quantum events do not, in fact, have causes, it would not affect premise 2. Here's why. Quantum events involve transitions from one state to another regarding things that already exist (electrons, atoms of uranium). But premise 2 of our argument involves the absolute coming-into-existence of something from nothing. So premise 2 does not really rest on the principle "Every event have a cause," but on the much more stringent principle "Every event *in which something comes into existence from nothing* has a cause."

Things don't just pop into existence from nothing with no cause. It is metaphysically absurd to think such a thing could happen. Remember, nothing is just that—nothing at all. A quantum vacuum, quantum ghost particles, or any other entity is something that actually exists, has certain characteristics that can be described, and so on. But nothingness is the absence of anything whatsoever. It is hardly a candidate for generating a universe!

Besides, if something could just pop into existence out of nothing without a cause, then there would be no reason why it would be a whole universe, a dog, a bucket of sand, a tomato, or anything else. Here's why. Coming into existence is not a process like walking into a room. When you walk into a room, you begin completely out of the room, then you are 10 percent in the room, 20 percent, and so on until you are completely in the room. Coming into existence isn't like that. It's not as though something starts out completely nonexistent, then it becomes 10 percent real and 90 percent unreal, then 50/50, and so on. Something either does or does not exist. Coming into existence from nothing is an instantaneous occurrence.

This means that *coming into existence from nothing cannot be governed by the laws of nature.* The laws of nature can govern only changes/transitions in things that already exist. If something pops into existence from nothing, then, there would be no reason why one thing rather than any other thing whatsoever came into existence as it did. Laws of nature do not apply. In fact, if you think about it, since we are imagining something popping into existence from absolute nothingness, then it would literally be nothing at all that could, in principle, be responsible for why such and such as opposed to thus and so came to be. This shows how bizarre the idea is.

Some may also object that if we hold that all events in which something comes to be need causes, then what caused God? But we can consistently hold that all such events need causes and that God does not need a cause because God is not an event. Furthermore, the question "What or who made God?" is a pointless category fallacy, like the question "What color is the note C?" The question "What made *x*?" can only be asked of $x$'s that are by definition, makeable. But God, if He exists at all, is a necessary being (a being which, if it exists, couldn't be such that it did not exist; the self-existent, uncreated Creator of all else who simply exists in and of Himself, period). This definition is what theists mean by "God" even if it turns out that no God exists. Atheists and theists typically agree about the definition of what God would be if He exists. They differ over whether or not anything exists that satisfies that definition. Now, *if that is what "God" means, then the question "What made God?" turns out to be "What made an entity, God, who is by definition, unmakeable?"*

It's important to bear in mind that my response does not presuppose that God actually exists; only that we have a certain concept of God that we are discussing. Suppose someone asked, "How big are the scales on a unicorn?" It would be appropriate to respond that the question is a pointless category fallacy. Why? Because the concept of a unicorn is about one-horned horses, and even if they do exist, given the concept, unicorns aren't the sorts of things that have scales. Fish do, but unicorns don't. In the same way, "Who made God?" is just a confusion.

But there's one more thing to be said here. The concept of God as a necessary being who is the self-existent, uncaused—indeed, uncauseable—Creator of everything else is far from arbitrary. To see why, we must take a brief look at something called a *vicious infinite regress*. Such a regress takes place when an analysis of something contains a covert appeal to the very thing being analyzed. A vicious infinite regress occurs because the analysis does not solve anything, but merely postpones a solution. No advance has been made. It is like a man without funds who writes checks from an empty account to cover his debts, and so on, forever.

Consider a chain of people borrowing an iPod. Whether or not the chain is vicious depends on one's analysis of the correct description of people at each stage in the chain. Suppose $a$ goes to $b$ to borrow an iPod and $b$ complies, claiming to have just what $a$ needs. If asked how $b$ has an iPod to loan, he claims to have borrowed it from $c$ who, having already borrowed one from *d*, has one to give to *b*. Allegedly, at each stage in the chain, the relevant person can be described as "a possessor of an iPod who can loan it to another." Thus, it could be alleged, the regress is not vicious: everyone will end up with an iPod.

But it is incomplete to describe each person as "a possessor of an iPod who can loan it to another." Rather, each person is "a possessor of an iPod who first had to borrow it from another in order to be able to loan it to another." At each stage, the person *qua* lender is such only because he is also a borrower. Thus, given the nature of the series, each stage cannot be adequately described without reference to the earlier stage. Because each member is a borrowing lender, no one will ever get an iPod unless the regress stops with someone who differs from all the other members of the series in being a lender who just has an iPod without having to borrow it. What we need is someone who just has an iPod, period.

Similarly, if *x* exists because it was made by *y*, and *y* exists because it was made by *z*, and so on, then at each state, the object is "a possessor of existence who first had to receive existence from something else in order to be able to give it to another." It is clear that this series cannot go on like this forever or else nothing would exist. Like the iPod series, this regress must stop with something that just exists, period—a necessary being, one that exists in itself without having to borrow existence from something else. It is clear that such a being cannot be any physical object or, indeed, the universe itself, since it did, in fact, come into existence. Something supernatural is the only appropriate candidate for the first being.

### Premise 3: The cause of the beginning of the universe was personal.

Whatever created the first event existed in an immaterial, timeless, changeless, immutable, spaceless state of affairs (all time, matter, change, and space resulted *from* the first event). How can an effect (the first event) be produced by such a state of affairs as its cause?

The world gives us examples of two basic types of efficient causes (the means that produce an effect). The first kind is the one that governs the behavior of physical or natural causal relationships and is the focus of science. It is called *event-event causation*. In general, this sort of causation involves one event (the cause) producing another event (the effect) in accordance with the laws of nature. An example is a brick breaking a glass or a ball hitting and moving another one.

Consider the brick and glass. Strictly speaking, the cause is not the brick, but rather a state or event realized in the brick, namely, the moving-of-the-brick (of course, hitting the glass, which is itself an event). The effect is the breaking-of-the-glass. The following are true of all examples of state-state causation: the cause is an event, the cause exists earlier than and simultaneous with the effect, and the transfer of power from the cause to the effect is a change requiring time.

It should be clear that the first event could not be produced by such a causal mechanism because the first event must be caused by something timeless, changeless, and which can spontaneously and immediately produce the first event. Event causal sequences presuppose time; thus, such a causal relation cannot itself account for the beginning of time and the coming-to-be of the first event itself. I should say that this is why science will never, in principle, be able to explain the first event. *Science cannot start explaining things without there already being objects, space, and time. The laws of nature govern changes in things that exist in space and time. Thus, science cannot explain the existence of the very thing that must already exist before science can start explaining things to begin with!*

There is a second type of efficient cause called *agent causation*. This type of causation occurs when a conscious person acts, say when I raise my arm or speak. The cause is a substance or thing (a self), not a temporally prior event or state inside a thing, and the effect (the raising of the arm) is produced immediately, directly, and spontaneously as the conscious self simply exercises and actualizes its causal powers to raise its arm. This type of causal relationship does not require an earlier temporal event to be the cause of an effect that exists a moment later, and thus, it is a good model for how a first event could have been generated. It follows, then, that the most reasonable explanation for the beginning of the universe is that it was the result of a free act of will by an immaterial, conscious agent who can exist outside of space and time.

In closing, I must say that the arguments of this and subsequent chapters are not merely intellectual exercises for me, and they should not be such for you. In my view, they are powerful, persuasive reasons for believing in a personal God. Well-known scientist Robert Jastrow mused about these and additional arguments to be mentioned in the next chapter. According to Jastrow, these arguments, especially the scientific aspects to them, have surged in prominence in the last sixty years or so. But for millennia, said Jastrow, people have known the truth of the statement "In the beginning, God created the heavens and the earth." Jastrow goes on to comment wryly that the discovery of theistic friendly evidence in the last sixty years has been a bad dream for the agnostic or atheistic scientist: "He has scaled the mountains of ignorance; he is about to conquer the highest peak; as he pulls himself over the final rock, he is greeted by a band of theologians who have been sitting there for centuries."[4]

# CHAPTER EIGHT

# THE QUESTION OF GOD (PART II)

Since the mid-1950s, the philosopher Antony Flew was the most influential, intellectually sophisticated defender of atheism in Western culture. He exercised a magisterial role in debates about God's existence for a half a century. But in 2004, Flew shocked the world by announcing that he had changed sides. From 2004 until his death in 2010, Flew became an ardent defender of belief in God.[1] As if this weren't newsworthy enough, his reasons for changing are important and deeply relevant to the conversation you and I are having. According to Flew, he had no particular interest in God, worship, and that sort of thing, nor did he have concerns about the afterlife. His change had absolutely nothing to do with wanting God to exist. Rather, his change resulted from following the evidence wherever it led, and his conversion was an intellectual one. Flew went so far as to say that if the arguments and evidence for God had been known fifty years ago, he and other prominent atheists of the twentieth century would have become believers decades ago.

Flew's change of mind is not an isolated incident. For at least twenty-five years there has been an explosion of intellectual activity on behalf of theism, particularly Christian theism, and more and more scholars have converted to or become more outspoken about Christian theism. The last chapter featured some of the evidence that was persuasive to Flew and others. In this chapter, I will discuss two additional lines of evidence that have likewise been significant.

## DESIGN

Human eyes are composed of more than two million working parts and can, under the right conditions, discern the light of a candle at a distance of fourteen miles. The human ear can discriminate among some 400,000 different sounds within a span of about ten octaves and can make the subtle distinction between music played by a violin or viola. The human heart pumps roughly one million barrels of blood during a normal lifetime, which would fill more than three super tankers. The eye bears a striking analogy to a telescope:

- The eye was made for vision; the telescope for assisting it.
- Both utilize a sophisticated lens to achieve its function and purpose.
- Both reflect and manipulate light.

Both are able to bring an object into proper focus. The muscles surrounding the soft lens of the eye move to bring objects into focus, while a telescope uses dials to move the lens. What are we to make of these facts? These and myriads of additional facts confirm what is obvious—we are the handiwork of a wise Designer. In fact, the evidence for God from design is most likely the most popular argument for God. I find at least four different sorts of evidence to be particularly powerful for justifying belief in God. Before I describe them, however, I should say a word about the basic structure of the design argument, which, as it turns out, is pretty commonsensical.

Each day we all try to explain the things that happen around us: Why did the water freeze? Why is it raining today? Why is the car parked on the street and not in the driveway? Why is the water boiling now? In these cases, we use two different forms of explanation: *natural law* and *personal explanations*. In a natural law explanation, we cite *a law of nature* and *physical conditions*. The water froze because water freezes at 32 degrees (the law) and it was 25 degrees last night (physical conditions). When the air reaches a certain saturation point it rains (law), and it is above that point today (conditions). By contrast, we often use a personal explanation to explain things. In this case, we cite *the ability of a person to do something; his motives, intentions, and so forth; and the means he used to carry out his purpose.* The car is in the street because Joe is able to drive (by contrast with Sammy the family's five-year-old), he wanted to play basketball last night, so he moved the car in order to clear out the driveway.

The design argument goes like this: *Certain facts about the world cannot be adequately explained by impersonal causes, conditions, and laws of nature. But they can be adequately explained by a personal explanation. There is no reason to treat these facts about the world as unexplainable brute facts. It is better to use a form of explanation—personal explanation—to explain them. Moreover, some of these facts have characteristics that clearly indicate and only come from intelligent agents. So the intelligent action of a Designing Person is the best explanation for these facts.*

The first type of evidence that impresses me greatly is *the ubiquitous existence of stunning, gratuitous beauty.* According to Christianity, the world is not the way it was intended to be. More specifically, death, disease, suffering, and other forms of evil are not part of God's ideal blueprint for the world. But in spite of evil, the world is still overwhelmingly filled with good things. In fact, the widespread presence of gratuitous beauty—beauty that seems to serve no additional function besides just being beautiful—is powerful evidence for a Grand Artist. Artists skillfully bring parts of a statue or painting together to form symmetry, elegance, and so forth. They effectively use just the right color coordination, the proper harmony of notes and sounds, to create beautiful things. But these features and more characterize the world far, far beyond the meager ability of humans to imitate them. In fact, design and beauty should not be discussed in the abstract. The power and force of beauty comes from carefully attending to specific cases of it: a butterfly, the way a baby is formed in the womb, the sunset over Maui, the Alps, the fish that fill the oceans. The world is teeming with overwhelming beauty.

There are three things about such cases that show why they are best explained by a Grand Artist. First, we all know where beauty frequently comes from—skilled artists who generate it day after day. There is no good reason to deny the analogy between human artifacts and the beauty of creation; thus, we should use the same sort of explanation (personal explanation) for the latter. Second, beauty is intrinsically good and valuable. If God does not exist, then the best atheistic account of how everything got here would be a strictly scientific account told in terms of chemistry and physics. But science can only tell a story of what is the case. It can say nothing about what ought to be the case; it cannot even use the category of intrinsic goodness or value, much less offer an explanation of how it came to be. But if God exists, the universe begins with a being who is intrinsically valuable, good, beautiful, wise, and so forth. So if God exists, we have a powerful explanation of how subsequent beauty could come to characterize our universe. But if God does not exist, we have no story of how this could be.

Some atheists think they can solve this problem by saying that at some point in the development of matter, beauty just emerged and that's the end of it. But "emergence" is just a name for the problem to be solved; it is not a genuine solution. Further, this sort of emergence is a case of something popping into existence out of nothing. Why? From the big bang until some stage at which matter reaches a certain complexity, matter can be fully described by its physical, chemical features. This sort of matter does not contain beauty or even the potential for beauty. Then all of a sudden, matter reaches a certain complexity and, presto, beauty squirts into existence. This borders on sheer magic—indeed, magic without a Magician!

Here's the third thing about these cases of beauty that provide evidence for the claim that they are best explained by a Grand Artist. To understand this factor, we need to distinguish primary and secondary qualities. Primary qualities are those thought to characterize matter: mass, size, shape, charge, location, being in motion or rest, solidity, wave characteristics (frequency, amplitude, length). Secondary qualities are colors, smells, sounds, tastes, textures. According to science, there (allegedly) really are no such things in the world as secondary qualities as commonsense people understand them. Secondary qualities should be reduced to primary qualities: colors are the same things as wavelengths; sounds are just vibrations, and so forth. But these reductions are all false. Colors may be correlated with wavelengths just as fire may be correlated with smoke. But fire is not the same thing as smoke and a color is not the same thing as a wavelength. A color is a stationary quality smoothly and continuously spread over an object's surface. By contrast, a wavelength is a colorless, rapidly vibrating, moving quantitative pattern.

Since the time of Newton, Boyle, and others in the seventeenth century, most scientists and philosophers have agreed that if secondary qualities were real, irreducible features of the world, there could never in principle be a scientific explanation for their origin or their regular, law-like correlation with primary qualities. The philosopher John Locke gave what is the only plausible explanation for their existence and regular appearance: these were due to God's good pleasure. I think Locke was right. But why God's pleasure instead of His justice or some other attribute of God? Because it is in virtue of secondary qualities that the world is beautiful and enjoyable. Think of how dull the world would be if it had no sounds, colors, tastes, and so forth, and only had particles and waves moving through space. It is both the sheer existence of secondary qualities and their crucial role in making the world beautiful that provide powerful evidence for God's existence, or so it seems to me and many others.

Scientist Michael Behe has recently called attention to a second and, in my view, impressive type of design called *irreducible complexity*. An irreducibly complex system is a system containing several well-matched, interacting parts that contribute to its basic function, and where the loss of any single part causes the system to cease functioning. Behe offers a simple illustration of an irreducibly complex system—a common mousetrap.

The mousetrap that one buys at the hardware store generally has a wooden platform to which all the other parts are attached. It also has a spring with extended ends, one of which presses against the platform, the other against a metal part called the hammer, which actually does the job of squashing the mouse. When one presses the hammer down, it has to be stabilized in that position until the mouse comes along, and that is the job of the holding bar. The end of the holding bar itself has to be stabilized, so it is placed into a metal piece called the catch.[2]

Behe then asks: How effective will the trap be if it's missing the spring? The hammer? The platform? Behe's answer: It won't catch anything! If *one* piece of the trap is missing, then it won't perform at all. Yet, evolution would seem to claim the mousetrap could evolve slowly, step-by-step. Thus, you would start with a platform, then a hammer, and then a spring, and so on. Here's the problem: according to Darwin, each piece of the mousetrap must be useful in and of itself in performing its function. If the purpose of a mousetrap is to catch mice, then what good is a block of wood (platform) or an isolated spring?

This same line of thinking concerning the mousetrap can be applied to the eye. What good is a retina by itself? Or, ocular muscles without a lens? As an irreducibly complex system, the eye must come as a package deal or it wouldn't be useful. Yet, according to Darwin the eye could not come as a package. If it did, it would violate the very criteria he established for his theory (that living structures had to be capable of evolving in small incremental steps; Darwin said that if a big jump in evolution occurred such that a complex structure "came as a package," that would be evidence of a miraculous act of the Deity).

But one does not need to turn to something as complicated as the eye to illustrate irreducible complexity. Indeed, the living world literally teems with it. Consider a much lower, "simpler" form of life: the bacterial flagellum.[3] A flagellum is a long hair-like filament that acts as a rotary propeller, enabling a bacterium to swim. The rotary propeller rotates at 100,000 rpms, it can stop on a dime and rotate at that speed in the opposite direction, and it contains at least fifty different parts that all have to be present and in exactly the right place or the structure does not function. And it exhibits a structure exactly the same as one that is engineered, and it conforms to the same requirements of functionality. The bacterial flagellum has studs, three different types of rings, a propeller, a universal joint, and much, much more.

When I ponder this structure—and it so often happens when I watch a PBS special on some living thing or ecosystem—I find it so obvious that the structure is designed by an Intelligence (and that is clear even if one does not know the means used by the Designer), that I cannot believe that an open-minded person can resist the same conclusion.

But other sorts of design are even more powerful, or so it seems to me. One of them—our third sort of design—is *specified complexity*. Recently, William Dembski wrote a book in which he analyzed cases where it is legitimate to infer that some phenomenon is the result of a purposive, intelligent act by an agent.[4] Among other things, Dembski analyzes cases in which insurance employees, police, and forensic scientists must determine whether a death was an accident (no intelligent cause) or brought about intentionally (done on purpose by an intelligent agent). According to Dembski, whenever three factors are present, investigators are rationally obligated to draw the conclusion that the event was brought about intentionally: (1) *the event was contingent, that is, even though it took place, it did not have to happen, no law of nature requires that the event happen* (unlike water, which, given the laws of nature, *must* freeze at a certain temperature); (2) *the event had a small probability of happening*; and (3) *the event is capable of independent specifiability* (capable of being identified as a special occurrence beside the simple fact that it did, in fact, happen).

To illustrate, consider a game of bridge in which two people receive a hand of cards. Let one hand be a random set of cards—call it hand A—and the other be a perfect bridge hand dealt to the dealer himself.

Now if that happened, we would immediately infer that while A was not dealt intentionally, the perfect bridge hand was, and, in fact, represents a case of cheating on the part of the dealer. What justifies our suspicion?

First, neither hand had to happen. There are no laws of nature, logic, or mathematics that necessitate that either hand had to come about in the history of the cosmos. In this sense, each hand, and, indeed, the card game itself, is a contingent event that did not have to take place. Second, since hand A and the perfect bridge hand have the same number of cards, each is equally improbable. So the small probability of an event is not sufficient to raise suspicions that the event came about by the intentional action of an agent.

The third criterion makes this clear. The perfect bridge hand can be specified as special independently of the fact that it happened to be the hand that came about, but this is not so for hand A. Hand A can be specified as "some random hand or other that someone happens to get." Now that specification applies to all hands whatever and does not mark out as special any particular hand that comes about. So understood, A is no more special than any other random deal. But this is not so for the perfect bridge hand. This hand can be characterized as a special sort of combination of cards by the rules of bridge independently of the fact that it is the hand that the dealer received. It is the combination of contingency (this hand did not have to be dealt), small probability (this particular arrangement of cards was quite unlikely to have occurred), and independent specifiability (according to the rules, this is a special hand for the dealer to receive) that justifies us in accusing the dealer of cheating.

Similarly, if a spouse happens to die at a young age in an unlikely manner even though that spouse is healthy, and if this happens just after the other spouse took out a large insurance policy on him or her or a week after proposing to a mistress, then the three factors that justify an intentional act by an intelligent designer are present.

What does all this have to do with the existence of God? In the last several years, scientists have made a shocking discovery. What is the discovery? In a phrase: the universe is precisely fine-tuned so life could appear. Over thirty independent, hard facts about the universe have been discovered in the form of basic constants of nature that are, scientifically speaking, brute facts and for which there is no further scientific explanation (the force of gravity in the universe, the charge of an electron, the rest mass of a proton, the rate of expansion resulting from the big bang). What blows the minds of so many is that if any single one of these — much less all thirty! — had been slightly larger or smaller on the order of a billionth of a percentage point, then no life could have appeared in the universe. *The universe is a razor's edge of precisely balanced life-permitting conditions.*

If gravity's force were infinitesimally stronger, all stars would burn too quickly to sustain life. If ever so slightly weaker, all stars would be too cold to support life-bearing planets. If the ratio of electron to proton mass were slightly larger or smaller, the sort of chemical bonding required to produce self-replicating molecules cannot take place. The same is true for the electromagnetic force in the universe. If the strong nuclear force were slightly larger, then the nuclei essential for life would be too unstable; if it were slightly larger, no elements but hydrogen would form. If the rate of the universe's expansion had been smaller by one part in a hundred thousand million million, the universe would have recollapsed and could not form or sustain life. Quantum laws are precisely what they need to be to prevent electrons from spiraling into atomic nuclei. If the Earth took *more* than twenty-four hours to rotate, temperatures on our planet would be too extreme between sunrise and sunset. If the rotation of the Earth were slightly *shorter,* wind would move at a dangerous velocity. If the oxygen level on our planet were *slightly less,* we would suffocate; if it were *slightly more,* spontaneous fires would erupt.

I could go on and on and on with additional facts. It should be clear why these discoveries shocked scientists and philosophers. These precisely balanced factors are: (1) contingent (it is easy to conceive of them being different; for example, that the mass of a proton or the expansion of the universe could have been quite different from what they actually are); (2) very, very improbable and balanced to an infinitesimally small degree; and (3) independently specfiable. Regarding this last point, for the longest time, scientists thought that these numbers could vary significantly with no impact on whether or not life could appear. But no longer. They now know that life-permitting universes have features that are precisely formulated within a range of billionths of a percentage point from what they actually are in the real world. Thus, the actual values fall within razor-thin ranges that are required for life to appear. These values are special (just as are the rules of a card game) quite independently of the fact that the universe's actual values correspond to them.

Think of it this way. Physicist Robin Collins imagines a scenario where human space travelers arrive on Mars and find a fully functioning, life-sustaining biosphere. When the astronauts enter the Martian biosphere, they find a panel that controls the environment.

> At the control panel they find that all the dials for its environment are set just right for life. The oxygen ratio is perfect; the temperature is seventy degrees; the humidity is fifty percent; there's a system for replenishing the air; there are systems for producing food, generating energy, and disposing of wastes. Each dial has a huge range of possible settings, and you can see if you were to adjust one or more of them just a little bit, the environment would go out of whack and life would be impossible.[5]

That's the universe we live in. There are over thirty independent dials (constants of nature, hard facts about the universe) — some estimate many, many more, and each has a wide range of alternate settings. Yet each dial is exactly set to precisely the correct setting so life can appear. It's no wonder that theoretical physicist Paul Davies acknowledged, "It is hard to resist the impression that the present structure of the universe, apparently so sensitive to minor alternation in the numbers, has been rather carefully thought out. . . . The seemingly miraculous concurrence of [these] numbers must remain the most compelling evidence for cosmic design."[6]

But as impressive as irreducible complexity and fine-tuning are, I believe there may be an even more powerful sort of design: *biological information*. To grasp the full force of this sort of design, we must first think for a moment about the SETI research program (the search for extra-terrestrial intelligence) begun in the early 1960s. Irrespective of what you think about SETI or its prospects for success, it is, nevertheless, a clearly formulated research project that has received millions of dollars of funding during the last half century.

Obviously, before SETI scientists look for intelligent life in outer space, they must first formulate criteria that will tell them when they have found it. And such they have. To grasp these criteria, we must distinguish among randomness, order, and information. Suppose we had a large pile of alphabet soup composed of numbers and letters of the alphabet, and I tossed a handful into the air resulting in this sequence scattered on my study desk: x, ½, an upside down g, %, +, @, xq17.5. This sequence is random and it has two characteristics: (1) *It is simple.* To generate a random sequence you would only have to give a computer two instructions: pick any symbol and repeat. (2) *It is not specific.* You tell the computer to pick *any* symbol and repeat with *any* symbol.

Now suppose I had 500 MEs in a row: ME ME ME . . . This sequence is ordered and it has four characteristics:

1. *It is simple.* To generate it, you would only have to give a computer three instructions: pick an M, then an E, and repeat.
2. *It is specific* (specifically pick an M then an E).
3. *It is iterative, or repeatable*—it consists in a unit repeated over and over (ME).
4. *The parts* (let's call each ME one part) *are prior to the whole* (which is just a sum of 500 MEs).

Here's a test you can perform to tell if the parts are prior to the whole: If you remove a part and it does not do anything to the rest of the whole, then the parts are prior to the whole. For example, if I removed the 75th ME, there would be a gap there, but the identity of the rest of the ME's would be unchanged. The 273rd ME would still be sitting there, quite indifferent to the presence or absence of the 75th ME.

If a SETI scientist received a signal from outer space that was random or ordered, the scientist would continue to sip his or her coffee. Such a signal would indicate nothing at all. But things change dramatically when one is confronted with the third category: information, for example, "John loves Mary." Information sequences have four characteristics:

1. *They are complex not simple.* To generate our sentence, one would have to tell a computer to produce fifteen specific symbols (including spaces) in a row. If we were dealing with the Gettysburg Address, the New Testament book of Romans, or the *Routledge Encyclopedia of Philosophy*, the complexity would be staggering.
2. *They are specific* (the computer must select very specific symbols).
3. *It is not simply composed of an iterative, repetitive unit.*
4. *The whole* (the thought expressed by the sentence that could be expressed in German or the precise sentence in English apt for expressing that thought) *is prior to the parts.*

Here's a test for determining when a whole is prior to its parts: If you remove or replace a part and the entire whole is destroyed. For example, if one replaces the "M" in "Mary" with the square root of minus one, you get unintelligible gibberish. If you replace that "M" with an "H" you have an entirely different whole—"John loves Hary."

The movie *Contact* based on a novel by Carl Sagan featured Jodie Foster as a SETI researcher, Dr. Eleanor "Ellie" Arroway. For a long time, Dr. Arroway only received random or simple ordered sequences. But one day she received a signal that told the world there was an intelligent designer behind the signal: one that represented the prime numbers from 2 to 101. It's easy to see that this signal satisfies the criteria for information. But why did Dr. Arroway correctly infer an intelligent designer/communicator as the cause of the signal? There's an assumption the SETI program makes that seems to me to be almost self-evident: information only comes from an intelligent agent/mind.

So far so good. But there's a punch line in all this: *Perhaps the single, most important discovery in twentieth-century biology was that living things contain a special molecule—DNA—that is composed not of order or randomness, but of information.* Indeed, the amount of information in the genetic code of a human being is more than all the information in all the books in the Library of Congress combined! Clearly, if the information in the prime numbers from 1 to 101—measly as it is—legitimately justifies an inference to an intelligent agent as its cause, then by parity of reasoning, an incredibly smart Intelligent Designer must stand behind the information in DNA. Note carefully that it is an intrinsic feature of information that indicates that it comes from intelligence. So if a critic of SETI claimed that given enough time, chance, and natural law, a signal bearing the prime numbers from 1 to 101 could easily be produced by natural processes, no one would take him seriously. If they did, then the entire rationale for SETI would vanish! Even if such an outcome *could* be produced naturally, it would be far more rational to conclude it came from intelligent life. The same sort of reasoning provides a fitting rejoinder to those who would make the same claim about the origin of information in DNA.

These considerations about beauty, irreducible complexity, specified complexity, and information have been defended in a more thorough, sophisticated way than I can do here. But for me, ordinary folk are correct in thinking that the existence of an Intelligent Designer is as plain as the nose on one's face, given the sort of world in which we live. In the remainder of this chapter, I want to share with you one further area of reflection that I believe provides grounds for the claim that we know there is a God: *various features of the moral life.*

## VARIOUS FEATURES OF THE MORAL LIFE

You don't have to be a rocket scientist to recognize that our society is in a state of moral chaos. The simple fact that Jerry Springer and his talk show competitors are such popular theaters of moral expression is enough to send shivers down the spine of anyone with an ounce of moral sensibility. This moral chaos should come as no surprise to anyone who acknowledges that there is a deep connection between the worldview of a culture and its moral beliefs and behaviors. The shift from a Judeo-Christian worldview to an atheistic, naturalistic one is what lies behind much of the moral chaos we now face. In April 1986, Steven Muller, the president of Johns Hopkins University, got it right when he warned that our crisis in moral values is due largely to the loss of a Judeo-Christian worldview and its replacement with secularism and naturalism.

Conversely, several features of the moral life and the objectivity of purpose in life are, in my view, best explained by the sort of monotheistic God the Bible describes and who creates human persons in His image:

- The fact that value properties exist and came to be exemplified in the world
- The imperatival force of moral law (they are commands, not mere facts or suggestions) that is best explained by a Moral Commander
- The existence and appropriateness of moral shame and guilt that goes beyond what is owed to other human persons
- The fact that human persons have incredibly high value compared with other entities in the cosmos and that they have equal value as human persons
- The fact that our faculties are such that we have knowledge of value

- The fact that our desire structure causes us to want to do what is right, even when it is not in our self-interests
- The fact that we are so constructed that we can actually make moral progress
- The fact that it is rational to adopt the moral point of view in the first place

Let's unpack some of these points a bit. We all know that *moral absolutes exist*. By a moral absolute I mean an objectively true moral prescription that, like the truths of math, science, and logic, we discover and do not invent. These prescriptions are true whether or not anyone believes them. "One ought not steal, murder, lie," "one ought not torture little babies for the fun of it," "one should be kind, just, and fair-minded" are examples of moral absolutes. If someone denies there are moral absolutes, claiming to subscribe to moral relativism, it is easy to show that the person is just posturing and not being honest. All you need to do is to find out what he or she deeply values, treat that issue as if it were arbitrary and relative, and you will see a absolutist come out of the closet every time!

For example, years ago I met a young man who claimed to be a relativist. After a bit of probing, I found out that he cared deeply for the environment. I then told him that I and four of my buddies had a monthly routine: We would each contribute fifty dollars to a kitty, buy a hundred gallon vat of sulfuric acid, drive to a local lake, dump in the acid, and see how many dead fish floated to the surface. The person whose guess was closest to the number of dead fish won the kitty. Well, you could see the blood vessels popping on his neck. He was enraged. I noted that from his body language, it seemed that he thought our monthly practice was, well, WRONG! This young man was a relativist in areas of his life in which relativism was convenient (for example, his sexual practices), but he was an absolutist when it came to the environment!

*The Nuremberg Trials* were a series of trials (1945–1949) held in Nuremberg, Germany, prosecuting leaders involved in the Nazi regime.

The most famous trial involved twenty-four key Nazi leaders charged with crimes against humanity. Individuals following the trial were shocked by how effective the Nazis' defense team was in arguing against the charges. How is that possible? What defense could be given for the indefensible? "The most telling defense offered by the accused was that they had simply followed orders or made decisions within the framework of their own legal system, in complete consistency with it, and that they therefore could not rightly be condemned because they deviated from the alien value system of their conquerors."[7]

The lawyers of the Nazis were simply appealing to a moral relativism to plead their case. After all, if morals are determined by culture, then how can you convict Germans for following the values, laws, and beliefs of German culture? If the Germans had won the war, there wouldn't even be a trial.

The trial came to a halt. How would the prosecution respond? The Chief Counsel of the United States, Robert Jackson, came up with an answer. The only way to judge any culture, he argued, was to appeal to a "law above the law." A "law above the law" transcends culture and applies to both the winners and losers of the war. The trial continued and justice was served. But from where does such an objective law come? Surely not from plasma or a cloud of electrons! Objective moral values do not come to us as a list of suggestions or simple statements of moral facts. No, they come as thundering imperatives, as commands: Do not murder! And so forth. That is what Jackson was saying. But commands only come from things with wills, that is, commanders. Thus, the best explanation for the "law above the law," something we all know is there, irrespective of what we claim in politically correct company, is that it represents the commands of a good, just, loving Commander.

Further, *when we violate this law, we feel a deep sense of shame and guilt that goes far beyond what we would experience in front of other human beings.* Somehow, we sense that we have done something wrong against—what? The universe itself or some abstract moral law is unconscious, impersonal, and it is not possible to be ashamed or have rational guilt feelings before it. No, the type of reasonable shame and guilt people feel the world over is best explained if there is a Personal Source of the absolute moral law and in front of whom we stand guilty.

Here's something else to think about. Consider the statement "The ball is hard." If this statement is true, it has implications for the way the world is. There is some specific ball that exists, and there is a real property, hardness, it possesses or exemplifies. Now consider the following value statements: "Mercy is a virtue." "Friendship is good." "Human beings have worth." Each of these statements is true and, common sensically, they ascribe non-natural, intrinsically normative value properties to mercy, friendship, and human beings. By a non-natural property I mean an attribute that is not a scientific, physical characteristic of physics or chemistry, for example, being a C fiber, having negative charge, being magnetic. By intrinsically normative I mean a property that is (1) valuable in and of itself and (2) something we ought to desire.

Now it is easy to explain how these properties could exist and "show up," as it were, in the spatio-temporal universe on a Christian view of things. For Christians, the most fundamental entity is not matter or energy or any other physical thing studied by science. It is God and among His attributes are those of moral and ontological excellence: wisdom, kindness, goodness, and the like. And God created the world to be a place where these values are exemplified and play a role in the course of things. Even if someone claims that value properties are forms that dwell, as it were, in Plato's heaven, it is wildly implausible to believe that if you start with a big bang, and the history of the cosmos amounts to the rearrangements of particles or waves according to the laws of chemistry and physics, that somehow these ordinary physical processes could reach up into Plato's heaven and pull these value-forms down into space and time. After all, science describes what is the case, not what ought to be the case; it can only give us descriptions, not prescriptions. Purely physical, natural states and laws amount to what is the case, and permit no reference at all to what ought to be the case. The simple fact is that *you can't get an "ought" from a mere "is."*

It is interesting to note that naturalist J. L. Mackie agreed and argued that *the emergence of moral properties would constitute a refutation of naturalism and evidence for theism*: "Moral properties constitute so odd a cluster of properties and relations that they are most unlikely to have arisen in the ordinary course of events without an all-powerful god to create them."[8]

Regarding our ability to know what has intrinsic value, if God exists and is as the the Bible depicts Him, then He made us to be able to know and live in light of real, objective, intrinsic values. But on a Darwinian atheistic account, the various brain mechanisms relevant to human behavior in general, and rational and ethical behavior in particular, are what they are because they aided (or at least did not hinder) their possessors in adapting to recurring problems over the long course of evolutionary history in feeding, reproducing, fighting, and fleeing, which in turn aided their possessors in the struggle for differential reproductive advantage. The blind processes of evolution selected sensory and mental faculties apt for interacting with the sense perceptible world under the demands of survival. However, the ability to be aware of intrinsic value goes far beyond sense experience (you can't see, hear, touch, taste, or smell a moral value) and, in any case, the accurate perception of value would be epiphenomenal (something is epiphenomenal if it is caused by something but does not itself cause anything; fire causes smoke but smoke is causally impotent) in a world whose successive states are governed entirely by the laws and states of physics. Thus, as evolutionary naturalist Michael Ruse notes,

Morality is a biological adaptation no less than are hands and feet and teeth. Considered as a rationally justifiable set of claims about an objective something, ethics is illusory. I appreciate that when somebody says "Love thy neighbor as thyself," they think they are referring above and beyond themselves. Nevertheless, such reference is truly without foundation. Morality is just an aid to survival and reproduction . . . and any deeper meaning is illusory.[9]

Penultimately, we all know that *there is a real difference between dysfunctional and properly functional behavior*. Child molestation, racist bigotry, and sociopathic narcissism are examples of the former, and behaving kindly, honestly, and lovingly are illustrations of the latter. Now, can a carburetor dysfunction? Of course it can. But suppose the Santa Ana winds blew a scattered pile of six leaves on my back porch. Would it make sense for me to say to my wife, "Honey, see the third leaf in the pile, the green one? That leaf is dysfunctional with respect to the whole pile of leaves."? It would not. Wherein lies the difference? When we say that the carburetor is dysfunctional, we mean that it isn't functioning the way it's supposed to function. And that means it isn't functioning the way it was designed to function. By contrast, since the green leaf was not designed to function a certain way in the pile of leaves—indeed, the entire pile was formed by chance and natural law—then there is no way that the leaf is supposed to function.

Thus, there is no such thing as a real dysfunctional/functional distinction for the leaf. It is only if there is a designer that the distinction makes sense. But we all know and act as if there really is such a distinction, and I believe this rational, accurate behavior makes the most sense if we were designed by God to function a certain way. In this case, there is such a thing as proper functioning and real dysfunctioning. By the way, this is why I think that far from counting as evidence against God's existence, evil actually provides evidence for God. How? Evil is when things aren't the way they are supposed to be or are the way they aren't supposed to be. You can't have real evil without there being a real way things are and are not supposed to be. But, again, this distinction is clear to me if there is a God. But if God does not exist, things just are. There is no way that things are supposed to be. Stuff happens and that's the end of the matter.

Finally, *Christian theism provides—and atheism utterly fails to provide—a satisfying answer to a question related to why we should care about the good life: Why should I be moral?* If I am trying to decide what my life plan will be—what I will care about, live for, spend my time seeking—and if I want my life plan to be rationally justified and sensible, then why is it reasonable for morality and the life of virtue to be a key part of my life plan? Why isn't it more reasonable to live a life of pure egoism, in which my own self-interests, defined any way I wish, are all that should matter to me, rationally speaking? Why should I not just pretend to care for morality when it is in my self-interests to do so, all the while not really adopting the moral point of view at all?

Christian theism says we should be moral because the moral life of virtue is real, we know some truths about it, and to live in disregard of the moral life is to live out of touch with a real and important part of reality made by God. Moreover, God made us to function best when we live the life of virtue. To live in disregard of morality and virtue is to live like a fish out of water, that is, to live contrary to our proper functioning. By contrast, naturalist atheism is too impoverished to be able to provide an answer to the question as to why I should be moral. Instead, its meager intellectual resources can only justify pure egoism, a grotesque philosophy of life in light of which even atheists cannot live consistently.

## SUMMARY AND PRELUDE

In the last two chapters, I have briefly provided some of the reasons why I take myself to know that God exists. But the arguments presented do not merely justify belief in God; they also provide information about what sort of being God is. From the arguments of the previous chapter (from the universe's beginning and dependency) we concluded that God is immaterial, capable of existing outside space and time, and possesses free will and, therefore, consciousness. From the design argument, we may conclude that God appreciates beauty, and He is extremely knowledgeable. From the moral argument, we may conclude that God is good and virtuous.

For three reasons, we should also conclude there is one personal God instead of many finite, polytheistic gods: (1) Finite gods (think of Greek gods or the multitude of Hindu gods) are capable of change, movement, and acting through a span of time and are, therefore, temporal; that is, they require the existence of time to exist. But the God who must exist to explain the facts of chapters 3 and 4 must exist outside of time (to be capable of causing time to begin). So a plurality of finite gods is ruled out. (2) If two explanations are equally successful, then all things being equal, one should prefer the simpler explanation. Solely for the sake of argument, let's assume that polytheism and monotheism are equally good explanations for the facts. Under these assumptions, simplicity considerations require us to prefer monotheism. (3) Any number of gods greater than one is explanatorily superfluous and impotent. To see this, take some arbitrary number of finite, polytheistic deities and call that number "n." Now, why are there n deities instead of n/2 or n+50, or . . . ? Any other number of finite deities will do just as well. If this is so, then no particular finite number over one will do a better job of explaining the facts than another number. Thus, any number greater than one is superfluous.

Besides the fact that there is one personal God, can we know anything more about God? The exciting answer is yes, and in the next chapter, we'll see why.

CHAPTER NINE

# THE EVIDENCE FOR JESUS

God exists. This much we know. And this is no small fact. It is, arguably, the single most important fact anyone could know. And knowledge of this fact should prod us to seek God with everything we have. But how do we go about such a thing? Where do we go from here?

## THREE CRITERIA FOR CHOOSING MY RELIGION

I think three criteria are central for choosing (and not losing!) one's religion:

*1. Does the depiction of the Supreme Being in a given religion harmonize with what we already know about God from creation,* for example, from the considerations about monotheism listed in chapters 3 and 4? If not, the religion is false; if so, it may be true. We do not bring a blank slate to the table when we assess various alleged revelation sources, and criterion (1) justifies religions that are forms of ethical monotheism. Note carefully, it is the explanatory demands of creation, not the Bible or some other alleged revelation, that justifies monotheism.

*2. Does that religion provide the most profound diagnosis of the human condition and the most adequate solution to that diagnosis?* Humans everywhere need help to overcome a threefold alienation (people are at odds with God, other people, and even themselves), relief from shame and guilt, meaning to life, hope for life with God and purposeful existence after death, guidance for living well, relational intimacy with God Himself, and empowerment to live the sort of life we all know we should live.

I cannot argue this point here, but while I admit that most religions have truths in them, the person, deeds, and teachings of Jesus of

Nazareth and His apostles, as inscripturated in the New Testament, simply tower over all other ideologies and religious systems. This is true both in the New Testament's intrinsic content and in its historical impact throughout generations. Regarding its intrinsic content, all one needs to do is to read the rich devotional, theological, and ethical literature in the history of Christianity to see that, when it accurately expounds the New Testament, this literature is without rival. Regarding historical influence, counter examples such as the Crusades, do not count as genuine counter examples because there are non-question-begging criteria—the teachings of the New Testament itself—to show that the counter examples are not genuine expressions of New Testament religion. Wherever genuine Christianity has thrived, human flourishing has flowered.

*3. Is the best explanation of both the origin and continued history of the religion one that employs supernatural activity on God's part?* Is the signature of the Divine on that religion? I am convinced by arguments from fulfilled Old Testament prophecy and historical evidence that the Bible is, indeed, a divine revelation and that Jesus of Nazareth is the risen Divine Son of God. The historical evidence for Jesus will occupy us in the remainder of this chapter.

How is it that a carpenter from obscure Nazareth commands the allegiance of hundreds of millions of people who have given and would give their lives to Him? The New Testament documents have an answer: Jesus was the very Son of God, that is, He was (and is) God the Son. Jesus was genuinely God and man, He was the incarnation of God, and He is the final, supreme revelation of God to the human race. He lived a sinless life, performed numerous miracles, and rose bodily from the dead three days after His crucifixion. I am convinced that this picture of Jesus is true, and I am going to present historical evidence to support that conviction. As I do, please keep something in mind. I will make reference from time to time to New Testament texts. However, I will not be assuming that the New Testament—or the Bible generally—is a true revelation from God, though I do believe that to be the case.

Instead, I will simply assume that the New Testament documents are first-century historical sources for the life of Jesus and the origins of Christianity. My task is to argue that these sources are solid and historically reliable.

## HISTORICAL EVIDENCE FOR JESUS

When we approach the topic of New Testament reliability, we are immediately confronted with a fact so significant that alone it shatters a widely held myth—that only simple-minded folk trust the New Testament and that intellectuals, on the other hand, are all convinced it is filled with legend. The fact to which I am referring is the simple truth that there are thousands of men and women with earned doctorates in history, New Testament studies, or first-century culture from world-class institutions who accept the reliability of the New Testament documents precisely because of (and not in spite of) their academic training. In fact, highly regarded intellectuals at elite universities who teach in this area of study are convinced by their investigation of the facts that the New Testament is reliable and that the traditional view of Jesus is true—for example (the universities in parentheses are where they teach), Richard Bauckham (University of St. Andrews, Scotland), James Dunn (University of Durham), Simon Gathercole (University of Aberdeen), Martin Hengel (University of Tubingen), Larry Hurtado (University of Edinburgh), Graham N. Stanton (Cambridge University), and N. T. Wright (former professor at Oxford). This does not prove the New Testament documents are historically reliable, but it does show that there must be a considerable case for their reliability, or else one would not find so many scholars, including many at the top of the field, who hold and have contended for this view. Let's look at some of the evidence.

### Evidence for Jesus Outside the New Testament

Roman and Greek historians during or shortly after Jesus' life were geographically distant from Judea and Galilee. Moreover, this location was considered to be a remote and unimportant outpost far, far away from Rome, so there was little interest in what happened there. And there were countless numbers of religious figures, social and political movements, great unrest and instability in Judea and Galilee, and little attention is paid to many key figures besides Jesus. Further, we must recall that much of ancient literature has been lost, so it is entirely plausible that Jesus was referred to more than He is in the documents we have.

In spite of all this and setting aside the New Testament documents, we have clear references to Jesus made by Roman, Jewish, and Greek historians. From these we get the following picture: Jesus was a Jewish teacher who had a group of disciples; He was a wonder worker of some sort, performing healings and exorcisms; He was rejected by the Jewish leaders and crucified by Pontius Pilate during the reign of Tiberius Caesar; the sky turned dark at the time of His crucifixion (the pagan historian Thallus explains this as an eclipse of the sun!); His followers claimed to have seen Him risen from the dead shortly after His crucifixion; and the Christian movement spread so rapidly that within a few decades it had taken root in Rome itself.[1] In AD 49, the Roman emperor Claudius expelled the Jews from Rome because they were disputing over "Chrestus," most likely because the preaching of Jesus in Roman synagogues created a large disturbance in Rome.

## The Time Factor

Let us use "*high Christology*" to refer to a picture of Jesus according to which He was God Incarnate, the miracle-working son of God who rose bodily from the dead; let's use "*low Christology*" to refer to a picture of Jesus according to which He was a mere man, though, of course, a charismatic leader and gifted teacher. The duration of time from Jesus' crucifixion in AD 33 until there is clearly a high Christology in the early church is too short for myth and legend to influence that portrait. The time factor is so short that it is implausible to disregard the early church's high Christology and its portraits of Jesus in the Gospels. Moreover, during this short time span, there were still plenty of friendly and hostile eyewitnesses to keep in check extravagant claims about Jesus. And the high Christological view of Jesus begins around the geographic area in which Jesus lived and ministered, not hundreds of miles away. This, too, provides grounds for trusting the New Testament picture of Jesus. Let me elaborate on these points.

Secular, classic historian A. N. Sherwin-White—an expert in the times prior to and during Jesus' day—claims that even though Roman and Greek historical sources are heavily biased and removed from the events they discuss by as much as two centuries, historians still use those sources successfully to reconstruct what actually happened. He also says that for the Gospels to be legendary, the rate of legendary development would have to be "unbelievable." Using Herodotus as a test case, Sherwin-White argues that *a span of even two generations is too short to allow legendary tendencies to sweep away the hard core of historical facts*.[2] Given this fact, let's consider the first three gospels: Matthew, Mark, and Luke.

Two facts are virtually beyond dispute: (1) The same person wrote Luke and Acts (based on style, grammar, vocabulary, themes, and so on). (2) Acts was written after Luke, and Luke was written after Matthew and Mark. It follows that if we can date the book of Acts, Luke should be dated earlier and Matthew and Mark earlier still. In my opinion, there is overwhelming evidence that *Acts should be dated around AD 60–62*.[3]

Here are three reasons for this dating:

1. Acts ends abruptly with Paul in prison in Rome and with no indication of what happened to him after his release. The ending of Acts has a distinctive feel of having been written at the same time of the events it recalls—Paul's imprisonment from AD 60–62.

2. The author of Luke and Acts focuses on events in and around Jerusalem more than the other gospels. For example, Jesus' resurrection appearances in Luke occur in Judea, but the ones in Matthew and Mark take place in Galilee. The city of Jerusalem and the church there play a prominent role in Acts. Jerusalem was surrounded by Gentile armies in

AD 66 and destroyed in AD 70, yet Acts makes no mention of this. The silence of Acts is even stranger when we realize that in Luke, Jesus predicts that Gentiles will surround and destroy Jerusalem. For the sake of argument, suppose the author made up this saying and placed it on Jesus' lips. What would be the purpose of such a fabrication if the "fulfillment" happened and was not duly noted? The only sensible explanation to me is that Acts was written before AD 66.

3. Acts is careful to record the martyrdoms of figures in the early church (for example, Stephen). The three key figures in Acts are James, Peter, and Paul. All three were martyred in the early to mid 60s, yet there is no mention of any of this in Acts. This is best explained if Acts was completed before the early 60s.

Given a date of AD 60–62, Luke should be dated from the early to late 50s (Luke was earlier than Acts, but no evidence exists that the two books were written in a continuous fashion; it is entirely possible that there was a time gap between the completion of Luke and the beginning of Acts), and Matthew and Mark from the early 40s to mid 50s.[4] And, of course, the material contained in these gospels was in wide circulation years before it was written down.

Besides the Gospels, we have thirteen of Paul's Epistles that were written over a sixteen-year period from AD 49–65. When we examine these letters, two facts become obvious: (1) Paul's view of Jesus is static; that is, there is no evolutionary development from a low Christology in his earlier letters to a high Christology is his later letters. Throughout this time period, Paul's view of Jesus remained constant. (2) Paul's Christology was uniformly high. He knows nothing of a mere sage or charismatic leader. From the beginning, Jesus is the incarnation of God Himself, a miracle worker, the Savior of the world who rose bodily from the dead. It is, therefore, a hard historical fact that sometime before AD 49, Paul's view of Jesus was solidified.

Some critics attempt to marginalize Paul by claiming he was in serious conflict with Peter such that Paul's Christology is not representative of the early church. However, this claim is a significant exaggeration for which there is no sufficient evidence. Peter and Paul's confrontation about certain issues (for example, separating from the Gentiles) hardly justifies this hasty generalization. *There is no evidence at all that Paul and Peter were involved in a major rift in the early church.* Moreover, not more than four years after the Crucifixion, Paul himself checked out his gospel and Christology with the early leaders of the Jerusalem church (Peter, John, James) to make sure it was in harmony with the rest of the early church (compare Galatians 1–2). And he explicitly states that his Christology was authoritative teaching in the early church that he received from others (1 Corinthians 15:1-7; Romans 1:1-4). This was entirely in keeping with the communitarian worldview of the Ancient Near East. That culture did not value Western individualism, so Lone Ranger Christianity—Christianity was started by the rogue Paul who individualistically stood by himself quite apart from the rest of the early Christian community—is a myth. *All this means that the early church had adopted a high Christology sometime before AD 49.*

But there's more. The letters of Paul and the others in the New Testament were written in Greek for Greek speakers in the Gentile world. The early Jewish followers of Jesus in the Jerusalem area during the first decade after AD 33 primarily spoke Aramaic and Hebrew (though many also knew Greek). Scholars have discovered various *hymns* and *creeds*—ranging from two to seven or eight verses—embedded in Pauline and other New Testament letters (for example, 1 Corinthians 15:3-8; Philippians 2:5-11). These texts are written in the form of Hebrew poetry, they translate easily from the Greek back into Aramaic, they contain Aramaic, Jewish phrases, and the vocabulary is sometimes different than the way Paul (Peter, John) typically speak.

These facts have led most New Testament scholars to the view that these are early hymns used in worship services and instruction among Aramaic-speaking Jewish followers of Jesus in the first decade after the Crucifixion—most likely, within three years—in and around Jerusalem. Paul and the others translate them into Greek and incorporate them into their letters. And get this: Every one of them is about Jesus Christ and they exalt Him to the status of God! These texts show two things: (1) The early Jewish Christian community had a high Christology at a very early date; within no longer than three to five years after the Crucifixion, Jesus was being worshipped by monotheistic Jews as God Almighty, and miracle-working deeds and the bodily Resurrection were ascribed to Jesus. (2) This early, high Christology was present in the very soil where Jesus was alleged to have performed miracles and risen from the dead. That is, it was present exactly where numerous friendly and hostile eyewitnesses lived!

New Testament scholar Larry Hurtado claims that within the first few months and, perhaps, within the first few weeks, these early Jewish converts not only accepted beliefs about Jesus as being God, they also engaged in devotional practices and worship that exalted Jesus to the status of being coequal with the Old Testament God of Israel. And Martin Hengel said that these hymns to Christ as God "grew out of the early services of the [primitive Jewish Christian] community after Easter, i.e., [they are] as old as the community itself."[5] Hymns were sung to Jesus; prayers were offered through and to Him; His name was called upon in healing and exorcism practices, even though the Old Testament explicitly commands that one call only on the name of the God of Israel; and Jesus was viewed as the Lord who stands in the middle of and unites the early community just as the God of Israel had done before Jesus' coming.[6] And all this is present from the earliest days after Jesus' crucifixion!

But there's even more!

1. It is beyond question that Paul wrote the book of Galatians and, in it, he states clearly that he received his high view of Jesus and his understanding of the gospel message at a time around AD 34 or 35. Paul states that he never deviated from this historical understanding and that it was identical to the views of the other apostles. Thus, *a high Christology was present within a year after the Crucifixion.*[7]

2. Acts records the history of the early church. According to Acts, chapters 1–12 are quite different from chapters 13–28. The former

feature Peter, and his speeches are delivered mostly to Aramaic, Hebrew-speaking Jews at a time when Christianity was still in its infancy. The latter feature Paul, and his speeches are delivered mostly to Greek-speaking Gentiles in subsequent years.

Now here's what I find interesting: Cambridge New Testament scholar G. N. Stanton discovered that the grammar, literary style, theological motifs and emphases, tone, and use of the Old Testament are different in Acts 1–12 compared to 13–28.[8] Moreover, the speeches in 1–12 contain a number of Semitic phrases and other features that indicate it is a Greek translation from an early Aramaic source. *This is exactly what one would expect if these narratives, particularly the speeches, were historically accurate.* Why? Because Peter is the speaker in Acts 1–12 and he is allegedly addressing Jews in Aramaic, whereas Paul is the speaker in Acts 13–28 and he is addressing Gentiles in Greek. This discovery by Stanton increases our confidence in the historical reliability and early dating of the speeches in Acts 1–12. And they express a high Christology.

3. Royce Gruenler has applied what is called *the criterion of dissimilarity* to the sayings (and actions) of Jesus with an interesting result.[9] The criterion of dissimilarity says that *if a parallel to a saying of Jesus can be found in the Jewish community in which Jesus lived or in the early church He founded (as evidenced by the New Testament materials besides the Gospels), then Jesus did not say it.* But if a saying passes this test, then it is so utterly unique (not bearing an analogy to sayings in the Jewish culture or the early church), that Jesus most likely said it, absent other reasons to suspect the saying. Now this criterion has always seemed crazy to me if it is taken as a necessary condition for accepting a saying as authentically coming from Jesus. Why? It drives a ridiculous wedge between Jesus and His culture—He can never agree with ideas in His culture—and a wedge between Jesus and His followers—He can't say anything that stuck with them, which they reiterate in their writings! The criterion is too harsh, too skeptical. If it were applied to historical figures besides Jesus, it would destroy much of what we hold to be accurate history.

But precisely because it is so skeptical, it seems to me that it is a sufficient condition for historical accuracy. That is, if a saying of Jesus passes this test, then it is irrational to treat the statement as a fabrication unless there are extremely strong independent reasons for doing so.

Gruenler uses this test to isolate a core of fifteen sayings of Jesus, ranging from one to twenty verses, that even the most radical skeptic must accept on pain of losing credibility as an honest historian. These core sayings accurately reflect the mind of the historical Jesus who actually lived. So, what do these sayings tell us? Jesus took Himself to be greater than Moses, Abraham, David, or anyone who had preceded Him. Even more, He took Himself to stand in the authority—indeed, the very place—of God, embodying in His person the power, presence, and authority of God's own kingdom, welcoming outcasts in God's name and offering forgiveness of sins, which only God could do. He also received worship and saw Himself as a divine-like figure who would judge the world—and each and every person in it—at the end of the age. So a high Christology goes back to Jesus of Nazareth Himself.

## Oral Tradition in First-Century Jewish Culture

Besides extrabiblical data and the time factor, another important issue in my confidence in the historical reliability of the New Testament documents, particularly the Gospels, resides in the nature and role of oral tradition in Jesus' day. Jesus lived in a predominantly oral culture, one which formulates, preserves, and passes down to subsequent generations its history, key events, central narrative, and core values largely through memorization and oral performance. Detailed studies have been done on such cultures, and we have learned that in contrast with contemporary Western culture, people were capable of memorizing a lot of information easily and passing it on carefully and without significant change.

Given that the materials about Jesus were preserved and passed on in an orally skilled culture during the ten to twenty years from Jesus' death until the first gospel was written, these materials would have been carefully preserved by people who were capable of such preservation. I find this to be powerful evidence for the historical reliability of the Gospels. However, there are four additional facts about this oral preservation that cement the Gospels' reliability. For one thing, the recollections of the early Christians of Jesus' teachings and deeds "were not individual memories but *collective* ones—confirmed by other eyewitnesses and burned into their minds by the constant retelling of the story. Thus, both the repetition of the stories about Jesus and the verification of such by other eyewitnesses served as checks and balances to the apostles' accuracy."[10] *The material about Jesus was recited in oral performances when the early church gathered for worship and instruction, and it was the collective memory of those who knew Jesus. The Gospels were not put together as a hodgepodge of the isolated memories of people scattered throughout the Ancient Near East.*

Second, the material was memorized, preserved, and circulated in the very area where Jesus had lived and ministered and, thus, among eyewitnesses. These eyewitnesses would have provided a check on the tradition when it went astray. Perhaps the leading expert on oral tradition is James D. G. Dunn. According to Dunn, the fact that a community of Jesus' followers gathered to preserve and spread this material in the first place, indicates that it was the material that formed the community and not vice versa:

> If, as I have argued, it was the impact of what Jesus said and did that first brought the disciple group together as disciples, it would follow that the tradition [about Jesus] that gave them their identity as a group of disciples would be treasured by them, particularly during the period of Jesus' continuing mission, during which . . . much of the tradition began to take its enduring shape.[11]

In other words, the oral tradition began during Jesus' ministry, was initially formulated by His disciples, and they would have served as guardians for preserving the accuracy of that tradition. *So the early origin of this oral tradition, along with the role of general eyewitnesses in the area and the influence of the apostles on the tradition,* count heavily in favor of its historical reliability.

Reference to the apostles provides a fitting occasion to mention the third point. According to Dunn, in oral cultures generally, *certain designated and recognized people were entrusted with the responsibility of performing/reciting and preserving the community's tradition.*[12] And in the Jewish culture of Jesus' day, it was customary for a rabbi to select certain pupils from among his students to designate them as authorities and give them the responsibility of memorizing his teachings/deeds and passing them on unchanged after the rabbi's death. These designated pupils were given the responsibility of settling disputes about the exact nature of the rabbi's teachings after his death. For several reasons, it seems clear that Jesus intentionally conformed to this pattern: (1) He was called "rabbi" and had pupils like other rabbis. (2) This broad pattern in rabbi/pupil relationships explains why Jesus selected twelve apostles in the first place. Indeed, their job was to serve as authorities in the community in a manner precisely parallel to the broader cultural pattern. (3) Designated rabbinic students had a specific way of referring to how they handled the tradition about the rabbi. They would "deliver over" to others what they had "received." The phrases "delivered over" and "received" were technical terms used to refer to the careful dissemination of the rabbi's sayings and deeds. But this is precisely how the apostles referred to their dissemination of the Jesus tradition (1 Corinthians 15:3-8; Galatians 2:1-10; Colossians 2:7; 1 Thessalonians 2:13). And Paul Barnett notes other key terms from the broader rabbinic practice that are used in the Gospels: "Jesus was called 'rabbi' and 'followed' by 'disciples' who 'sat at his feet,' 'learned from him,' took his 'yoke' upon them."[13]

(4) It is highly probable that the apostles took notes and used written compilations of these notes alongside the oral tradition that would serve as an additional check for preserving its accuracy. For one thing, we now know that it was customary for disciples of a rabbi to do just this—engage in note taking. These notes were sometimes taken on

wax tablets. Tax collectors in Jesus' day often knew three languages and, in fact, had their own form of shorthand, so it may be no accident that Jesus selected a tax collector (Matthew) to be among the Twelve. It is also significant that the early Jesus movement and its transmission of the Jesus tradition flow from urban Jerusalem and not rural Galilee. This reinforces the idea that a rabbi/pupil relationship is the correct context for understanding the Jesus tradition, along with the note taking that was a part of rabbinic dissemination. Further, the Jesus tradition was passed on in the first decade or so in a synagogue-based, Jewish context. In such a context, public reading of Jesus' sayings and deeds would have been important, and as with the synagogue, written texts of Jesus' sayings and deeds would have arisen quickly to be read along with oral recitation.

The cumulative weight of this evidence provides substantial grounds for taking the Gospels to be reliable historical sources. Interestingly, when we examine the Gospels, we find exactly what one would expect if Jewish oral tradition and note taking form the background prior to their writing. Much of Jesus' teaching is in poetic form in which there is parallelism, alliteration, and other techniques that aid memorization. In fact, it has been estimated that 80 percent of Jesus' teaching is in rhythmic, easily memorized poetic form. In addition, there are sixty-four examples of easy-to-memorize threefold sayings (for example, "ask, seek, knock"). All this provides hard evidence for the historical reliability of the Gospels.

### Miscellaneous Features of the Gospels That Underscore Their Historical Accuracy

It has always impressed me that the Gospels and Acts were written by people who knew the difference between fact and fiction, who attempted to write accurate history that recorded what actually happened, and who were quite capable of success—and actually did succeed—in this aim. In several places in the New Testament, the importance of eyewitness testimony is acknowledged (for example, Luke 1:1-4; John 21:24-25;

Acts 1:21-26; 1 Corinthians 15; Galatians 1; 2 Peter 1:16; 1 John 1:1-4). And in these and other places, the New Testament writers tell us that they are being careful to record the exact truth of what happened. Of course they could have been lying or incompetent, but I believe there is considerable evidence that they intended to record the truth and did a good job of doing so. There are at least four lines of evidence for this claim.[14]

*1. The inclusion of self-damaging or embarrassing details.* Historians agree that if a document contains details that are embarrassing to or harm the author's purpose for writing, then the details are likely to be historically reliable since there would be strong motivation to exclude them. The Gospels have numerous passages that cast doubt on Jesus' divinity, character, or competence and make the leaders of the early church look like fools. For example, Jesus' baptism by John (John only baptized sinners, yet Jesus was supposed to be sinless), the betrayal by Judas (Why would Jesus seemingly incompetently pick someone like Judas? Why would a close associate turn against Jesus?), Peter's denial (this makes the leader of the early church look like an immoral coward and eviscerates his moral authority), Jesus' crucifixion (which was reserved for criminals).

Paul Rhodes Eddy and Gregory A. Boyd add these (all references are to the gospel of Mark): Jesus' own family questioned His sanity (3:21); Jesus could not perform many miracles in His own town (6:5); Jesus was rejected by people in His hometown (6:3); some thought Jesus was in collusion with, and even possessed by, the Devil (3:22,30); Jesus at times seemed to rely on common medicinal techniques (7:33; 8:23); Jesus' healings were not always instantaneous (8:22-25); Jesus' disciples were not always able to exorcise demons (9:18), and Jesus' own exorcisms were not always instantaneously successful (5:8); Jesus seemingly suggested He was not "good" (10:18); Jesus associated with people of ill repute (2:14-16); Jesus was sometimes rude to people (7:27); Jesus seemed to disregard Jewish laws, customs, and cleanliness codes (2:23-25); Jesus often spoke and acted in culturally "shameful" ways (3:31-35);

Jesus cursed a fig tree for not having any fruit when He was hungry, even though it was not even the season for bearing fruit (11:13-14); the disciples who were to form the foundation of the new community consistently seemed dull, obstinate, and eventually cowardly (8:32-33; 10:35-37; 14:37-40,50). There are answers to these cases, but that is not the point. That these are even present significantly increases the credibility of the Gospels.

**2. The omission of relevant information and the inclusion of irrelevant information.** If the Gospels were largely legendary creations by the church from AD 50–85 (when they were written; I am including the latest dating possible for the first three gospels), then how would the authors or their communities decide what to create and what not to create? Clearly, they would invent material and place it into the Gospel narratives that met the needs of the churches during the time (AD 50–85) when they were invented. For example, if believers were starting to die (and Jesus had not returned yet), then — on this mythological view — sayings of Jesus were invented and placed on His lips that addressed this situation by giving hope to those who died before the Second Coming.

But there are two problems with this scenario, and each points to the historical reliability of the Gospels. First, there are a number of important issues facing the churches from AD 50–85 for which it would have been wonderful to have (an invented) saying of Jesus, yet Jesus is strangely silent about them: what "Jewish" Gentiles must do to be accepted into the new community, the nature of spiritual gifts and how they were to be used in assembly meetings, how congregations were to be organized and run, the role of women in the early church, what attitude disciples should have toward meat sacrificed to idols, several ministries of the Holy Spirit, and church-state relations. Perhaps the single biggest omission is the presence of "Paulinisms" (statements that reflect the way Paul thought and spoke). Many of the churches from AD 50–85 were planted by Paul and the others were heavily influenced by him. This means that their way of thinking and talking about their faith would be influenced by Paul. But the Jesus of the Gospels, while not contradicting the teachings of Paul, does not sound like him. If many of Jesus' sayings were inventions of the early church, the Jesus of the Gospels should think and sound a lot like Paul, but He does not.

Not only is there a lack of teaching by Jesus that was relevant to what the church was facing in AD 50–85, there is the presence of a lot of material that was, frankly, irrelevant to what they were facing. In this case, there would be no motive for including them in the Gospels besides the fact that they were things Jesus had actually said and, even though they were not particularly helpful to their pressing issues, the church retained them in the Gospels because they were accurate: Jesus' attitude of favor toward Israel and its privileged place in God's plan, Jesus' use of "the son of Man" and parables, His controversies with the Pharisees about distinctively Jewish issues (for example, keeping the Sabbath).

**3. The presence of Aramaisms and personal names.** The Gospels were written in Greek predominantly to those who spoke that language. But Jesus most likely spoke Aramaic (though He also knew and on occasion used Greek). Now, there are a number of occasions when an Aramaic phrase occurs in the Gospels, and this most likely is retained even though the Greek reader would not know what it meant because it was historically accurate. There is no other good explanation for their presence. For example, *"talitha koum"* (Mark 5:41), *"Ephphatha"* (Mark 7:34), *"Golgotha"* (Mark 15:22). When Jesus says that the Pharisees "strain out a gnat but swallow a camel" (Matthew 23:24), He was making a play on Aramaic words (the Aramaic for "gnat" is *galma* and for "camel" is *gamla*). There are a number of other cases where this occurs.

There are two things of significance about the widespread use of personal names in the Gospels and Acts. For one thing, it is a feature of legend that eyewitnesses to events contained therein are not usually named, but the Gospels name them quite frequently. Second, Richard Bauckham recently published an incredible study of the personal names in the Gospels, and he has identified two facts that, he claims (correctly, in my view), provide strong evidence that the Gospels are factual accounts written by eyewitnesses.[15]

Here's the first fact: Historians have discovered grocery lists, letters, and other documents from Jesus' day and, on that basis, have developed a database of hundreds and hundreds of individuals' names, along with the frequency of use each name enjoyed in the culture. That frequency is different for the strictly Palestinian Jewish community, the Diaspora (the scattered Gentile Jewish) community, and the strictly Gentile community. Incredibly, Bauckham discovered that the relative frequency of the various names used in the Gospels corresponds accurately with the three thousand names from the Palestinian Jewish community in the database, but not with the other two communities. If the names were inventions prior to or at the time of the Gospels' writing, then the name frequency should correspond to the latter two communities (since they were the location where and provided the context for the writing of the Gospels). On the other hand, if the Gospels were eyewitness accounts of Jesus' life as it unfolded in the Palestinian Jewish setting, one would expect the names to refer to real people and the frequency of usage to correspond to that of the Palestinian Jewish community. And that is what we have discovered.

Here's the second fact: Since there were more people than names, a way had to be developed to distinguish several people with the same name, say, "Simon." Several strategies were, in fact, developed (for example, by adding the father's name — "John son of Zacharias"). When compared to the database, the strategies used in the Gospels and the frequency of their usage fit and only fit the Palestinian Jewish community. According to Bauckham, all this evidence indicates the implausibility of random invention of the names and underscores the eyewitness nature of the Gospels.

*4. Archaeological confirmation of irrelevant details in the Gospels.* Over and over again, archaeologists have made discoveries that confirm completely irrelevant, "picky little" details in Gospel stories. If one is writing a legend, one does not take pains to get small details accurate, especially if they have nothing to do with the reason for writing the account in the first place. Such confirmation shows that the Gospel writers were trying to get it right, even down to the level of insignificant details. Here are two examples of this selected from a much larger pool of candidates.

In John 5:1-15, Jesus is supposed to have healed a man at a place called the pool of Bethesda. The passage says that the pool was surrounded by five porticos (rows of columns supporting a roof). Until the 1890s, critics dismissed the entire narrative on the grounds that no one had ever discovered the pool. But, then, archaeologists discovered the pool, and it had exactly five porticoes, just as John said.

Here's a second example: The author of Luke and Acts was concerned about the geographical area of Jerusalem and surrounding Judea as opposed to Galilee. Thus, the resurrection appearances in Luke occur in Judea and the Galilean appearances are omitted. Accordingly, Luke is familiar with and interested in customs and events in Judea. Now, in Luke 7:11-17, the story is told of Jesus raising the widow of Nain's son from the dead when He comes upon the funeral procession. It is significant that Jesus speaks to the mother first, and then goes back to the coffin. This corresponds exactly to the custom in Galilee (the province containing Nain). In Galilean funeral processions, people walked in front of the casket. But in Judea, people walked behind the casket. If the account were a fabrication, one would expect the funeral to be described according to Judean practices. But it is not. Rather, it is accurately described, and this is what one would expect if the account were historically correct.

I wish I had time to discuss the accuracy of the book of Acts. There are literally hundreds of cases in which tiny details in Acts accurately capture geographical details, local customs, titles given to local governors, army units, major routes, descriptions of agricultural data, length of time to travel from one place to another, typical weather conditions of different locations, topology, and on and on and on.[16] Acts is one of the most accurate pieces of historical writing we have from the ancient world.

## THE RESURRECTION OF JESUS FROM THE DEAD

I close this chapter with reflections on what I consider to be not only the very heart of Christianity, but also an event so well attested that only personal or philosophical bias could justify its rejection. I am speaking of Jesus' bodily resurrection from the dead three days after His execution. I am particularly impressed with four lines of evidence for this fact. First, the length of time from Jesus' death until there was widespread belief in His resurrection can be dated to within five years, and many scholars would say a few months or even weeks, after the Crucifixion. *There is not enough time for legend to develop.* Some of the time factors cited above are relevant here. But I cannot resist adding one more consideration. Atheists and Christians agree that Paul wrote 1 Corinthians. Here is one of Paul's assertion from 1 Corinthians 15:3-8:

> For I delivered to you as of first importance what I also received, that Christ died for our sins according to the Scriptures, and that He was buried, and that He was raised on the third day according to the Scriptures, and that He appeared to Cephas, then to the twelve. After that He appeared to more than five hundred brethren at one time, most of whom remain until now, but some have fallen asleep; then He appeared to James, then to all the apostles; and last of all, as to one untimely born, He appeared to me also. (NASB)

There are three key facts about this text: (1) It is preceded by the "deliver to," "received" phrases that indicate the transmission of memorized material to be treated along the lines of oral tradition. (2) It is usually dated in the mid 30s because of the oral formula, the fact that this is in the form of a Hebrew poem and translates back into Aramaic nicely (making it an early hymn/creed), the fact that the primitive Jewish "Cephas" and "the twelve" are used instead of "Peter" and "the apostles," which was more typical as time went on, and the fact that the term "sins" is in the plural, yet Paul usually uses "sin" in the singular (indicating that this is a text given to Paul, not one of his own writing). (3) Jesus appeared to five hundred people at once, many of whom were still alive and, by clear indication, could and should be interrogated by folks who had doubts.

The second and third facts are the empty tomb of Jesus and the resurrection appearances to the disciples. In his hernia-inducing, 817-page defense of the Resurrection, N. T. Wright argues that one cannot explain the origin of Christianity, especially the belief that Jesus had risen, without both facts.[17] Given pagan and Jewish beliefs about life after death in those days, neither by itself can explain the early belief that Jesus was raised. If the empty tomb was a fact but there were no resurrection experiences, then the early church would have been taken to indicate that Jesus' body was stolen, and His crucifixion and empty tomb would have been seen as a puzzle and a tragedy. If the resurrection appearances had occurred without the empty tomb, they would have been construed as visions or hallucinations. Let me say a bit more about each fact.

Several lines of evidence convince me that Jesus' tomb was, indeed, empty three days after His burial. (1) The Gospel narratives are simple, unadorned, and do not exhibit later reflection. (2) The fact that women are alleged to be the first to witness and bear testimony to the empty tomb and to have undergone resurrection appearances simply must be accurate. A woman's testimony was considered worthless in those days and, indeed, a woman could not testify in a court of law unless certain circumstances occurred (for example, a male from her family would back her testimony). The presence of women as the first witnesses would be highly counterproductive; it would raise doubt and suspicion among those who were being evangelized, and it represented an embarrassment to the early church. The only rational explanation for their presence is that this is what actually happened. (3) The description of Jesus' tomb comports with archaeological finds of tombs around Jerusalem in Jesus' day, and Joseph of Arimathea is most likely a real historical figure (you don't invent a name for someone in the Sanhedrin because everyone knew who the members of this body were; being a rich man, Joseph would have had such a tomb, and the tomb would have been like those discovered by archaeologists). (4) The earliest Jewish response to the Resurrection proclamation was to say Jesus' body was stolen, a response that grants the empty tomb. (5) In Jesus' day, at least fifty tombs of holy men were sites of yearly veneration by the rabbi's/priest's followers, yet Jesus' tomb was never used this way. This could only be taken as a sign of disrespect for Jesus, unless, of course, the early church did not associate Jesus' tomb with the place where Jesus was. Indeed, the early church did have such times of veneration, but they did not venerate Jesus' character or teachings. They celebrated the fact that He had been killed! This is odd, unless they did not think He was still dead. The veneration took place, of course, in the regular practice of baptism and the Lord's Supper, both of which celebrate the Resurrection.

Regarding the resurrection appearances, almost all scholars agree that the disciples had "resurrection appearances of Jesus" after His death. They were obviously sincere in their proclamation of Jesus' resurrection, they clearly did not invent what they preached, they suffered lives of hardship, they were martyred for their belief, and they subjected themselves to damnation in hell if they fabricated something that Jehovah God had done and falsely and intentionally bore witness to a lie. Remember, they believed in the existence of hell and the God of the Old Testament, and they were not about to lie in this way. People often die for mistaken beliefs, but that is not what we have here. We have people dying for something they saw, heard, and physically touched. That's very different.

These experiences could not reasonably have been hallucinations. For one thing, Jesus appeared to several groups of people, including five hundred folks at once, and these people were not anticipating Jesus' showing up after He was killed. There was no wish fulfillment involved. And if the early followers of Jesus had, in fact, undergone hallucination, they would never have interpreted them as experiences of a resurrected person. Here's why: In those days, it was universally believed that there was one and only one resurrection at the end of the age at which time everyone was raised from the dead all at once. There was no concept of a solo resurrection by an individual prior to that end-time event. So they would never have thought of the category of "resurrection" to interpret their hallucinatory experiences. Not only that, but there were other categories understood to be quite distinct from "resurrection" that they would have used to interpret "experiences of Jesus" after His death: resuscitations (the individual comes back to life in a mortal body that will die again, whereas the end-time resurrection involves an immortal body) and translations directly to heaven (as they believed had happened to Enoch), which were considered to be entirely different from a resurrection. In my view, the best explanation for these experiences is that Jesus had actually risen from the dead and appeared to various individuals and groups.[18]

There is an additional line of evidence for Jesus' resurrection that serves, as it were, double duty. It not only provides additional evidence, but it helps to answer the "So what?" question. I am referring to the fact that for two thousand years, millions of pilgrims have encountered the risen Jesus and had their lives transformed as a result. If you have not already done so, you should perform a devotional experiment in which you place your trust in Jesus, cast yourself on Him and His kindness, and seek Him with all your heart. Begin to attempt to do what He taught, and you will begin to see the power of His presence and kingdom manifest itself in, through, and around you. This will be the final confirmation that a life of discipleship unto the luminous Nazarene is, indeed, entrance into the Way, the Truth, and the Life.[19]

# PART FOUR

# GUARANTEEING A FUTURE FOR THE CHRISTIAN MIND

# CHAPTER TEN

# RECAPTURING THE INTELLECTUAL LIFE IN THE CHURCH

Saint Paul tells us that the church—not the university, the media, or the public schools—is the pillar and support of the truth (1 Timothy 3:15). But you would never know it by actually examining our local church practices week by week or by observing the goals and objectives set by many parachurch ministries. We evangelicals need to ask ourselves three very important and painful questions.

First, why is our impact not proportionate to our numbers? If the evangelical community is even one-third the size polls tell us it is, we should be turning this culture upside down. Second, why are ministers no longer viewed as the intellectual and cultural leaders in their communities that they once were? Compared to pastors of the past, contemporary ministers have lost much of their authority among both unbelievers and the members of their own flocks. Third, how is it possible for a person to be an active member of an evangelical church for twenty or thirty years and still know next to nothing about the history and theology of the Christian religion, the methods and tools required for serious Bible study, and the skills and information necessary to preach and defend Christianity in a post-Christian, neopagan culture?

I cannot offer a full response to these questions here, even if I were adequate for the task (which I am not). But forty years of ministry have convinced me of this: *Among a small handful of factors foundational to such a response is the hostility or indifference to the development of an intellectual life in the way we go about our business in the church.* Having planted two churches and four Campus Crusade ministries from scratch, pastored in two other congregations, and spoken in hundreds of churches during the last quarter century, I have become convinced that we evangelicals neither value nor have a strategy for developing every member of our congregations to one degree or another as a Christian thinker. To convince yourself of this you need only look regularly at the types of books that show up on the Christian booksellers' top-ten list. Since the 1960s, we have experienced an evolution in what we expect a local church pastor to be. Forty years ago he was expected to be a resident authority on theology and biblical teaching. Slowly this gave way to a model of the pastor as the CEO of the church, the administrative and organizational leader. Today the ministers we want are Christianized pop therapists who are entertaining to listen to.

In the midst of all this, the church has become primarily a hospital to soothe empty selves instead of a war college to mobilize and train an army of men and women to occupy territory and advance the kingdom until the King returns. Of course, the church should actually be *both* hospital and war college and, in fact, much, much more. But there is no question that we are not succeeding in mobilizing such an army and training them with the intellectual and spiritual skills necessary to enter deeply and profoundly into the spiritual life and to destroy speculations and every lofty thing raised up against the knowledge of God. A church incompetent cannot effectively be a church militant. And make no mistake, like it or not, we are in a war for the hearts, minds, and destinies of men and women all around us.

Because the stakes are so high, we simply cannot afford to tolerate this situation any longer. I am not suggesting that we evangelicals are not making progress or doing well in a number of areas. But neither is my head in the sand. We must recommit ourselves to developing richer, deeper, more powerful churches for Jesus Christ and the good of others and ourselves. And as philosopher Roger Trigg points out, it is a matter of common sense that "Any commitment, it seems, depends on two distinct elements. It presupposes certain beliefs [to be true] and it also involves a personal dedication to the actions implied by them."[1] This means that we must become convinced that change is needed and we must be willing to pay the price to bring about that change.

Change is not valuable for its own sake, and I have no interest in novelty just to be novel. Many of the things we do in the local church are good and should remain a part of our philosophy of ministry. *But no business, movement, or group will survive and flourish if its resistance to relevant and important change is rooted in the idea that we should keep doing something simply because that's the way we've always done it.* The purpose of this chapter is to rouse discussion among us and to provide some practical suggestions with which to experiment in our churches. If you don't agree with the ideas and suggestions to follow, then at least argue about them among your brothers and sisters. Find out where and why you think I am wrong and come up with better suggestions.

I offer one word of caution before we proceed. If what I am about to say is true, then we need to change a number of things we are currently doing in the church. Unfortunately, people can get hurt in the way we bring about change, and it is all too easy to look for people to blame for things that are going wrong. These harmful approaches and attitudes are foreign to the Spirit of Christ, so read what follows with a tender spirit as well as with a tough mind.

## REFURBISHING THE LOCAL CHURCH
### Philosophy of Ministry
*1. No senior pastors.* Any local church or any individual believer should have a philosophy of ministry — that is, a view about the purpose, objectives, structures, and methods of ministry that ought to characterize a local church ministry. In my view, any philosophy of local church ministry ought to be clear about three very crucial ideas. First, the local church in the New Testament contained a plurality of elders (Acts 14:23; 20:28; Philippians 1:1; Hebrews 13:17). The New Testament knows nothing about a senior pastor. In my opinion, the emergence of the

senior pastor in the local church is one of the factors that has most significantly undermined the development of healthy churches.

Think about it. More and more people go into the pastorate to get their own significance needs met, and congregations are increasingly filled with empty selves, as we saw in chapter 4. Given these facts, the senior-pastor model actually produces a codependence that often feeds the egos of senior pastors while allowing parishioners to remain passive. None of this is intentional, but the effects are still real. The senior pastor model tends to create a situation in which we identify the church as "Pastor Smith's church" and parishioners come to support his ministry. If a visitor asks where the minister is, instead of pointing to the entire congregation (as the New Testament would indicate, since we are all ministers of the New Covenant), we actually point to Pastor Smith. On the other hand, poor Pastor Smith increasingly gets isolated from people and peer accountability, and eventually, he dries up spiritually if he is not careful.

The local church should be led and taught by a plurality of voices called elders, and these voices should be equal. If so-called lay elders (I dislike the word *lay*!) do not have the seminary training possessed by those paid to be in "full-time" local church ministry, then the church needs to develop a long-term plan to give them that training in the church itself or elsewhere. No one person has enough gifts, perspective, and maturity to be given the opportunity disproportionately to shape the personality and texture of a local church. If Christ is actually the head of the church, our church structures ought to reflect that fact, and a group of undershepherds, not a senior pastor, should collectively seek His guidance in leading the congregation.

*2. What the pastoral staff and elders should be doing.* Second, Ephesians 4:11-16 may well be the most critical section in the entire New Testament for informing the nature of local church leadership. In that passage, the apostle Paul tells us that God has given the church evangelists and pastors-teachers (among other persons) who have a very specific function in the body. Their job description is to equip others for ministry, not to do the ministry themselves and have others come and passively support them. For example, the test of the gift of evangelism is not how effective you are at winning others to Christ, but rather, your track record at training others to evangelize. The senior-pastor model tends to centralize ministry around the church building and the pastor himself. Where he is, is where the action is. We bring people to him to evangelize, to counsel, and so forth. In this view, there is little need to actually equip parishioners to develop their own gifts, talents, and ministries because their job is to support *the* minister.

But according to Ephesians 4, this tradition has it backward. New Testament ministry is *decentralized*, and *the function of pastors-teachers is to equip others to do the ministry.* If we were more serious about this approach, we would do a better job of providing theological, biblical, philosophical, psychological, and other forms of training in our churches because without it, the ministers (that is, the members of the church) would not be adequately equipped to do the ministry.

**3. *The distinction between forms and functions.*** Third, we need to make a careful distinction between forms and functions in the church. *A New Testament function is an absolute biblical mandate that every church must do*—for example, edify believers, worship God, evangelize the lost, and so forth. Functions are unchanging nonnegotiables.

By contrast, *a form is a culturally relative means of fulfilling biblical functions.* Forms are valuable as a means to accomplish those functions and should be constantly evaluated, kept, or replaced in light of their effectiveness. Examples of forms are the existence of youth directors, Sunday school classes, vacation Bible schools, the order used in the worship service along with the kinds of music utilized, and so forth. We must keep in mind that we are free—genuinely and honestly *free* in Christ—to adjust our forms any way we wish, under the constraints of common sense, biblical teaching, and effectiveness. If the way a specific church conducts Sunday school classes is not effective in fulfilling the function of teaching people in the faith, then we should change it.

Serious harm has been done to our churches by confusing forms and functions and by clinging to the former just because we have always done them a certain way. We have no right to adjust our functions, but we have a duty to examine constantly our forms. A church that does not do this will have a lot to answer for at the judgment seat of the Head of the church.

Before I offer several suggestions for refurbishing the local church that, in one way or another, express these three core components of philosophy of ministry, I want to summarize more precisely what I am claiming. The local church ought to be led by a plurality of elders whose main job is to develop the ministries of others. They are to see to it that members of the body discover their spiritual gifts and natural talents and receive the training and equipping necessary to be good at their ministries individually and corporately. The elders are free to do whatever is necessary to the forms in the church in order to succeed in equipping the saints to accomplish biblical functions for the church. *If this is correct, then the church must see herself as an educational institution, and the development of the Christian mind will be at the forefront of the church's ministry strategy of equipping the saints.*

## Practical Suggestions

Here are a number of practical suggestions for making this philosophy of ministry a reality in the local church. I have actually done most of these in my own ministry and have witnessed their effectiveness firsthand.

*1. Sermons.* We must overhaul our understanding of the sermon along with our evaluation of what counts as a good one. The filling station approach (people come each week to get filled up until next week) is itself running out of gas. Yet we persist in viewing the sermon as a popular message that ought to be grasped easily by all who attend and evaluated solely on the basis of its pleasurableness, entertainment value, and practical orientation. Unfortunately, twenty years of exposure to these types of messages result in a congregation filled with people who have learned very little about their religion and who are inappropriately dependent upon someone else to tell them what to believe each week.

I do not dispute that sermons should be interesting and of practical value. But when most people say they want a sermon to be practical, I don't think they really mean how-tos and religious formulas as opposed to reasoned sermons that argue a case and actually cause people to learn something new. After all, most practicing Christians sense deep in their hearts that they know far too little about their faith and are embarrassed about it. *They want to be stretched to learn something regularly and cumulatively over the years by the sermons they hear.* What people really want when they say they desire practical sermons is this: They want passion and deep commitment to come through the message instead of a talk that sounds like it was hurriedly put together the day before.

How can we improve the quality of the sermons in our churches? I have three suggestions. First, we need to be more thoughtful and serious about supplementary material for the sermon. A small bulletin insert with three points is inadequate if, in fact, the sermon is a teaching vehicle. Instead, a detailed handout of two or three pages on regular-sized paper ought to be given to people. It should include detailed, structured notes following the sermon structure; a set of study exercises on the last page; recommendations for further reflection that week; and a bibliography. After a series is completed, these could be put together (with sermon CDs) to form a nice minicourse on the series topic for later study or distribution to those not attending the church.

Further, before a series begins, a book or commentary should be selected, order forms passed out, and copies sold the week before the series begins. Reading assignments could be given each week during the series. I once preached a series on 1 Peter, and seventy-five copies of a good commentary on the book were purchased by the congregation. I listed each week's text along with the relevant page numbers in the commentary on a sheet of paper the first week of the series. A number of people came to the sermon prepared to think about what I was teaching since they had read the commentary on the text prior to the message. Among other things, this forced me to work harder on my messages because people were not taking my word for it about the meaning of a passage! Can you imagine! They had their own ideas about the text!

Anything we can do with supplementary materials to get people reading and thinking about a series topic will enhance learning and growth.

Second, from time to time a minister should intentionally pitch a message to the upper one-third of the congregation, intellectually speaking. This may leave some people feeling a bit left out and confused during the sermon, which is unfortunate, but the alternative (which we follow almost all the time) is to dumb down our sermons so often that the upper one-third get bored and have to look elsewhere for spiritual and intellectual food. The intellectual level of our messages ought to be varied to provide more of a balance for all of the congregation. Furthermore, such an approach may motivate those in the lower two-thirds to work to catch up!

Finally, for two reasons I do not think a single individual ought to preach more than half (twenty-six) the Sundays during the year. First, no one person ought to have a disproportionate influence through the pulpit because, inevitably, the church will take on that person's strengths, weaknesses, and emphases. Now, who among us is adequate for this? No one. By rotating speakers, the body gets exposure to God's truth being poured through a number of different personalities, and that is more healthy. If one person is a better speaker than the others, he should train (equip) the rest over the years to be more adequate. As a result, the local church will have a growing number of competent leaders able to preach and consequently not be so dependent on one person.

Here is an important question: Would it inordinately impact your church's attendance and effectiveness if the main preacher went to another church? If the answer is yes, your church is going about its business in the wrong way. Leaders are not being developed in the body, and the pulpit is not being adequately shared.

Second, no one who preaches week after week can do adequate study for a message or deeply process and internalize the sermon topic spiritually. What inevitably happens is that a pastor will rely on his speaking ability and skills at putting together a message. Unfortunately, I have been in this situation myself, and my messages started sounding hollow and packaged. After several weeks of preaching, I started giving talks instead of preaching my passions and feeding others the fruits of my own deep study. In one church where I was a pastor-teacher, we rotated preaching among four people and each of us knew that he would have a four- to eight-week series coming up in, say, three months. That gave us the chance to work on a subject for a long time. By the time our turn on the calendar arrived, we were well prepared intellectually and spiritually.

**2. The church library.** Those in charge of the church library should see their job to be one of enlisting a growing number of church members into an army of readers and learners who, over the years, are becoming spiritually mature, clearly thinking believers who know what and why they believe. The church library ought to be large, and it should contain intellectual resources and not just self-help books. I recognize that building the church library costs money, but our investment of funds should reflect our values and we should value intellectual resources enough to pay for them.

In one church where I was a pastor-teacher, we had a library of twelve thousand volumes. As with most church libraries, its location was off the beaten path. So every single Sunday different volunteers on a rotating basis set up tables in the foyer, placed five hundred books on those tables, and actually greeted people at the door and invited them to check out a book or purchase a minicourse from a previous sermon series. Hundreds of books were regularly checked out and read that would have stayed on the shelf if we had simply left them in the out-of-sight-out-of-mind church library.

Church librarians should see to it that book reviews are regularly inserted into the bulletin and that each month several copies of a featured book are secured on consignment and sold in the lobby. For several years, the railroad industry all but died in this country because it wrongly defined its purpose. Railroad employees should have seen themselves in the transportation industry, not the railroad industry per se. Likewise, those who work in the church library must ask themselves what they are about. They do not serve to process books and keep the library open. They serve to enhance the development of a thinking, reading, literate congregation.

*3. Sunday school and study centers.* For many churches, the main purpose for a Sunday school class is to enfold, not to educate. A Sunday school class provides a place of contact with a mid-sized group numbering somewhere between the large congregational meeting and the small group. So understood, Sunday school classes require no preparation and little commitment to study on the part of their participants, and, if judged by their effects over several years, they accomplish little by way of actual education. Now it may surprise you to know that I do not think that this situation is bad in and of itself. More specifically, I think some vehicle for enfolding people and building group cohesion at a mid-sized-level church is appropriate, and Sunday school may well be that vehicle.

What we need, however, is to develop alternative, parallel classes that have a distinctively educational focus, so people can choose one or the other or alternate between the two. Years ago I colabored at Grace Fellowship Church in Baltimore for three years in what we called the Grace Discovery Center. We developed a set of course offerings that changed each quarter of the year. A few weeks prior to a change in church quarter, we passed out a list of course offerings and signed people up for the study center classes.

Courses cost from $25 to $75 depending on the number of hours of classroom instruction required. We varied the times of meeting. Some Discovery Center classes met on Wednesday nights from 7:00 to 9:00 p.m., some met for three hours on four consecutive Saturday mornings, some lasted from 7:00 to 9:30 Friday evening and from 9:00 a.m. to

4:00 p.m. the following day with a lunch break, others ran parallel to the Sunday school hour. Each course had a syllabus, required texts, and assignments (papers, letters to the editor, etc.), and grades were given out. We had classes in Greek, counseling, systematic theology, church history, apologetics, the history of philosophy, various vocations (medical ethics, Christianity and science, education and childhood development), and other areas. We used books written by unbelievers as well as believers and published by companies ranging from Oxford University Press to standard evangelical houses. If your church doesn't have the teaching resources for such a study center, you should band together with two or three other churches and form a jointly sponsored study center.

The Discovery Center also sponsored focused weekend retreats not of interest to everyone. For example, a group of around forty adults in the church had a special interest in Christianity and politics. So the Discovery Center responded to the need to equip these saints by hosting a weekend conference on the topic and flying in a Christian scholar who could address it competently, and we required that all attenders purchase and read a specific book on the topic (and state on a three-by-five-inch card they had done so) before they could attend.

The simple fact is that Sunday school as it's currently practiced is not doing the job of developing the Christian mind, and there may be more pressing, legitimate objectives (enfolding) for such classes. If this is so, we need to develop other ways of seeing to it that the local church develops Christian thinkers equipped to do the work of ministry. At the church in Baltimore, one group of twenty people studied psychology and pastoral counseling for a whole year under a local Christian psychologist. One Sunday morning, we called them all up to the front of the church and passed out a list of their names and phone numbers to the congregation, and the elders laid hands on them to dedicate this group to the body as those responsible for the counseling ministry in the church. None of us who were elders or paid staff members were especially gifted in this area, but we saw our biblical mandate to be that of ensuring the job was done by equipping others. Among other things, this freed us up to do more work in leadership development in the church while those with the training and desire to counsel fulfilled that role in the body.

Likewise, eighteen engineers and scientists in the body went through an eighteen-month study of science and Christianity. One Sunday morning we dedicated this group in front of the church just as we had the counseling group. These scientists and engineers were looked to by the body as people who could help families if issues in creation and evolution arose. For the first time in their lives, what these men and women had studied in college and chosen as a vocation became relevant to their discipleship unto Jesus and their ministry in the body! We need to offer more courses in church partitioned along vocational lines to tap into natural motivation, opportunity, and talent.

*4. Deepening the value of the intellectual life and raising the visibility of Christian intellectuals and intellectual work.* A group's values will largely determine the corporate and individual behavior of the group. And a group must find ways to foster, sustain, and propagate its values among its members. If the local church is to overcome its anti-intellectualism, it must find ways to raise conscious awareness of the value of the intellectual life among its members. Most believers know the names of leading Christian speakers and radio personalities. But how many of us know our Christian intellectuals, celebrate their accomplishments on our behalf, pray regularly for the intellectual war they wage, and hold them forth as heroes and vocational role models among our teenagers? If we do this for missionaries, why don't we do it for Christian intellectuals? We should, because we are in a struggle about ideas and need to raise up a new generation of Christian scholars. In our master of arts program in philosophy and ethics at Talbot School of Theology, one of our goals is to help raise up one hundred men and women in the next twenty-five years who will study under us, go on for their PhD, and become evangelical university professors at schools all across the country. The local church needs to be more intentional about fostering the intellectual life and mobilizing a new generation of Christian intellectuals. Here are some suggestions for doing this.

First, we should regularly incorporate vocational or apologetical testimonies and book reports on timely topics into our services. Selected worshippers should be given five minutes to share how they are growing to think more Christianly as a businessperson, a teacher, or whatever. They should share what they are reading, the issues with which they are grappling, and the progress they are making. People should share occasions where apologetics has aided their own ministry of evangelism and discipleship. Once a month we ought to entertain a brief book review of a key new book, some of which should be written by influential unbelievers. We can do a better job of encouraging a life of reading, apologetical argumentation, and vocational integration during our services.

Second, we ought to identify intellectual leaders who are associated with the evangelical community or historic Christianity more broadly conceived and find ways to hold forth their lifework as possible vocations for our young people. Further, Christian intellectuals, especially university professors, sometimes feel a bit estranged from the sociological ambience of their local churches and from the anti-Christian ideas of their colleagues. We need to do a better job of recognizing, celebrating, enfolding, and aiding these intellectuals in their work. An occasional bulletin announcement to pray for professor so-and-so who labors for Christ at a local college would be a wonderful thing. We get upset because we are underrepresented in the university. But how many churches have taken specific steps to encourage the university professors (and graduate students soon to be university professors) among their membership to be faithful to orthodoxy and to be bold in their vocation?

Third, we need to prepare teenagers for the intellectual world they will face in college. The summer after high school graduation, it would be a good idea to hold a summer institute in apologetics and try to offer some worldview instruction to prepare our young brothers and sisters to think more carefully about what they will study at the university. Such an institute could also be used to challenge teens with the ideal of vocation as the point of college in the first place. Having worked with college students for twenty-six years, I can testify that our churches are not preparing young people for what they will face intellectually in their college years, and we simply must be more intentional about this.

Fourth, we should be more proactive in supporting and enfolding members of the body who go to graduate school. Many churches have a number of people each year who engage in graduate studies. Often, these people begin to identify with their department of study in such a way that they are sociologized out of a vibrant evangelical commitment. Why should we abandon these students in this way? Graduate students do not simply need the same sort of fellowship as everyone else in the church. They need intellectual support as well. I think each August we should print a list of students heading off for graduate school that includes their names, universities, addresses, and majors. These students should be brought before the congregation, admonished to develop Christian minds in their graduate work, and dedicated to the Lord by the laying on of hands by the elders. If possible, they should be paired up with someone in the church who is engaged in the same vocation, and this person could be available for support through letters, phone conversations about issues in the discipline, and so forth. Can you imagine the extent to which the Christian mind would emerge in this culture if thousands of churches began to practice this?

Finally, we need to increase our individual and congregational giving to support Christian scholarship. When I speak in a church, I sometimes challenge people to ask themselves just how much of their individual giving or church budget goes to support the development of Christian scholarship? Most people have never even thought of such an idea. Evangelical colleges and seminaries are grossly underfunded. As a result, many such schools are tuition driven and their faculties are underpaid, strapped with inordinate teaching loads, and left with inadequate library resources and funds for professional conferences compared to their secular counterparts. And we expect those schools and their faculties to compete in the war of ideas!

Moreover, there is less scholarship money available to students who attend evangelical colleges and seminaries compared to those who attend secular institutions. When I did my doctorate at USC, I received $10,000 a year for three years. The university knew that if I (and other graduate students) had time to spend in the library and on academic work, this would increase my chances of getting a teaching job and making a contribution in the academic world, and eventually, would bode well for USC. Unfortunately, students at evangelical seminaries face high tuitions and, therefore, must work at part-time jobs when they could be in the library improving their educational experience and ministerial training. If we evangelicals are tired of being underrepresented in the media, the university, and the government, then we need to support evangelical scholarship, especially solid evangelical colleges and seminaries, because such institutions nurture the intellectual leaders of the future.

## SUMMARY

The morning I began to write this chapter, I picked up the newspaper and read the editorial page. One of the featured editorials was a defense of Promise Keepers against feminist and liberal critiques of that movement.[2] The article was articulate, carefully written, overtly evangelical, and powerfully presented. And it was read by millions of people. What really stirred my heart, however, was not just the substance of the article but who wrote it—Brad Stetson. This may not mean much to you, but it was symbolic to me. I have met Dr. Stetson. He is a young, dedicated evangelical who did his PhD in social ethics concurrently with two of my faculty colleagues and he is symbolic of a new and, I hope, growing breed of younger evangelical intellectuals. I was encouraged to see a faithful, well-trained evangelical scholar impact the public marketplace of ideas that is available to laypeople in the community.

What I am saying in this chapter is that we need one hundred thousand Brad Stetsons to write editorials, penetrate secular universities, write books, speak on talk shows, and much, much more. The local church needs to be more intentional in finding and developing the young Brad Stetsons now in her ranks. May almighty God help us to do just that.

# APPENDICES OF RESOURCES AND ORGANIZATIONS

## Developed by Joseph E. Gorra, Biola University

Our world is exploding with information. Credible curators can beneficially guide and encourage focus in the midst of a plentitude of information options. These appendices were developed with this value in mind. They do not try to be comprehensive, but at least representative of recommendations in light of some of the perspectives, values, and interests of *Love Your God with All Your Mind*. These recommendations do not necessarily entail an endorsement from J. P. Moreland or his Eidos Christian Center, as much as they are encouraged companions to help learning and thinking seriously about a topic. More recommendations and resources are available at www.jpmoreland.com.

Joseph E. Gorra
joseph.gorra@gmail.com

# RECOMMENDED RESOURCES

Resources are classified according to the following reading level categories:

- **Beginner:** Identifies content representative of at least a high school degree level of comprehension. It is intended for a thoughtful general audience. It may also reflect introductory content about a topic.
- **Intermediate:** Identifies content representative of at least a college degree level of comprehension. It is intended for an educated general audience.
- **Advanced:** Identifies content representative of at least a graduate degree level of comprehension with some specialist interests.

Categories A–M reflect basic areas of biblical worldview development, regardless of one's calling/profession, interests, or expertise. Categories N–T represent applied areas of interest. Recommended resources include mostly books, academic journals, periodicals, and some curriculum and Internet-based materials. You may wish to think about the following resources as the basis toward building your own curriculum for growth and enrichment.

## A. INTELLECTUAL AND CHARACTER DEVELOPMENT
*Beginner Resources*
Armstrong, William. *Study Is Hard Work: The Most Accessible and Lucid Text Available on Acquiring and Keeping Study Skills Through a Lifetime.* 2nd ed. Boston: David R. Godine, 2010.

Benner, David G. *The Gift of Being Yourself: The Sacred Call to Self-Discovery.* Downers Grove, IL: InterVarsity, 2004.

Craig, William Lane, and Paul Gould, eds. *The Two Tasks of the Christian Scholar: Redeeming the Soul, Redeeming the Mind.* Wheaton, IL: Crossway, 2007.

Ford, David F. *The Shape of Living: Spiritual Directions for Everyday Life.* 2nd ed. Grand Rapids, MI: Baker, 2004.

Guinness, Os. *The Call: Finding and Fulfilling the Central Purpose of Your Life.* Nashville: Thomas Nelson, 2003.

Kostenberger, Andreas J. *Excellence: The Character of God and the Pursuit of Scholarly Virtue.* Wheaton, IL: Crossway, 2011.

McEntyre, Marilyn. *Caring for Words in a Culture of Lies.* Grand Rapids, MI: Eerdmans, 2009.

Piper, John, and David Mathis. *Thinking. Loving. Doing.: A Call to Glorify God with Heart and Mind.* Wheaton, IL: Crossway, 2011.

Schall, James. *The Life of the Mind: On the Joys and Travails of Thinking.* Wilmington, DE: ISI Books, 2008.

Voskamp, Ann. *One Thousand Gifts: A Dare to Live Fully Right Where You Are.* Grand Rapids, MI: Zondervan, 2010.

***Intermediate Resources***

Casey, Michael. *Sacred Reading: The Ancient Art of Lectio Divina.* Liguori, MO: Triumph Books, 1996.

Kass, Leon. *Being Human: Core Readings in the Humanities.* New York: Norton, 2004.

Kreeft, Peter. *Socratic Logic: A Logic Text Using Socratic Method, Platonic Questions, and Aristotelian Principles.* South Bend, IN: St. Augustine's Press, 2010.

Naugle, David K. *Reordered Love, Reordered Lives: Learning the Deep Meaning of Happiness.* Grand Rapids, MI: Eerdmans, 2008.

Noll, Mark. *Jesus Christ and the Life of the Mind.* Grand Rapids, MI: Eerdmans, 2011.

Pieper, Josef. *Happiness and Contemplation.* South Bend, IN: St. Augustine's Press, 1998.

Pieper, Josef. *Tradition: Concept and Claim.* Wilmington, DE: ISI Books, 2008.

Ten Elshof, Gregg A. *I Told Me So: Self-Deception and the Christian Life.* Grand Rapids, MI: Eerdmans, 2009.

Williams, Clifford. *The Divided Soul: A Kierkegaardian Exploration.* Eugene, OR: Wipf & Stock, 2009.

Wright, N. T. *After You Believe: Why Christian Character Matters.* New York: HarperOne, 2010.

### Advanced Resources

Agee, Bob R., and Douglas V. Henry. *Faithful Learning and the Christian Scholarly Vocation.* Grand Rapids, MI: Eerdmans, 2003.

Annas, Julia. *Intelligent Virtue.* Oxford: Oxford University Press, 2011.

Meek, Esther Lightcap. *Longing to Know.* Grand Rapids, MI: Brazos, 2003.

Meek, Esther Lightcap. *Loving to Know: Covenant Epistemology.* Eugene, OR: Cascade Books, 2011.

Moser, Paul K., ed. *Jesus and Philosophy: New Essays.* Cambridge: Cambridge University Press, 2009.

Roberts, Robert C., and W. Jay Wood. *Intellectual Virtues: An Essay in Regulative Epistemology.* New York: Oxford University Press, 2009.

Sertillanges, James. *The Intellectual Life: Its Spirit, Conditions, Methods.* Translated by Mary Ryan. Washington, DC: Catholic University Press, 1998.

Sire, James W. *Habits of the Mind: Intellectual Life as a Christian Calling.* Downers Grove, IL: InterVarsity, 2000.

Sowell, Thomas. *Intellectuals and Society.* New York: Basic Books, 2009.

Zagzebski, Linda T. *Virtues of the Mind: An Inquiry into the Nature of Virtue and the Ethical Foundations of Knowledge.* Cambridge: Cambridge University Press, 1996.

To read further in this area, please consult *Anamnesis, Books & Culture, Book Forum, City Journal, Claremont Review of Books, Christian Scholar's Review, Daedalus, The Common Review, Critical Inquiry, First Things, The Hedgehog Review, The New Atlantis, The City, Lapham's Quarterly, The Mars Hill Audio Journal, The Times Literary Supplement,* and *The University Bookman,* along with the diverse learning resources available from iTunesU, The Teaching Company, and the recommendations in Appendix 2. Please also see Don King with Perry Glanzer, David Hoekema, Jerry Pattengale, Todd Ream, and Todd Steen, eds. *Taking Every Thought Captive: Forty Years of the Christian Scholar's Review* (Abilene, TX: Abilene Christian University Press, 2011).

## B. BIBLICAL WORLDVIEW INTEGRATION

### Beginner Resources

Carter, Joe, and John Coleman. *How to Argue Like Jesus: Learning Persuasion from History's Greatest Communicator.* Wheaton, IL: Crossway, 2009.

Colson, Charles, and Nancy Pearcey. *How Now Shall We Live?* Wheaton, IL: Tyndale, 1999.

Hewitt, Hugh. *In, but Not Of: A Guide to Christian Ambition and the Desire to Influence the World.* Nashville: Thomas Nelson, 2003.

Issler, Klaus, and J. P. Moreland. *In Search of a Confident Faith.* Downers Grove, IL: InterVarsity, 2008.

Marshall, Paul. *Heaven Is Not My Home: Living in the Now of God's Creation.* Nashville: Thomas Nelson, 1999.

Moreland, J. P. *The God Question: An Invitation to a Life of Meaning.* Eugene, OR: Harvest House, 2009.

Piper, John, and D. A. Carson. *The Pastor as Scholar and the Scholar as Pastor.* Wheaton, IL: Crossway, 2011.

Stott, John R. W. *Your Mind Matters to God.* Downers Grove, IL: InterVarsity, 2006.

Wilkens, Steve, and Mark L. Sanford. *Hidden Worldviews: Eight Cultural Stories That Shape Our Lives.* Downers Grove, IL: IVP Academic, 2009.

Wolters, Albert M. *Creation Regained: Biblical Basis for a Reformational Worldview.* Grand Rapids, MI: Eerdmans, 2005.

### Intermediate Resources

Berger, Peter, and Anton Zijderveld. *In Praise of Doubt: How to Have Convictions Without Becoming a Fanatic.* New York: HarperOne, 2009.

Davis, John Jefferson. *Worship and the Reality of God: An Evangelical Theology of Real Presence.* Downers Grove, IL: IVP Academic, 2010.

Frye, Northrop. *The Educated Imagination.* Toronto, Ontario: CBC Enterprise, 1988.

Goheen, Michael W., and Craig Bartholomew. *Living at the Crossroads: An Introduction to Christian Worldview.* Grand Rapids, MI: Baker Academic, 2008.

Green, Bradley. *The Gospel and the Mind.* Wheaton, IL: Crossway, 2010.

Houston, James M. *The Mentored Life: From Individualism to Personhood.* Colorado Springs, CO: NavPress, 2002.

Moreland, J. P. *The Kingdom Triangle: Recover the Christian Mind, Renovate the Soul, Restore the Spirit's Power.* Grand Rapids, MI: Zondervan, 2007.

Morris, Thomas V. *Making Sense of It All: Pascal and the Meaning of Life.* Grand Rapids, MI: Eerdmans, 1992.

Plantinga, Cornelius. *Engaging God's World: A Primer for Students.* Grand Rapids, MI: Eerdmans, 2002.

Sire, James W. *The Universe Next Door: A Basic Worldview Catalog.* 5th ed. Downers Grove, IL: IVP Academic, 2009.

### Advanced Resources

Bovell, Carlos, ed. *Interdisciplinary Perspectives on the Authority of Scripture: Historical, Biblical, and Theoretical Perspectives.* Eugene, OR: Pickwick Publications, 2011.

Corduan, Winfried. *Handmaid to Theology: An Essay in Philosophical Prolegomena.* Eugene, OR: Wipf & Stock, 2009.

Gundry, Stanley N., ed. *Four Views on Moving Beyond the Bible to Theology.* Grand Rapids, MI: Zondervan, 2009.

Hiebert, Paul G. *Transforming Worldviews: An Anthropological Understanding of How People Change.* Grand Rapids, MI: Baker, 2008.

Himmelfarb, Gertrude. *The De-moralization of Society: From Victorian Virtues to Modern Values.* New York: Vintage Books, 1996.

Naugle, David K. *Worldview: The History of a Concept.* Grand Rapids, MI: Eerdmans, 2002.

Paul II, Pope John. *Restoring Faith in Reason: A New Translation of the Encyclical Letter "Faith and Reason" of Pope John Paul II.* Together with a commentary and discussion. Notre Dame, IN: University of Notre Dame Press, 2002.

Smith, James K. A. *Desiring the Kingdom: Worship, Worldview, and Cultural Formation, Cultural Liturgies.* Grand Rapids, MI: Baker Academic, 2009.

VanDrunen, David. *Natural Law and the Two Kingdoms: A Study in the Development of Reformed Social Thought.* Grand Rapids, MI: Eerdmans, 2009.

Werther, David, and Mark D. Linville. *Philosophy and the Christian Worldview: Analysis, Assessment, and Development.* New York: Continuum Press, 2012.

To read further in this area, please consult *Books & Culture, Comment, First Things, The Hedgehog Review, Christian Scholar's Review, Salvo, The Mars Hill Audio Journal, Philosophia Christi,* and *The Other Journal,* and see the multi-volume CHRISTIAN WORLDVIEW INTEGRATION series from InterVarsity, coedited by J. P. Moreland and Francis J. Beckwith.

## C. SPIRITUAL TRANSFORMATION AND CHRISTIAN DISCIPLESHIP

### Beginner Resources

Andrews, Alan, gen. ed. *The Kingdom Life: A Practical Theology of Discipleship and Spiritual Formation.* Colorado Springs, CO: NavPress, 2010.

Bass, Dorothy, and Susan Briehl. *On Our Way: Christian Practices for Living a Whole Life.* Nashville: Upper Room, 2010.

Best, Gary. *Naturally Supernatural: God May Be Closer Than You Think.* Capetown, South Africa: Vineyard International Publishing, 2007.

Calhoun, Adele Ahlberg. *Spiritual Disciplines Handbook: Practices That Transform Us.* Downers Grove, IL: InterVarsity, 2005.

Foster, Richard J. *Celebration of Discipline: The Path to Spiritual Growth.* 25th anniversary ed. New York: HarperCollins, 2003.

Issler, Klaus. *Living into the Life of Jesus: The Formation of Christian Character.* Downers Grove, IL: IVP Academic, 2012.

Johnson, Jan. *Abundant Simplicity: Discovering the Unhurried Rhythms of Grace.* Downers Grove, IL: InterVarsity, 2011.

McMinn, Lisa Graham. *The Contented Soul: The Art of Savoring Life.* Downers Grove, IL: InterVarsity, 2006.

Peterson, Eugene. *A Long Obedience in the Same Direction: Discipleship in an Instant Society.* Downers Grove, IL: InterVarsity, 2000.

Renovare. *25 Books Every Christian Should Read: A Guide to the Essential Spiritual Classics.* New York: HarperOne, 2011.

### Intermediate Resources

Anderson, Matthew Lee. *Earthen Vessels: Why Our Bodies Matter to Our Faith.* Minneapolis: Bethany, 2011.

Benner, David G. *Soulful Spirituality: Becoming Fully Alive and Deeply Human.* Grand Rapids, MI: Brazos, 2011.

DeYoung, Rebecca Konyndyk. *Glittering Vices: A New Look at the Seven Deadly Sins and Their Remedies.* Grand Rapids, MI: Brazos, 2009.

Foster, Richard J. *Streams of Living Water: Celebrating the Great Traditions of Christian Faith.* New York: HarperOne, 2001.

Gundry, Stanley N. *Five Views on Sanctification.* Grand Rapids, MI: Zondervan, 1996.

Hildebrand, Dietrich von. *Transformation in Christ: On the Christian Attitude.* San Francisco: Ignatius Press, 2001.

Peterson, Eugene H. *Eat This Book: A Conversation in the Art of Spiritual Reading.* Grand Rapids, MI: Eerdmans, 2004.

Storms, Sam. *Signs of the Spirit: An Interpretation of Jonathan Edwards' Religious Affections.* Wheaton, IL: Crossway, 2007.

Wilhoit, James. *Spiritual Formation as if the Church Mattered.* Grand Rapids, MI: Baker Academic, 2008.

Willard, Dallas. *Renovation of the Heart: Putting On the Character of Christ.* Colorado Springs, CO: NavPress, 2002.

### Advanced Resources

Alston, William P. *Perceiving God: The Epistemology of Religious Experience.* Ithaca, NY: Cornell University Press, 1991.

Corduan, Winfried. *Mysticism: An Evangelical Option?* Grand Rapids, MI: Zondervan, 2009.

Howard, Evan B., ed. *The Brazos Introduction to Christian Spirituality.* Grand Rapids, MI: Brazos, 2008.

Jones, Cheslyn, Geoffrey Wainwright, and Edward Yarnold. *The Study of Spirituality.* Oxford: Oxford University Press, 1986.

McIntosh, Mark A. *Discernment and Truth: The Spirituality and Theology of Knowledge.* Chestnut Ridge, NY: The Crossroad Publishing, 2004.

McIntosh, Mark A. *Mystical Theology: The Integrity of Spirituality and Theology.* Malden, MA: Wiley-Blackwell, 1998.

Moser, Paul K. *The Evidence for God: Religious Knowledge Reexamined.* Cambridge: Cambridge University Press, 2009.

Roberts, Robert C. *Spiritual Emotions: A Psychology of Christian Virtues.* Grand Rapids, MI: Eerdmans, 2007.

von Hildebrand, Dietrich. *The Heart: An Analysis of Human and Divine Affectivity.* South Bend, IN: St. Augustine Press, 2007.

von Hildebrand, Dietrich. *The Nature of Love.* South Bend, IN: St. Augustine Press, 2009.

To read further in this area, please consult *Conversations: A Forum for Authentic Transformation, Journal of Spiritual Formation and Soul Care, Reflective Practice: Formation and Supervision in Ministry,* and *Spiritus,* and see the fruitful Inter-Varsity APPRENTICE series by James Bryan Smith and also the SOUL'S LONGING series by James M. Houston (Colorado Springs, CO: David C. Cook).

## D. BIBLICAL STUDIES
### Beginner Resources

Bartholomew, Craig G., and Michael W. Goheen. *The Drama of Scripture: Finding Our Place in the Biblical Story.* Grand Rapids, MI: Baker Academic, 2004.

Fee, Gordon, and Mark L. Strauss. *How to Choose a Translation for All Its Worth: A Guide to Understanding and Using Bible Versions.* Grand Rapids, MI: Zondervan, 2007.

Hendricks, Howard, and William D. Hendricks. *Living by the Book: The Art and Science of Reading the Bible.* Chicago: Moody, 2007.

Kang, Joshua Choonmin. *Scripture by Heart: Devotional Practices for Memorizing God's Word.* Downers Grove, IL: InterVarsity, 2010.

Keller, Timothy. *King's Cross: The Story of the World in the Life of Jesus.* New York: Dutton, 2011.

Lubeck, Ray. *Read the Bible for a Change: Understanding and Responding to God's Word.* Eugene, OR: Wipf & Stock, 2009.

McLean, Max, and Warren Bird. *Unleashing the Word: Rediscovering the Public Reading of Scripture.* Grand Rapids, MI: Zondervan, 2009.

Russell, Walt. *Playing with Fire: How the Bible Ignites Change in Your Soul.* Colorado Springs, CO: NavPress, 2000.

Ryken, Leland. *The Word of God in English: Criteria for Excellence in Bible Translation*. Wheaton, IL: Crossway, 2002.

Wright, Christopher J. H. *The Mission of God's People: A Biblical Theology of the Church's Mission*. Grand Rapids, MI: Zondervan, 2010.

### Intermediate Resources

Bruce, F. F. *The Canon of Scripture*. Downers Grove, IL: IVP Academic, 1988.

Carson, D. A. *Exegetical Fallacies*. Grand Rapids, MI: Baker Academic, 1996.

Carson, D. A., and Douglas J. Moo. *An Introduction to the New Testament*. Grand Rapids, MI: Zondervan, 2005.

Duvall, J. Scott, and J. Daniel Hays. *Grasping God's Word*. Grand Rapids, MI: Zondervan, 2005.

Gundry, Robert H. *A Survey of the New Testament*. Grand Rapids, MI: Zondervan, 2003.

Harbin, Michael A. *The Promise and the Blessing: A Historical Survey of the Old and New Testaments*. Grand Rapids, MI: Zondervan, 2005.

Klein, William K., Craig L. Blomberg, and Robert I. Hubbard Jr. *Introduction to Biblical Interpretation*. Revised and updated. Nashville: Thomas Nelson, 2004.

Longman III, Tremper, and Raymond B. Dillard. *An Introduction to the Old Testament*. Grand Rapids, MI: Zondervan, 2006.

Wegner, Paul D. *A Student's Guide to Textual Criticism of the Bible*. Downers Grove, IL: IVP Academic, 2006.

Wright, Christopher J. H. *The Mission of God's People: A Biblical Theology of the Church's Mission*. Grand Rapids, MI: Zondervan, 2010.

### Advanced Resources

Beale, G. K. *We Become What We Worship: A Biblical Theology of Idolatry*. Downers Grove, IL: IVP Academic, 2008.

Fee, Gordon D. *God's Empowering Presence: The Holy Spirit in the Letters of Paul*. Reprint ed. Grand Rapids, MI: Baker Academic, 2009.

Firth, David G., and Paul D. Wegner, eds. *Presence, Power, and Promise: The Role of the Spirit of God in the Old Testament*. Downers Grove, IL: IVP Academic, 2011.

Hawthorne, Gerald F. *The Presence and the Power*. Eugene, OR: Wipf & Stock, 2003.

Hubbard, Moyer V. *Christianity in the Greco-Roman World: A Narrative Introduction*. Peabody, MA: Hendrickson Publishers, 2010.

Keener, Craig S. *Miracles: The Credibility of the New Testament Accounts*. Grand Rapids, MI: Baker Academic, 2011.

Keener, Craig S. *The Historical Jesus of the Gospels*. Grand Rapids, MI: Eerdmans, 2009.

Lunde, Jonathan. *Following Jesus, the Servant King: A Biblical Theology of Covenantal Discipleship*. Grand Rapids, MI: Zondervan, 2010.

Lyle Jeffrey David, and C. Stephen Evans, eds. *The Bible and the University*. Grand Rapids, MI: Zondervan, 2007.

Studzinski, Raymond. *Reading to Live: The Evolving Practice of Lectio Divina*. Collegeville, MN: Cistercian Publications/Liturgical Press, 2009.

Wright, N. T. *The Resurrection of the Son of God*. Minneapolis: Fortress, 2003.

To read further in this area, please consult *Currents in Biblical Research, Journal of the Evangelical Theological Society, Journal of Religious & Theological Information, Biblical Interpretation, Biblical Research, Bulletin of Biblical Research, Horizons in Biblical Theology, Journal of Biblical Literature, International Journal of Practical Theology.*

For helpful bibliographies, see David R. Bauer, *An Annotated Guide to Biblical Resources for Ministry* (Eugene, OR: Wipf & Stock, 2011); John Glynn, *Commentary and Reference Survey*, 9th ed. (Grand Rapids, MI: Kregel, 2003); D. A. Carson, *New Testament Commentary Survey*, 6th ed. (Grand Rapids, MI: Baker Academic, 2007); Tremper Longman III, *Old Testament Commentary Survey*, 4th ed. (Grand Rapids, MI: Baker Academic, 2007); Scot McKnight and Grant Osborne, eds., *The Face of New Testament Studies* (Grand Rapids, MI: Baker Academic, 2004); David W. Baker and Bill T. Arnold, eds., *The Face of Old Testament Studies* (Grand Rapids, MI: Baker Academic, 1999). Please also see the entire INSTITUTE OF BIBLICAL RESEARCH bibliography series published by Baker Academic.

## E. THEOLOGICAL STUDIES
### Beginner Resources

Banks, Robert. *Redeeming the Routines: Bringing Theology to Life*. Grand Rapids, MI: Baker Academic, 2001.

DeYoung, Kevin, and Greg Gilbert. *What Is the Mission of the Church?: Making Sense of Social Justice, Shalom, and the Great Commission*. Wheaton, IL: Crossway, 2011.

Dorman, Ted. *A Faith for All Seasons*. Nashville: B&H Academic, 2001.

Grenz, Stanley J., and Roger E. Olson. *Who Needs Theology?: An Invitation to the Study of God*. Downers Grove, IL: IVP Academic, 1996.

Kraft, Charles H. *Christianity with Power: Your Worldview and Your Experience of the Supernatural*. Eugene, OR: Wipf & Stock, 2005.

MacArthur, John. *Slave: The Hidden Truth About Your Identity in Christ*. Nashville: Thomas Nelson, 2010.

McKnight, Scot. *The King Jesus Gospel: The Original Good News Revisited.* Grand Rapids, MI: Zondervan, 2011.

Packer, J. I. *Knowing God.* 20th anniversary ed. Downers Grove, IL: InterVarsity, 1993.

Sanders, Fred. *The Deep Things of God: How the Trinity Changes Everything.* Wheaton, IL: Crossway, 2010.

Williams, Don. *Start Here: Kingdom Essentials for Christians.* Ventura, CA: Regal, 2006.

### Intermediate Resources

Davis, John Jefferson. *Worship and the Reality of God: An Evangelical Theology of Real Presence.* Downers Grove, IL: IVP Academic, 2010.

Dembski, William A. *The End of Christianity: Finding a Good God in an Evil World.* Nashville: B&H Academic, 2009.

Harper, Brad, and Paul Louis Metzger. *Exploring Ecclesiology: An Evangelical and Ecumenical Introduction.* Grand Rapids, MI: Brazos, 2009.

Lewis, Gordon R., and Bruce A. Demarest. *Integrative Theology.* Grand Rapids, MI: Zondervan, 1996.

Marshall, Howard. *New Testament Theology: Many Witnesses, One Gospel.* Downers Grove, IL: IVP Academic, 2004.

Morphew, Derek J. *Breakthrough: Discovering the Kingdom.* Capetown, South Africa: Vineyard International Publishing, 2007.

Oden, Thomas C. *Classic Christianity: A Systematic Theology.* New York: HarperOne, 2009.

Plantinga Jr., Cornelius. *Not the Way It's Supposed to Be: A Breviary of Sin.* Grand Rapids, MI: Eerdmans, 1995.

Tennent, Timothy C. *Theology in the Context of World Christianity: How the Global Church Is Influencing the Way We Think About and Discuss Theology.* Grand Rapids, MI: Zondervan, 2007.

Waltke, Bruce K., and Charles Yu. *An Old Testament Theology: An Exegetical, Canonical, and Thematic Approach.* Grand Rapids, MI: Zondervan, 2007.

### Advanced Resources

Clark, David K., and John S. Feinberg. *To Know and Love God: Method for Theology.* Wheaton, IL: Crossway, 2010.

Corduan, Winfried. *Handmaid to Theology: An Essay in Philosophical Prolegomena.* Eugene, OR: Wipf & Stock, 2009.

Craig, William Lane, and J. P. Moreland, eds. *The Blackwell Companion to Natural Theology.* Malden, MA: Wiley-Blackwell, 2009.

Crisp, Oliver D. *God Incarnate: Explorations in Christology.* London: T&T Clark International, 2009.

Flint, Thomas P., and Michael C. Rea, eds. *The Oxford Handbook of Philosophical Theology.* Oxford: Oxford University Press, 2011.

McCall, Thomas, and Michael C. Rea, eds. *Philosophical and Theological Essays on the Trinity.* Oxford: Oxford University Press, 2010.

McDermott, Gerald, ed. *The Oxford Handbook of Evangelical Theology.* Oxford: Oxford University Press, 2010.

Naselli, Andrew David, and Collin Hansen, eds. *Four Views of on the Spectrum of Evangelicalism.* Grand Rapids, MI: Zondervan, 2011.

Rea, Michael C., ed. *Oxford Readings in Philosophical Theology.* Vol. 1–2. Oxford: Oxford University Press, 2009.

Stump, Eleonore. *Wandering in Darkness: Narrative and the Problem of Suffering.* Oxford: Oxford University Press, 2010.

To read further in this area, please consult *Anglican Theological Review, Calvin Theological Journal, Criswell Theological Review, Journal of the Evangelical Theological Society, American Journal of Theology and Philosophy, Evangelical Review of Theology, Philosophia Christi, Theology Today, Southwestern Journal of Theology, Scottish Journal of Theology, Practical Theology, Modern Theology, Medieval Philosophy and Theology, Literature and Theology, Wesleyan Theological Journal, Westminster Theological Journal.*

For comparison of theological views on various topics, see the multi-view series of books from Zondervan, Baker Academic, IVP Academic, Kregel, and the Oxford Handbooks of Theology series. See also the IVP Bible Dictionary Series and the Ancient Christian Commentary Series by Inter-Varsity, along with Donald K. McKim's *Dictionary of Major Biblical Interpreters* (Downers Grove, IL: IVP Academic, 2007). See also the multi-series Scripture and Hermeneutics volumes by Zondervan.

Useful theological dictionaries include: Walter A. Elwell, ed., *Evangelical Dictionary of Theology,* 2nd ed. (Grand Rapids, MI: Baker Academic, 2001); Richard A. Muller, *Dictionary of Latin and Greek Theological Terms* (Grand Rapids, MI: Baker, 2006); Kelly James Clark, Richard Lints, and James K. A. Smith, *101 Key Terms in Philosophy and Their Importance for Theology* (Louisville, KY: John Knox, 2004); Donald K. McKim, *Westminster Dictionary of Theological Terms* (Louisville, KY: John Knox, 1996).

For laity theological training, see the certificate and bachelor's degree earning program of the Vineyard Bible Institute, which offers seasoned training in a theology of the kingdom and its implications for leadership in the church and in the world (www.vineyardbibleinstitute.org).

## F. PHILOSOPHY

### Beginner Resources

Ayer, A. J., and Jane O'Grady, eds. *A Dictionary of Philosophical Quotations.* Malden, MA: Wiley-Blackwell, 1994.

Baggett, David, Gary R. Habermas, and Jerry L. Walls. *C. S. Lewis as Philosopher: Truth, Goodness, and Beauty.* Downers Grove, IL: IVP Academic, 2008.

Baggini, Julian, and Peter S. Fosl. *The Philosopher's Toolkit: A Compendium of Philosophical Concepts and Methods.* Malden, MA: Wiley-Blackwell, 2010.

Clark, Kelly James, ed. *Philosophers Who Believe: The Spiritual Journeys of 11 Leading Thinkers.* Downers Grove, IL: InterVarsity, 1997.

DeWeese, Garrett J., and J. P. Moreland. *Philosophy Made Slightly Less Difficult: A Beginner's Guide to Life's Big Questions.* Downers Grove, IL: InterVarsity, 2005.

Ganssle, Gregory E. *Thinking About God: First Steps in Philosophy.* Downers Grove, IL: InterVarsity, 2004.

Groothuis, Douglas. *On Jesus.* Florence, KY: Wadsworth, 2002.

Kreeft, Peter. *Socratic Logic: A Logic Text Using Socratic Method, Platonic Questions, and Aristotelian Principles.* South Bend, IN: St. Augustine's Press, 2010.

Pieper, Josef. *Happiness and Contemplation.* South Bend, IN: St. Augustine's Press, 1998.

Sparks, A. W. *Talking Philosophy: A WordBook.* London: Routledge, 1991.

### Intermediate Resources

Cowan, Steven B., and James S. Spiegel. *The Love of Wisdom: A Christian Introduction to Philosophy.* Nashville: B&H Academic, 2009.

DeWeese, Garrett J. *Doing Philosophy as a Christian.* Downers Grove, IL: IVP Academic, 2011.

DeYoung, Rebecca Konyndyk. *Glittering Vices: A New Look at the Seven Deadly Sins and Their Remedies.* Grand Rapids, MI: Brazos, 2009.

Downey, Patrick. *Desperately Wicked: Philosophy, Christianity and the Human Heart.* Downers Grove, IL: IVP Academic, 2009.

Geisler, Norman L., and Ronald M. Brooks. *Come, Let Us Reason: An Introduction to Logical Thinking.* Grand Rapids, MI: Baker, 1990.

Geivett, R. Douglas, and James S. Spiegel. *Faith, Film and Philosophy: Big Ideas on the Big Screen.* Downers Grove, IL: IVP Academic, 2007.

Hadot, Pierre. *Philosophy as a Way of Life.* Malden, MA: Wiley-Blackwell, 1995.

Moreland, J. P., and William Lane Craig. *Philosophical Foundations for a Christian Worldview.* Downers Grove, IL: IVP Academic, 2003.

Morris, Thomas V., ed. *God and the Philosophers: The Reconciliation of Faith and Reason.* Oxford: Oxford University Press, 1996.

Moser, Paul K., ed. *Jesus and Philosophy: New Essays.* Cambridge: Cambridge University Press, 2009.

### Advanced Resources

Audi, Robert. *Epistemology: A Contemporary Introduction to the Theory of Knowledge.* London: Routledge, 2010.

Boghossian, Paul. *Fear of Knowledge: Against Relativism and Constructivism.* Oxford: Oxford University Press, 2006.

Craig, William Lane, and J. P. Moreland, eds. *The Blackwell Companion to Natural Theology.* Malden, MA: Wiley-Blackwell, 2009.

Crosby, John F. *The Selfhood of the Human Person.* Washington, DC: Catholic University Press, 1996.

Evans, C. Stephen. *Natural Signs and Knowledge of God: A New Look at Theistic Arguments.* Oxford: Oxford University Press, 2010.

Geivett, R. Douglas, and Brendan Sweetman, eds. *Contemporary Perspectives on Religious Epistemology.* Oxford: Oxford University Press, 1993.

Koons, Robert C., and George Bealer, eds. *The Waning of Materialism.* Oxford: Oxford University Press, 2010.

Lowe, E. J. *A Survey of Metaphysics.* Oxford: Oxford University Press, 2002.

Moreland, J. P. *Metaphysics.* Montreal, Quebec: McGill-Queen's University Press, 2001.

Moser, Paul K. *The Elusive God: Reorienting Religious Epistemology.* Cambridge: Cambridge University Press, 2009.

To read further in this area, please consult *Australasian Journal of Philosophy, Ethical Theory and Moral Practice, Ethics, Husserl Studies, Journal of Moral Philosophy, Journal of Religious Ethics, Journal of the Society of Christian Ethics, Studies in Christian Ethics, Philosophia Christi, Faith & Philosophy, Religious Studies* (Cambridge), *International Journal for Philosophy of Religion, Philosophy Compass.* Consider any of the resourceful OXFORD HANDBOOKS or CAMBRIDGE COMPANIONS or CONTINUUM COMPANIONS series of books. See also the various volumes in the BLACKWELL PHILOSOPHY ANTHOLOGIES series published by Wiley-Blackwell.

For graduate work in Christian philosophy, please consider the Master of Arts in Philosophy of Religion and Ethics at Biola University's Talbot School of Theology (talbot.edu/philosophy). For a historical overview of key philosophical ideas, see the course "Great Ideas of Philosophy" (2nd ed.) by Daniel N. Robinson (thegreatcourses.com).

## G. ETHICS
*Beginner Resources*

Evans, Jeremy A., and Daniel Heimbach. *Taking Christian Moral Thought Seriously: The Legitimacy of Religious Beliefs in the Marketplace of Ideas.* Nashville: B&H Academic, 2011.

Geisler, Norman L. *Christian Ethics: Contemporary Issues and Options.* 2nd ed. Grand Rapids, MI: Baker Academic, 2010.

Grenz, Stanley J., and Jay T. Smith. *Pocket Dictionary of Ethics.* Downers Grove, IL: IVP Academic, 2003.

Holmes, Arthur F. *Ethics: Approaching Moral Decisions.* 2nd ed. Downers Grove, IL: IVP Academic, 2007.

Horner, David. *Mind Your Faith: A Student's Guide to Thinking and Living Well.* Downers Grove, IL: IVP Academic, 2011.

Hunter, James Davison. *The Death of Character: Moral Education in an Age Without Good or Evil.* New York: Basic Books, 2001.

Kreeft, Peter. *Back to Virtue: Traditional Moral Wisdom for Modern Moral Confusion.* San Francisco: Ignatius Press, 1992.

Long, D. Stephen. *Christian Ethics: A Very Short Introduction.* Oxford: Oxford University Press, 2010.

Wilkens, Steve. *Beyond Bumper Sticker Ethics: An Introduction to Theories of Right and Wrong.* 2nd ed. Downers Grove, IL: IVP Academic, 2011.

Wright, N. T. *After You Believe: Why Christian Character Matters.* New York: HarperOne, 2010.

*Intermediate Resources*

Davis, John Jefferson. *Evangelical Ethics: Issues Facing the Church Today.* Phillipsburg, NJ: P&R Publishing, 2004.

Hare, John. *Why Bother Being Good?: The Place of God in the Moral Life.* Eugene, OR: Wipf & Stock, 2011.

Meilaender, Gilbert. *Neither Beast nor God: The Dignity of the Human Person.* Jackson, TN: Encounter Books, 2009.

O'Donovan, Oliver. *Common Objects of Love: Moral Reflection and the Shaping of Community.* Grand Rapids, MI: Eerdmans, 2009.

Peters, James R. *The Logic of the Heart: Augustine, Pascal, and the Rationality of Faith.* Grand Rapids, MI: Baker Academic, 2009.

Rae, Scott B. *Moral Choices: An Introduction to Ethics.* 3rd ed. Grand Rapids, MI: Zondervan, 2008.

Stassen, Glen H., and David P. Gushee. *Kingdom Ethics: Following Jesus in Contemporary Context.* Downers Grove, IL: IVP Academic, 2003.

Walls, Jerry, and David Baggett. *Good God: The Theistic Foundations of Morality.* Oxford: Oxford University Press, 2011.

Wolterstorff, Nicholas. *Justice in Love.* Grand Rapids, MI: Eerdmans, 2011.
Wright, Christopher J. H. *Old Testament Ethics for the People of God.* Downers Grove, IL: IVP Academic, 2004.

### Advanced Resources
Adams, Robert Merrihew. *A Theory of Virtue: Excellence in Being for the Good.* Oxford: Oxford University Press, 2009.
Annas, Julia. *Intelligent Virtue.* Oxford: Oxford University Press, 2011.
Evans, C. Stephen. *Kierkegaard on Faith and the Self: Collected Essays.* Waco, TX: Baylor University Press, 2009.
Meilaender, Gilbert. *The Oxford Handbook of Theological Ethics.* Oxford: Oxford University Press, 2007.
O'Donovan, Oliver. *Resurrection and Moral Order: An Outline for Evangelical Ethics.* Grand Rapids, MI: Eerdmans, 1994.
Rae, Scott B., and D. Joy Riley. *Outside the Womb: Moral Guidance for Assisted Reproduction.* Chicago: Moody, 2011.
Spaemann, Robert. *Happiness and Benevolence.* Translated by Jeremiah Alberg. Notre Dame, IN: University of Notre Dame Press, 2000.
von Hildebrand, Dietrich. *The Nature of Love.* Translated by John F. Crosby and John Henry Crosby. South Bend, IN: St. Augustine's Press, 2009.
Wannenwetsch, Bernd. *Political Worship: Ethics for Christian Citizens.* Translated by Margaret Kohl. Oxford: Oxford University Press, 2004.
Waters, Brent. *This Mortal Flesh: Incarnation and Bioethics.* Grand Rapids, MI: Brazos, 2009.

To read further in this area, please consult *British Journal of Aesthetics, Journal of Aesthetics and Art Criticism, Ethical Theory and Moral Practice, Ethics, Journal of Moral Philosophy, Journal of Religious Ethics, Journal of the Society of Christian Ethics, Studies in Christian Ethics, Journal of Markets and Morality, Philosophia Christi, International Journal of Ethics, Christian Bioethics, New Atlantis.*

There are numerous helpful anthologies: Robert Rakestraw and David Clark, eds., *Readings in Christian Ethics*, 2 vol. (Grand Rapids, MI: Baker Academic, 1994, 1995). See also the various volumes in the BLACKWELL PHILOSOPHY ANTHOLOGIES series published by Wiley-Blackwell. For beginner matter, see Chuck Colson's Center for Christian Worldview's product, *Doing the Right Thing: A Six-Part Exploration of Ethics* DVD series and study guide (www.doingtherightthing.com).

## H. Apologetics and Evangelism

### Beginner Resources

Copan, Paul. *When God Goes to Starbucks: A Guide to Everyday Apologetics.* Grand Rapids, MI: Baker, 2008.

Craig, William Lane. *On Guard: Defending Your Faith with Reason and Precision.* Colorado Springs, CO: David C. Cook, 2010.

Geisler, Norman, and Patrick Zuckeran. *The Apologetics of Jesus: A Caring Approach to Dealing with Doubters.* Grand Rapids, MI: Baker, 2009.

Hazen, Craig. *Five Sacred Crossings: A Novel Approach to a Reasonable Faith.* Eugene, OR: Harvest House, 2008.

Keller, Timothy. *The Reason for God: Belief in an Age of Skepticism.* New York: Dutton, 2008.

Koukl, Gregory. *Tactics: A Game Plan for Discussing Your Christian Convictions.* Grand Rapids, MI: Zondervan, 2009.

McDowell, Sean, ed. *Apologetics for a New Generation: A Biblical and Culturally Relevant Approach to Talking About God.* Eugene, OR: Harvest House, 2009.

Moreland, J. P., and Klaus Issler. *In Search of a Confident Faith: Overcoming Barriers to Trusting in God.* Downers Grove, IL: InterVarsity, 2008.

Newman, Randy. *Bringing the Gospel Home: Witnessing to Family Members, Close Friends, and Others Who Know You Well.* Wheaton, IL: Crossway, 2011.

Newman, Randy. *Questioning Evangelism: Engaging People's Hearts the Way Jesus Did.* Grand Rapids, MI: Kregel, 2004.

Zacharias, Ravi. *Is Your Church Ready?: Motivating Leaders to Live an Apologetic Life.* Grand Rapids, MI: Zondervan, 2003.

### Intermediate Resources

Boa, Kenneth, and Robert M. Bowman. *Faith Has Its Reasons: Integrative Approaches to Defending the Christian Faith.* Waynesboro, GA: Paternoster, 2006.

Clark, David K. *Dialogical Apologetics: A Person-Centered Approach to Christian Defense.* Grand Rapids, MI: Baker, 1999.

Coppenger, Mark. *Moral Apologetics for Contemporary Christians: Pushing Back Against Cultural and Religious Critics.* Nashville: B&H Academic, 2011.

Corduan, Winfried. *No Doubt About It: The Case for Christianity.* Nashville: B&H, 1997.

Green, Michael. *Evangelism in the Early Church.* Revised edition. Grand Rapids, MI: Eerdmans, 2004.

Horner, David. *Mind Your Faith: A Student's Guide to Thinking and Living Well.* Downers Grove, IL: IVP Academic, 2011.

Root, Jerry, and Stan Guthrie. *The Sacrament of Evangelism.* Chicago: Moody, 2011.

Willard, Dallas. *Knowing Christ Today: Why We Can Trust Spiritual Knowledge.* New York: HarperOne, 2009.

Williams, Clifford. *Existential Reasons for Belief in God: A Defense of Desires and Emotions for Faith.* Downers Grove, IL: IVP Academic, 2011.

Wooddell, Joseph. *The Beauty of the Faith: Using Aesthetics for Christian Apologetics.* Eugene, OR: Wipf & Stock, 2010.

### Advanced Resources

Baggett, David, and Jerry L. Walls. *Good God: The Theistic Foundations of Morality.* Oxford: Oxford University Press, 2011.

Copan, Paul. *Is God a Moral Monster?: Making Sense of the Old Testament God.* Grand Rapids, MI: Baker Academic, 2010.

Copan, Paul, and Mark D. Linville. *Moral Argument.* New York: Continuum, 2012.

Cowan, Steven, gen. ed. *Five Views on Apologetics.* Grand Rapids, MI: Zondervan, 2000.

Craig, William Lane. *Reasonable Faith: Christian Truth and Apologetics.* 3rd ed. Wheaton, IL: Crossway, 2009.

Craig, William Lane, and J. P. Moreland, eds. *The Blackwell Companion to Natural Theology.* Malden, MA: Wiley-Blackwell, 2009.

Groothuis, Doug. *Christian Apologetics: A Comprehensive Case for Biblical Faith.* Downers Grove, IL: IVP Academic, 2011.

Habermas, Gary R., and Michael R. Licona. *The Case for the Resurrection of Jesus.* Grand Rapids, MI: Kregel, 2004.

Licona, Michael R. *The Resurrection of Jesus: A New Historiographical Approach.* Downers Grove, IL: IVP Academic, 2010.

Wright, N. T. *The Resurrection of the Son of God.* Minneapolis: Fortress, 2003.

To read further in this area, please consult *Christian Research Journal, Philosophia Christi, Salvo, Areopagus Journal, Christian Apologetics Journal, Journal of Christian Apologetics.* For a worthwhile beginner series, see Lee Strobel's "Case" books (for example, *Case for Christ*) published by Zondervan. Please also note Ted Cabal, gen. ed., *The Apologetics Study Bible* (Nashville: Holman Bible Publishers, 2007).

For intermediate and advanced general reference resources, see the "readers" and "anthology" multi-volumes that showcase primary sources in

Christian apologetics by Chad Meister and Khaldoun Sweis and then William Edgar and Scott Oliphant (Zondervan, Crossway), respectively. See also Louis Markos, *Apologetics for the Twenty-First Century* (Wheaton, IL: Crossway, 2010); Norman Geisler, *Baker Encyclopedia of Christian Apologetics* (Grand Rapids, MI: Baker, 1999).

In recent years, there have been some fruitful autobiographical accounts written in order to show conversion from some non-Christian worldview (for example, atheism) to Deism or Christianity. See Peter Hitchens, *The Rage Against God: How Atheism Led Me to Faith* (Grand Rapids, MI: Zondervan, 2010); Holly Ordway, *Not God's Type: A Rational Academic Finds a Radical Faith* (Chicago: Moody, 2010); Antony Flew with Roy Abraham Varghese, *There Is a God: How the World's Most Notorious Atheist Changed His Mind* (New York: HarperOne, 2008); J. P. Moreland, *The God Question: An Invitation to a Life of Meaning* (Eugene, OR: Harvest House, 2009).

For certificate and graduate level work in Christian apologetics, please consider the offerings from Biola University's Christian Apologetics program (biola.edu/apologetics).

## I. HISTORY
### Beginner Resources
Fischer, David Hackett. *Historians' Fallacies: Toward a Logic of Historical Thought*. New York: Harper Torchbook, 1970.

Foster, Paul. *Early Christian Thinkers: The Lives and Legacies of Twelve Key Figures*. Downers Grove, IL: IVP Academic, 2010.

Green, Bradley G., ed. *Shapers of Christian Orthodoxy: Engaging with Early and Medieval Theologians*. Downers Grove, IL: IVP Academic, 2010.

Jenkins, Philip. *The Next Christendom: The Coming of Global Christianity*. Revised and updated. New York: Oxford University Press, USA, 2011.

Noll, Mark A. *Turning Points: Decisive Moments in the History of Christianity*. Grand Rapids, MI: Baker Academic, 2001.

Schmidt, Alvin J. *How Christianity Changed the World*. Grand Rapids, MI: Zondervan, 2004.

Shelley, Bruce L. *Church History in Plain Language*. 3rd ed. Nashville: Thomas Nelson, 2008.

Stark, Rodney. *Cities of God: The Real Story of How Christianity Became an Urban Movement and Conquered Rome*. New York: HarperOne, 2007.

Stark, Rodney. *The Victory of Reason: How Christianity Led to Freedom, Capitalism, and Western Success*. New York: Random House, 2006.

Trueman, Carl. *Histories and Fallacies: Problems Faced in the Writing of History*. Wheaton, IL: Crossway, 2010.

### Intermediate Resources

Breisach, Ernst. *Historiography: Ancient, Medieval, and Modern.* 3rd ed. Chicago: University of Chicago Press, 2007.

Gilderhus, Mark T. *History and Historians.* 7th ed. New York: Prentice-Hall, 2009.

Gonzalez, Justo. *Story of Christianity.* Volumes 1–2. 2nd ed. New York: HarperOne, 2010.

Herrera, Robert A. *Reasons for Our Rhymes: An Inquiry into the Philosophy of History.* Grand Rapids, MI: Eerdmans, 2001.

McGrath, Alister. *Historical Theology: An Introduction to the History of Christian Thought.* Oxford: Wiley-Blackwell, 1998.

Meister, Chad, and James Stump. *Christian Thought: A Historical Introduction.* London: Routledge, 2010.

Noll, Mark A. *The New Shape of World Christianity: How American Experience Reflects Global Faith.* Downers Grove, IL: IVP Academic, 2009.

Noll, Mark A. *The Old Religion in a New World: The History of North American Christianity.* Grand Rapids, MI: Eerdmans, 2002.

Olson, Roger E. *The Mosaic of Christian Belief: Twenty Centuries of Unity and Diversity.* Downers Grove, IL: IVP Academic, 2002.

Reynolds, John Mark. *When Athens Met Jerusalem: An Introduction to Classical and Christian Thought.* Downers Grove, IL: IVP Academic, 2009.

### Advanced Resources

Bentley, Michael. *Modern Historiography: An Introduction.* London: Routledge, 1999.

Dawson, Christopher. *Dynamics of World History.* 3rd ed. Wilmington, DE: ISI Books, 2002.

Gillespie, Michael Allen. *The Theological Origins of Modernity.* Chicago: University of Chicago Press, 2008.

Harlan, David. *The Degradation of American History.* Chicago: University of Chicago Press, 1997.

Keillor, Steven J. *God's Judgments: Interpreting History and the Christian Faith.* Downers Grove, IL: IVP Academic, 2007.

Kidd, Thomas S. *God of Liberty: A Religious History of the American Revolution.* New York: Basic Books, 2010.

Middelmann, Udo. *Neither Necessary nor Inevitable: History Needn't Have Been Like That.* Eugene, OR: Wipf & Stock, 2011.

Noll, Mark A. *America's God, from Jonathan Edwards to Abraham Lincoln.* Oxford: Oxford University Press, 2002.

O'Malley, John W. *Four Cultures of the West.* Cambridge, MA: Harvard University Press, 2004.

Smith, Christian, ed. *The Secular Revolution: Power, Interests, and Conflict in the Secularization of American Public Life.* Berkeley, CA: University of California Press, 2003.

To read further in this area, please consult *Journal of Church and State, Church History, Fides et historia, Reviews in American History, Journal of American History, The Historian, The American Historical Review.* For reference resources, see Henry Bettenson and Chris Maunder, *Documents of the Christian Church,* 3rd ed. (Oxford: Oxford University Press, 1999) and Alister E. McGrath, *The Christian Theology Reader,* 4th ed. (Malden, MA: Wiley-Blackwell, 2011).

## J. CULTURE MAKING AND CHRISTIAN SOCIAL RESPONSIBILITY

### Beginner Resources

Crouch, Andy. *Culture Making: Recovering Our Creative Calling.* Downers Grove, IL: InterVarsity, 2008.

Keller, Timothy. *Generous Justice: How God's Grace Makes Us Just.* New York: Penguin Books, 2010.

McCracken, Brett. *Hipster Christianity: When Church and Cool Collide.* Grand Rapids, MI: Baker, 2010.

Mouw, Richard B. *Uncommon Decency: Christian Civility in an Uncivil World.* Downers Grove, IL: InterVarsity, 2010.

Mouw, Richard J. *Abraham Kuyper: A Short and Personal Introduction.* Grand Rapids, MI: Eerdmans, 2011.

Myers, Ken. *All God's Children and Blue Suede Shoes.* Updated introduction. Wheaton, IL: Crossway, 2012.

Staub, Dick. *The Culturally Savvy Christian: A Manifesto for Deepening Faith and Enriching Popular Culture in an Age of Christianity-Lite.* San Francisco: Jossey-Bass, 2008.

Stott, John. *Christian Mission in the Modern World.* Downers Grove, IL: InterVarsity, 2008.

Swanson, Eric, and Sam Williams. *To Transform a City: Whole Church, Whole Gospel, Whole City.* Grand Rapids, MI: Zondervan, 2010.

Volf, Miroslav. *A Public Faith: How Followers of Christ Should Serve the Common Good.* Grand Rapids, MI: Brazos, 2011.

### Intermediate Resources

Dickson, John. *The Best Kept Secret of Christian Mission: Promoting the Gospel with More Than Our Lips.* Grand Rapids, MI: Zondervan, 2010.

Goheen, Michael W. *A Light to the Nations: The Missional Church and the Biblical Story.* Grand Rapids, MI: Baker, 2011.

Hegeman, David B. *Plowing in Hope: Toward a Biblical Theology of Culture.* Moscow, ID: Canon Press, 2007.

Hicks, Douglas A. *With God on All Sides: Leadership in a Devout and Diverse America.* Oxford: Oxford University Press, 2008.

Kraft, Charles H., and Marquerite G. Kraft. *Christianity in Culture: A Study in Dynamic Biblical Theologizing in Cross-Cultural Perspective.* 25th anniversary ed. MaryKnoll, NY: Orbis Books, 2005.

Moore, T. M. *Culture Matters: A Call for Consensus on Christian Cultural Engagement.* Grand Rapids, MI: Baker Academic, 2007.

Muehlhoff, Tim, and Todd Lewis. *Authentic Communication: Christian Speech Engaging Culture.* Downers Grove, IL: IVP Academic, 2010.

Stark, Rodney. *The Rise of Christianity: How the Obscure, Marginal Jesus Movement Became the Dominant Religious Force in the Western World in a Few Centuries.* New York: HarperCollins, 1996.

Stark, Rodney. *What Americans Really Believe.* Waco, TX: Baylor University Press, 2008.

Vanhoozer, Kevin J., Charles A. Anderson, and Michael J. Sleasman, eds. *Everyday Theology: How to Read Cultural Texts and Interpret Trends.* Grand Rapids, MI: Baker Academic, 2007.

### *Advanced Resources*

Boersma, Hans. *Heavenly Participation: The Weaving of a Sacramental Tapestry.* Grand Rapids, MI: Eerdmans, 2011.

Calhoun, Craig, Mark Juergensmeyer, and Jonathan VanAntwerpen, eds. *Rethinking Secularism.* New York: Oxford University Press, USA, 2011.

Chaplin, Jonathan. *Herman Dooyeweerd: Christian Philosopher of State and Civil Society.* Notre Dame, IN: University of Notre Dame Press, 2010.

Gay, Craig M. *The Way of the (Modern) World: Or, Why It's Tempting to Live as if God Doesn't Exist.* Grand Rapids, MI: Eerdmans, 1998.

Hunter, James Davison. *To Change the World: The Irony, Tragedy, and Possibility of Christianity in the Late Modern World.* New York: Oxford University Press, USA, 2010.

Smith, Steven D. *The Disenchantment of Secular Discourse.* Cambridge, MA: Harvard University Press, 2010.

Taylor, Charles. *A Secular Age.* Cambridge, MA: Belknap Press/Harvard University Press, 2007.

Volf, Miroslav. *Exclusion and Embrace: A Theological Exploration of Identity, Otherness, and Reconciliation.* Nashville: Abingdon, 1996.

Warner, Michael, Jonathan VanAntwerpen, and Craig Calhoun, eds. *Varieties of Secularism in a Secular Age.* Cambridge, MA: Harvard University Press, 2010.

Wolterstorff, Nicholas. *Hearing the Call: Liturgy, Justice, Church, and World.* Edited by Mark R. Gornik and Gregory Thompson. Grand Rapids, MI: Eerdmans, 2011.

To read further in this area, please consult *Books & Culture, Christianity Today, Cultural Encounters: A Journal for the Theology of Culture, First Things, Modern Age, The Intercollegiate Review, Mars Hill Review, Mars Hill Audio Journal, The Other Journal, WORLD* magazine.

## K. COMPARATIVE WORLDVIEW AND WORLD RELIGION ANALYSIS

### Beginner Resources

Bertrand, J. Mark. *(Re)Thinking Worldview: Learning to Think, Live, and Speak in This World.* Wheaton, IL: Crossway, 2007.

Corduan, Winfried. *A Tapestry of Faiths: The Common Threads Between Christianity and World Religions.* Eugene, OR: Wipf & Stock, 2009.

Corduan, Winfried. *Neighboring Faiths: A Christian Introduction to World Religions.* Downers Grove, IL: IVP Academic, 1998.

Halverson, Dean. *The Compact Guide to World Religions.* Minneapolis: Bethany, 1996.

Kärkkäinen, Veli-Matti. *An Introduction to the Theology of Religions: Biblical, Historical, and Contemporary Perspectives.* Downers Grove, IL: IVP Academic, 2003.

Lilla, Mark. *The Stillborn God: Religion, Politics, and the Modern West.* New York: Random House, 2008.

McDermott, Gerald R. *The Baker Pocket Guide to World Religions.* Grand Rapids, MI: Baker, 2008.

Robinson, Thomas A., and Hillary Rodrigues, eds. *World Religions: A Guide to the Essentials.* Peabody, MA: Hendrickson Publishers, 2006.

Sire, James W. *Why Should Anyone Believe Anything at All?* Downers Grove, IL: InterVarsity, 1994.

Spiegel, James S. *The Making of an Atheist: How Immorality Leads to Unbelief.* Chicago: Moody, 2010.

### Intermediate Resources

Carson, D. A. *The Gagging of God: Christianity Confronts Pluralism.* 15th anniversary ed. Grand Rapids, MI: Zondervan, 2002.

Craycraft Jr., Kenneth R. *The American Myth of Religious Freedom.* Dallas: Spence Publishing, 1999.

Nash, Ronald H. *Is Jesus the Only Savior?* Grand Rapids, MI: Zondervan, 1994.

Netland, Harold. *Encountering Religious Pluralism: The Challenge to Christian Faith and Mission.* Downers Grove, IL: IVP Academic, 2001.

Okholm, Dennis L., and Timothy R. Phillips, eds. *Four Views on Salvation in a Pluralistic World*, COUNTERPOINT Series. Grand Rapids, MI: Zondervan, 1995.

Ott, Craig, and Harold A. Netland, eds. *Globalizing Theology: Belief and Practice in an Era of World Christianity.* Grand Rapids, MI: Baker Academic, 2006.

Owen, J. Judd. *Religion and the Demise of Liberal Rationalism: The Foundational Crisis of the Separation of Church and State.* Chicago: University of Chicago Press, 2001.

Post, Stephen G. *Human Nature and the Freedom of Public Religious Expression.* Notre Dame, IN: University of Notre Dame Press, 2003.

Rieff, Philip. *The Triumph of the Therapeutic: Uses of Faith After Freud.* Wilmington, DE: ISI Books, 2007.

Sire, James W. *The Universe Next Door: A Basic Worldview Catalog.* 5th ed. Downers Grove, IL: IVP Academic, 2009.

## Advanced Resources

Basinger, David. *Religious Diversity: A Philosophical Assessment.* Burlington, VT: Ashgate, 2002.

Eddy, Paul R. *John Hick's Pluralist Philosophy of World Religions.* Burlington, VT: Ashgate, 2002.

Griffiths, Paul J. *Problems of Religious Diversity.* Malden, MA: Wiley-Blackwell, 2001.

Hart, D. G. *The University Gets Religion: Religious Studies in American Higher Education.* Baltimore, MD: Johns Hopkins University, 1999.

Johnson, Keith E. *Rethinking the Trinity and Religious Pluralism: An Augustinian Assessment.* Downers Grove, IL: IVP Academic, 2011.

Meister, Chad V. *The Oxford Handbook of Religious Diversity.* New York: Oxford University Press, USA, 2010.

Pavlischeck, Keith J. *John Courtney Murray and the Dilemma of Religious Toleration.* Kirksville, MO: Thomas Jefferson University Press, 1994.

Quinn, Philip L., and Kevin Meeker. *The Philosophical Challenge of Religious Diversity.* New York: Oxford University Press, USA, 2000.

Vanhoozer, Kevin J., ed. *The Trinity in a Pluralistic Age: Theological Essays on Culture and Religion.* Grand Rapids, MI: Eerdmans, 1997.

Werther, David, and Mark D. Linville. *Philosophy and the Christian Worldview: Analysis, Assessment, and Development.* New York: Continuum Press, 2012.

To read further in this area, please consult the sources mentioned above in the Apologetics and Philosophy sections. In addition, please see *Christian Scholar's Review, The Review of Faith & International Affairs, First Things, Evangelical Interfaith Dialogue, The Christian Century, Cross Currents, Theology Today, Journal of Religion, Journal of Religion and Popular Culture*.

## L. WORK-LIFE ROUTINES
### Beginner Resources
Allen, David. *Making It All Work: Winning at the Game of Work and Business of Life*. New York: Viking, 2008.

Fields, Leslie Leyland. *The Spirit of Food: 34 Writers on Feasting and Fasting Toward God*. Eugene, OR: Wipf & Stock, 2010.

Guinness, Os, Ginger Koloszyc, and Karen Lee-Thorp, eds. *Entrepreneurs of Life: Faith and the Venture of Purposeful Living*. Colorado Springs, CO: NavPress, 2001.

Hanna, Frank. *What Your Money Means: And How to Use It Well*. Chestnut Ridge, NY: Crossroad Publishing, 2008.

Jones, Timothy. *Workday Prayers: On the Job Meditations for Tending Your Soul*. Chicago: Loyola Press, 2001.

Morris, Thomas. *Art of Achievement: Mastering the 7Cs of Success in Business and Life*. Kansas City, MO: Andrews McMeel Publishing, 2002.

Nelson, Tom. *Work Matters: Connecting Sunday Worship to Monday Work*. Wheaton, IL: Crossway, 2011.

Schuurman, Douglas J. *Vocation: Discerning Our Callings in Life*. Grand Rapids, MI: Eerdmans, 2003.

Stevens, R. Paul, and Alvin Ung. *Taking Your Soul to Work: Overcoming the Nine Deadly Sins of the Workplace*. Grand Rapids, MI: Eerdmans, 2010.

Witherington III, Ben. *Work: A Kingdom Perspective on Labor*. Grand Rapids, MI: Eerdmans, 2011.

### Intermediate Resources
Alexander, Robert William. *Professionals: Men and Women Partnering with the Trinity in Everyday Life*. Seattle: CreateSpace, 2009.

Banks, Robert. *Redeeming the Routines: Bringing Theology to Life*. Grand Rapids, MI: Baker Academic, 2001.

Bonzo, J. Matthew, and Michael R. Stevens. *Wendell Berry and the Cultivation of Life*. Grand Rapids, MI: Baker Academic, 2009.

Crawford, Matthew. *Shop Class as Soulcraft: An Inquiry into the Value of Work*. New York: Penguin Books, 2010.

Harvey, Dave. *Rescuing Ambition*. Wheaton, IL: Crossway, 2010.

Placher, William C. *Callings: Twenty Centuries of Christian Wisdom on Vocation.* Grand Rapids, MI: Eerdmans, 2005.

Ryken, Leland. *Work and Leisure in Christian Perspective.* Eugene, OR: Wipf & Stock, 2002.

Stevens, R. Paul. *The Other Six Days: Vocation, Work, and Ministry in Biblical Perspective.* Grand Rapids, MI: Eerdmans, 2000.

Veith, Gene Edward. *God at Work: Your Christian Vocation in All of Life.* Wheaton, IL: Crossway, 2002.

Wirzba, Norman. *Food and Faith: A Theology of Eating.* Cambridge: Cambridge University Press, 2011.

***Advanced Resources***

Andreou, Chrisoula, and Mark D. White, eds. *The Thief of Time: Philosophical Essays on Procrastination.* New York: Oxford University Press, USA, 2010.

Charry, Ellen T. *Inquiring After God: Classic and Contemporary Readings.* Malden, MA: Wiley-Blackwell, 2000.

Cosden, Darrell. *A Theology of Work: Work and the New Creation.* Eugene, OR: Wipf & Stock, 2006.

Haney, Mitchell R., and A. David Kline. *The Value of Time and Leisure in a World of Work.* Lanham, MD: Lexington Books, 2010.

Kanigel, Robert. *The One Best Way: Frederick Winslow Taylor and the Enigma of Efficiency.* Cambridge, MA: MIT Press, 2005.

Marshall, Paul. *A Kind of Life Imposed on Man: Vocation and Social Order from Tyndale to Locke.* Toronto, Ontario: University of Toronto Press, 1996.

Pieper, Josef. *Leisure: The Basis of Culture.* San Francisco: Ignatius Press, 2009.

Ranft, Patricia. *The Theology of Work: Peter Damian and the Medieval Religious Renewal Movement.* New York: Palgrave MacMillan, 2006.

Sorg, Dom Rembert. *Holy Work: Toward a Benedictine Theology of Manual Labor.* Naperville, IL: Source Books, 2003.

Volf, Miroslav. *Work in the Spirit: Toward a Theology of Work.* Eugene, OR: Wipf & Stock, 2001.

To read further in this area, please consult *International Journal of Practical Theology.* See also the Fortress Press series CHRISTIAN EXPLORATIONS OF DAILY LIVING, and Robert Banks and R. Paul Stevens, eds., *The Complete Book of Everyday Christianity: An A–Z Guide to Following Christ in Every Aspect of Life* (Grand Rapids, MI: Eerdmans, 1997).

## M. LEADERSHIP FORMATION AND FRIENDSHIP
### Beginner Resources

Barton, Ruth Haley. *Strengthening the Soul of Your Leadership: Seeking God in the Crucible of Ministry.* Downers Grove, IL: InterVarsity, 2006.

Belcher, Jim. *Deep Church: A Third Way Beyond Emerging and Traditional.* Downers Grove, IL: InterVarsity, 2009.

Benner, David G. *Sacred Companions: The Gift of Spiritual Friendship and Direction.* Downers Grove, IL: InterVarsity, 2004.

Bonhoeffer, Dietrich. *Life Together: The Classic Exploration of Faith in Community.* New York: HarperOne, 1978.

Epstein, Joseph. *Friendship: An Exposé.* Boston, MA: Houghton Mifflin, 2007.

Fryling, Robert A. *The Leadership Ellipse: Shaping How We Lead by Who We Are.* Downers Grove, IL: InterVarsity, 2010.

Nouwen, Henri J. M. *Creative Ministry.* Garden City, NY: Doubleday, 1991.

Nouwen, Henri J. M. *The Wounded Healer: Ministry in Contemporary Society.* Garden City, NY: Doubleday, 1979.

Peterson, Eugene H. *The Pastor: A Memoir.* New York: HarperCollins, 2011.

Workman, Dave. *The Outward Focused Life: Becoming a Servant in a Serve-Me World.* Grand Rapids, MI: Baker, 2008.

### Intermediate Resources

Banks, Robert, and Bernice Ledbetter. *Reviewing Leadership: A Christian Evaluation of Current Approaches.* Grand Rapids, MI: Baker Academic, 2004.

Brennen, Dan. *Sacred Unions, Sacred Passions: Engaging the Mystery of Friendship Between Women and Men.* Elgin, IL: FaithDance Publishing, 2010.

Hagberg, Janet O. *Real Power: Stages of Personal Power in Organizations.* 3rd ed. Salem, WI: Sheffield Publishing, 2003.

Heuertz, Christopher L., and Christine D. Pohl. *Friendship at the Margins: Discovering Mutuality in Service and Mission.* Downers Grove, IL: InterVarsity, 2010.

Jacobsen, Eric O. *The Three Tasks of Leadership: Worldly Wisdom for Pastoral Leaders.* Grand Rapids, MI: Eerdmans, 2009.

Lewis, C. S. *Four Loves.* New York: Harcourt, 1960.

Lingenfelter, Sherwood G. *Leading Cross-Culturally: Covenant Relationships for Effective Christian Leadership.* Grand Rapids, MI: Baker Academic, 2008.

Pohl, Christine D. *Making Room: Recovering Hospitality as a Christian Tradition.* Grand Rapids, MI: Eerdmans, 1999.

Richard, Lucien. *Living the Hospitality of God.* New York: Paulist Press, 2000.

Swanson, Eric, and Rick Rusaw. *The Externally Focused Quest: Becoming the Best Church for the Community.* San Francisco: Jossey-Bass, 2010.

### Advanced Resources

Branson, Mark Lau, and Juan F. Martinez. *Churches, Cultures and Leadership: A Practical Theology of Congregations and Ethnicities*. Downers Grove, IL: IVP Academic, 2011.

Chemers, Martin M. *An Integrative Theory of Leadership*. New York: Psychology Press, 1997.

Healy, Nicholas. *Church, World, and the Christian Life: Practical-Prophetic Ecclesiology*. Cambridge: Cambridge University Press, 2000.

Kierkegaard, Søren. *Works of Love*. New York: Harper Perennial Modern Classics, 2009.

Meilaender, Gilbert. *Friendship: A Study in Theological Ethics*. Notre Dame, IN: University of Notre Dame Press, 1985.

Moschella, Mary Clark. *Ethnography as a Pastoral Practice*. Cleveland, OH: Pilgrim Press, 2008.

Reinders, Hans S. *Receiving the Gift of Friendship: Profound Disability, Theological Anthropology, and Ethics*. Grand Rapids, MI: Eerdmans, 2008.

Reynolds, Thomas E. *Vulnerable Communion: A Theology of Disability and Hospitality*. Grand Rapids, MI: Brazos, 2008.

Tan, Siang-Yang. *Full Service: Moving from Self-Serve Christianity to Total Servanthood*. Grand Rapids, MI: Baker, 2006.

Wadell, Paul J. *Friendship and the Moral Life*. Notre Dame, IN: University of Notre Dame Press, 1989.

To read further in this area, please consult *Leadership Journal, Journal of Religious Leadership*, and *Harvard Business Review*, along with the resources mentioned in the Ethics section.

## N. BUSINESS, ECONOMICS, URBANISM, AND ENVIRONMENT

### Beginner Resources

Bouma-Prediger, Steven. *For the Beauty of the Earth: A Christian View for Creation Care*. Grand Rapids, MI: Baker Academic, 2010.

Cavanaugh, William T. *Being Consumed: Economics and Christian Desire*. Grand Rapids, MI: Eerdmans, 2008.

Hanna, Frank. *What Your Money Means: And How to Use It Well*. Chestnut Ridge, NY: Crossroad Publishing, 2008.

Hazlitt, William. *Economics in One Lesson*. 50th anniversary ed. New York: Laissez Faire Books, 2008.

Hill, Alexander. *Just Business: Christian Ethics for the Marketplace*. Revised edition. Downers Grove, IL: IVP Academic, 2008.

Jacobsen, Eric O. *Sidewalks in the Kingdom: New Urbanism and the Christian Faith*. Grand Rapids, MI: Brazos, 2003.

Keller, Timothy J. *Center Church: Doing Balanced, Gospel-Centered Ministry in Your City*. Grand Rapids, MI: Zondervan, 2012.

Kotkin, Joel. *The City: A Global History*. New York: Modern Library, 2006.

Rae, Scott, and Austin Hill. *The Virtues of Capitalism*. Chicago: Northfield Publishing, 2010.

van Duzer, Jeff. *Why Business Matters to God*. Downers Grove, IL: IVP Academic, 2010.

### Intermediate Resources

Claar, Victor V., and Robin J. Klay. *Economics in Christian Perspective: Theory, Policy, and Life Choices*. Downers Grove, IL: IVP Academic, 2007.

Gregg, Samuel. *Economic Thinking for the Theologically Minded*. Lanham, MD: University Press of America, 2002.

Morse, Jennifer Roback. *Love and Economics: Why the Laissez-Faire Family Doesn't Work*. Dallas: Spence Publishing, 2004.

Richards, Jay. *Money, Greed, and God: Why Capitalism Is the Solution and Not the Problem*. New York: HarperOne, 2009.

Rundle, Steve, and Tom Steffen. *Great Commission Companies: The Emerging Role of Business in Mission*. Downers Grove, IL: IVP Academic, 2011.

Sowell, Thomas. *Basic Economics: A Common Sense Guide to the Economy*. 4th ed. New York: Basic Books, 2011.

Sowell, Thomas. *Economic Facts and Fallacies*. New York: Basic Books, 2011.

Stevens, R. Paul. *Doing God's Business: Meaning and Motivation for the Marketplace*. Grand Rapids, MI: Eerdmans, 2006.

Wong, Kenman L., and Scott Rae. *Beyond Integrity: A Judeo-Christian Approach to Business Ethics*. Grand Rapids, MI: Zondervan, 2012.

Wong, Kenman L., and Scott Rae. *Business for the Common Good: A Christian Vision for the Marketplace*. Downers Grove, IL: IVP Academic, 2011.

### Advanced Resources

Bartholomew, Craig. *Where Mortals Dwell: A Christian View of Place for Today*. Grand Rapids, MI: Baker Academic, 2011.

Bess, Philip. *Till We Have Built Jerusalem: Architecture, Urbanism, and the Sacred*. Wilmington, DE: ISI Books, 2006.

Chafuen, Alejandro A. *Faith and Liberty: The Economic Thought of the Late Scholastics*. Lanham, MD: Lexington Books, 2003.

Gorringe, T. J. *A Theology of the Built Environment: Justice, Empowerment, Redemption*. Cambridge: Cambridge University Press, 2002.

Gregg, Samuel. *The Commercial Society: Foundations and Challenges in a Global Age*. Lanham, MD: Lexington Books, 2007.

Inge, John. *A Christian Theology of Place*. Burlington, VT: Ashgate, 2003.

Mueller, John D. *Redeeming Economics: Rediscovering the Missing Element*. Wilmington, DE: ISI Books, 2010.

Ropke, Wilhelm. *A Humane Economy: The Social Framework of the Free Market*. 3rd ed. Wilmington, DE: ISI Books, 1999.

Schneider, John. *The Good of Affluence: Seeking God in a Culture of Wealth*. Grand Rapids, MI: Eerdmans, 2002.

Stark, Rodney. *The Victory of Reason: How Christianity Led to Freedom, Capitalism, and Western Success*. New York: Random House, 2006.

For further reading, see *Journal of Markets and Morality, Business & Society, Business Ethics Magazine, Business Ethics Quarterly, Business & Society Review, Comment Magazine, Ethix, Faith & Economics, Journal of Biblical Integration in Business, Journal of Business Ethics, Journal of Faith in Business and the Industrial Christian Fellowship, Journal of Management, Spirituality and Religion.*

For resources on economics, see the Acton Institute's *Effective Stewardship* DVD and study guide (www.effectivestewardship.com), Acton Institute's *The Call of the Entrepreneur* DVD and study guide, and "The Cornwall Declaration on Environmental Stewardship" (www.cornwallalliance.org).

## O. POLITICS, LAW, AND SOCIAL THEORY
### Beginner Resources

Forni, P. M. *Choosing Civility: The Twenty-Five Rules of Considerate Conduct*. New York: St. Martin's Press, 2004.

George, Robert P. *The Clash of Orthodoxies: Law, Religion, and Morality in Crisis*. Wilmington, DE: ISI Press, 2001.

Gerson, Michael, and Peter Wehner. *City of Man: Religion and Politics in a New Era*. Chicago: Moody, 2010.

Grudem, Wayne. *Politics—According to the Bible: A Comprehensive Resource for Understanding Modern Political Issues in Light of Scripture*. Grand Rapids, MI: Zondervan, 2010.

Guinness, Os. *The Case for Civility: And Why Our Future Depends on It*. New York: HarperOne, 2008.

Mahoney, Daniel J. *The Conservative Foundations of the Liberal Order: Defending Democracy Against Its Modern Enemies and Immoderate Friends*. Wilmington, DE: ISI Books, 2011.

Mansfield, Harvey C. *Tocqueville: A Very Short Introduction*. Oxford: Oxford University Press, 2010.

Marty, Martin. *Building Cultures of Trust*. Grand Rapids, MI: Eerdmans, 2010.

Mitchell, Mark T., and Nathan Schlueter. *The Humane Vision of Wendell Berry.* Wilmington, DE: ISI Books, 2011.

Sommerville, John C. *Religion in the National Agenda: What We Mean by Religious, Spiritual, Secular.* Waco, TX: Baylor University Press, 2009.

**Intermediate Resources**

Beckwith, Francis J. *Politics for Christians: Statecraft as Soulcraft.* Downers Grove, IL: IVP Academic, 2010.

Budziszewski, J. *The Line Through the Heart: Natural Law as Fact, Theory, and Sign of Contradiction.* Wilmington, DE: ISI Books, 2009.

Carey, George W. *Freedom and Virtue: The Conservative/Libertarian Debate.* Wilmington, DE: ISI Books, 1998.

Forsythe, Clarke D. *Politics for the Greatest Good: The Case for Prudence in the Public Square.* Downers Grove, IL: IVP Academic, 2009.

Guerra, Marc D. *Christians as Political Animals: Taking the Measure of Modernity and Modern Democracy.* Wilmington, DE: ISI Books, 2010.

Lindsay, D. Michael. *Faith in the Halls of Power: How Evangelicals Joined the American Elite.* New York: Oxford University Press, USA, 2007.

O'Donovan, Oliver. *Bonds of Imperfection: Christian Politics, Past and Present.* Grand Rapids, MI: Eerdmans, 2003.

Sweetman, Brendan. *Why Politics Needs Religion: The Place of Religious Arguments in the Public Square.* Downers Grove, IL: InterVarsity, 2006.

Taylor, Charles. *Modern Social Imaginaries.* Durham, NC: Duke University Press, 2003.

VanDrunen, David. *Natural Law and the Two Kingdoms: A Study in the Development of Reformed Social Thought.* Grand Rapids, MI: Eerdmans, 2010.

**Advanced Resources**

Audi, Robert, and Nicholas Wolterstorff. *Religion in the Public Square: The Place of Religious Convictions in Political Debate.* Lanham, MD: Rowman & Littlefield, 1997.

Bartholomew, Craig, Jonathan Chaplin, Robert Song, and Al Wolters, eds. *A Royal Priesthood? The Use of the Bible Ethically and Politically: A Dialogue with Oliver O'Donovan.* Grand Rapids, MI: Zondervan, 2002.

Gregg, Samuel. *On Ordered Liberty: A Treatise on the Free Society.* Lanham, MD: Lexington Books, 2003.

Gregory, Eric. *Politics and the Order of Love: An Augustinian Ethic of Democratic Citizenship.* Chicago: University of Chicago Press, 2010.

Hunter, James Davison. *To Change the World: The Irony, Tragedy and Possibility of Christianity in the Late Modern World.* New York: Oxford University Press, USA, 2010.

Laycock, Douglas. RELIGIOUS LIBERTY Series. Grand Rapids, MI: Eerdmans, 2010.

Mahoney, Daniel J. *Bertrand De Jouvenel: Conservative Liberal and Illusions of Modernity.* Wilmington, DE: ISI Books, 2005.

Matthewes, Charles. *The Republic of Grace: Augustinian Thoughts for Dark Times.* Grand Rapids, MI: Eerdmans, 2010.

Matthewes, Charles. *A Theology of Public Life.* Cambridge: Cambridge University Press, 2008.

O'Donovan, Oliver, and Joan Lockwood O'Donovan. *From Irenaeus to Grotius: A Sourcebook in Christian Political Thought.* Grand Rapids, MI: Eerdmans, 1999.

Porter, Jean. *Ministers of the Law: A Natural Law Theory of Legal Authority.* Grand Rapids, MI: Eerdmans, 2010.

To read more in this area, please consult *Claremont Review of Books, City Journal, Faith and International Affairs, Journal of Markets and Morality, First Things, Perspectives on Political Science, Political Science Reviewer, Society.* For helpful primary sources on Catholic Social Thought, see www.thesocial agenda.com. For ancient, medieval, renaissance, and modern political primary sources, see The Liberty Fund (http://oll.libertyfund.org).

The writings of John Witte Jr. on law and human rights are worthwhile. For example, see John Witte Jr. and Frank S. Alexander, *Christianity and Human Rights: An Introduction* (Cambridge: Cambridge University Press, 2011); with John A. Nichols, *Religion and the American Constitutional Experiment* (Boulder, CO: Westview Press, 2010); *Christianity and Law: An Introduction* (Cambridge: Cambridge University Press, 2008); with Frank S. Alexander, *The Teaching of Modern Christianity on Law, Politics, and Human Nature*, 2 vol. (New York: Columbia University Press, 2005, 2007); *God's Joust, God's Justice: Law and Religion in the Western Tradition* (Grand Rapids, MI: Eerdmans, 2006).

## P. COMMUNICATION STUDIES, TECHNOLOGY, AND MEDIA ECOLOGY

### Beginner Resources

Challies, Tim. *The Next Story: Life and Faith After the Digital Explosion.* Grand Rapids, MI: Zondervan, 2011.

Muehlhoff, Timothy M., and J. P. Moreland. *The God Conversation: Using Stories and Illustrations to Explain Your Faith.* Downers Grove, IL: InterVarsity, 2007.

Powers, William. *Hamlet's BlackBerry: Building a Good Life in the Digital Age.* New York: Harper, 2011.

Reynolds, Gregory Edward. *The Word Is Worth a Thousand Pictures: Preaching in the Electronic Age.* Eugene, OR: Wipf & Stock, 2001.

Schultze, Quintin J. *An Essential Guide to Public Speaking: Serving Your Audience with Faith, Skill, and Virtue.* Grand Rapids, MI: Baker Academic, 2006.

Schultze, Quintin J. *Communicating for Life: Christian Stewardship in Community and Media.* Grand Rapids, MI: Baker Academic, 2000.

Siegel, Lee. *Against the Machine: Being Human in the Age of the Electronic Mob.* New York: Spiegel & Grau, 2008.

Sommerville, C. John. *How the News Makes Us Dumb: The Death of Wisdom in an Information Society.* Downers Grove, IL: InterVarsity, 1999.

Stark, Rodney. *What Americans Really Believe.* Waco, TX: Baylor University Press, 2008.

Woods, Robert H., Jr. *Prophetically Incorrect: A Christian Introduction to Media Criticism.* Grand Rapids, MI: Brazos, 2010.

**Intermediate Resources**

Aboujaoude, Elias. *Virtually You: The Dangerous Powers of the E-Personality.* New York: Norton, 2011.

Badaracco, Claire H. *Quoting God: How Media Shape Ideas About Religion and Culture.* Waco, TX: Baylor University Press, 2004.

Dickerson, Matthew. *The Mind and the Machine: What It Means to Be Human and Why It Matters.* Grand Rapids, MI: Brazos, 2011.

Dyer, John. *From the Garden to the City: The Redeeming and Corrupting Power of Technology.* Grand Rapids, MI: Kregel, 2011.

Kallenberg, Brad J. *God and Gadgets: Following Jesus in a Technological Age.* Eugene, OR: Cascade Books, 2011.

Marshall, Paul, Lela Gilbert, and Roberta Green-Ahmanson, eds. *Blind Spot: When Journalists Don't Get Religion.* New York: Oxford University Press, USA, 2008.

Muehlhoff, Tim, and Todd Lewis. *Authentic Communication: Christian Speech Engaging Culture.* Downers Grove, IL: IVP Academic, 2010.

Schultze, Quentin. *Habits of the High-Tech Heart: Living Virtuously in the Information Age.* Grand Rapids, MI: Baker Academic, 2004.

Song, Felicia Wu. *Virtual Communities: Bowling Alone, Online Together.* New York: Peter Lang, 2009.

Turkle, Sherry. *Alone Together: Why We Expect More from Technology and Less from Each Other.* New York: Basic Books, 2011.

### Advanced Resources

Borgmann, Albert. *Power Failure: Christianity in the Culture of Technology.* Grand Rapids, MI: Brazos, 2003.

Borgmann, Albert. *Technology and the Character of Contemporary Life: A Philosophical Inquiry.* Chicago: University of Chicago Press, 1987.

Brock, Brian. *Christian Ethics in a Technological Age.* Grand Rapids, MI: Eerdmans, 2010.

Campbell, Heidi. *When Religion Meets New Media.* London: Routledge, 2010.

Melzer, Arthur M., Jerry Weinberger, and M. Richard Zinman, eds. *Technology in the Western Political Tradition.* Ithaca, NY: Cornell University Press, 1993.

Peters, John Durham. *Speaking into the Air: A History of the Idea of Communication.* Chicago: University of Chicago Press, 1999.

Postman, Neil. *Technopoly: The Surrender of Culture to Technology.* New York: Vintage Books, 1993.

Scharff, Robert, and Val Dusek. *Philosophy of Technology: The Technological Condition, An Anthology.* Malden, MA: Wiley-Blackwell, 2003.

Swearengen, Jack Clayton. *Beyond Paradise: Technology and the Kingdom of God.* Eugene, OR: Wipf & Stock, 2007.

Zengotita, Thomas de. *Mediated: How the Media Shapes Our World and the Way We Live in It.* New York: Bloomsbury, 2006.


To read more in this area, please consult *Communication Research Trends, Journal of Communication and Religion, New Atlantis, Technology and Culture, Charleston Advisor, Wired magazine, Fast Company, GizMag.com*. See also the relevant resources in Appendix 2.

## Q. EDUCATION

### Beginner Resources

Bauer, Susan Wise. *The Well-Educated Mind: A Guide to the Classical Education You Never Had.* New York: Norton, 2003.

Bauer, Susan Wise, and Jessie Wise. *The Well-Trained Mind: A Guide to Classical Education at Home.* 3rd ed. New York: Norton, 2009.

Budziszewski, J. *How to Stay Christian in College.* Colorado Springs, CO: NavPress, 2004.

Chediak, Alex. *Thriving at College: Make Great Friends, Keep Your Faith, and Get Ready for the Real World.* Wheaton, IL: Tyndale, 2011.

Garber, Steven. *The Fabric of Faithfulness: Weaving Together Belief and Behavior.* Expanded edition. Downers Grove, IL: InterVarsity, 2007.

Melleby, Derek. *Make College Count: A Faithful Guide to Life + Learning.* Grand Rapids, MI: Baker, 2011.

Morrow, Jonathan. *Welcome to College: A Christ-Follower's Guide for the Journey.* Grand Rapids, MI: Kregel, 2008.

Opitz, Donald, and Derek Melleby. *The Outrageous Idea of Academic Faithfulness: A Guide for Students.* Grand Rapids, MI: Brazos, 2007.

Wartenberg, Thomas E. *Big Ideas for Little Kids: Teaching Philosophy Through Children's Literature.* Lanham, MD: Rowman & Littlfield Education, 2009.

Wilson, Douglas. *The Case for Classical Christian Education.* Wheaton, IL: Crossway, 2003.

### *Intermediate Resources*

Estep, James, Michael Anthony, and Greg Allison. *A Theology for Christian Education.* Nashville: B&H Academic, 2008.

Habermas, Ronald T. *Introduction to Christian Education and Formation: A Lifelong Plan for Christ-Centered Restoration.* Grand Rapids, MI: Zondervan, 2008.

Issler, Klaus, and Ronald T. Habermas. *How We Learn: A Christian Teacher's Guide to Educational Psychology.* Eugene, OR: Wipf & Stock, 2002.

Kronman, Anthony T. *Education's End: Why Our Colleges and Universities Have Given Up on the Meaning of Life.* New Haven, CT: Yale University Press, 2007.

Littlejohn, Robert, and Charles T. Evans. *Wisdom and Eloquence: A Christian Paradigm for Classical Learning.* Wheaton, IL: Crossway, 2006.

Parrett, Gary A., and S. Steven Kang. *Teaching the Faith, Forming the Faithful: A Biblical Vision for Education in the Church.* Downers Grove, IL: IVP Academic, 2009.

Smith, Christian, Kari Christoffersen, Hilary Davidson, and Patricia Snell-Herzog. *Lost in Transition: The Dark Side of Emerging Adulthood.* New York: Oxford University Press, USA, 2011.

Smith, Christian, and Patricia Snell. *Souls in Transition: The Religious and Spiritual Lives of Emerging Adults.* New York: Oxford University Press, USA, 2009.

Smith, David I., and James K. A. Smith. *Teaching and Christian Practices: Reshaping Faith and Learning.* Grand Rapids, MI: Eerdmans, 2011.

Sommerville, C. John. *Religious Ideas for Secular Universities.* Grand Rapids, MI: Eerdmans, 2009.

### *Advanced Resources*

Budde, Michael L., and John Wright, eds. *Conflicting Allegiances: The Church-Based University in a Liberal Democratic Society.* Grand Rapids, MI: Brazos, 2004.

Gamble, Richard. *The Great Tradition: Classic Readings on What It Means to Be an Educated Human Being.* Wilmington, DE: ISI Books, 2009.

Graham, Gordon. *The Institution of Intellectual Values: Realism and Idealism in Higher Education.* Charlottesville, VA: Imprint Academic, 2007.

Knight, George R. *Philosophy and Education: An Introduction in Christian Perspective.* 4th ed. Berrien Springs, MI: Andrews University Press, 2006.

Marsden, George M. *The Soul of the American University: From Protestant Establishment to Established Nonbelief.* New York: Oxford University Press, USA, 1994.

Mooney, Brian, and Mark Nowacki. *Understanding Teaching and Learning: Classic Texts on Education by Augustine, Aquinas, Newman and Mill.* Charlottesville, VA: Imprint Academic, 2011.

Peterson, Michael L. *With All Your Mind: A Christian Philosophy of Education.* Notre Dame, IN: University of Notre Dame Press, 2001.

Reuben, Julie A. *The Making of the Modern University: Intellectual Transformation and the Marginalization of Morality.* Chicago: University of Chicago Press, 1996.

Smith, James K. A. *Desiring the Kingdom: Worship, Worldview, and Cultural Formation.* Grand Rapids, MI: Baker Academic, 2009.

Spears, Paul D., and Steven R. Loomis. *Education for Human Flourishing: A Christian Perspective.* Downers Grove, IL: IVP Academic, 2009.

To read more in this area, please consult *Christian Education Journal, Christian Scholar's Review, Comparative Education Review, Educational Policy, Journal of Moral Education, Religious Education, Journal of General Education, Journal of Education and Christian Belief, Religion.* See also the Crossway series RECLAIMING THE CHRISTIAN INTELLECTUAL TRADITION, edited by David S. Dockery. See also David S. Dockery, *Renewing Minds: Serving Church and Society Through Christian Higher Education*, revised and updated (Nashville: B&H Academic, 2008). All philosophy and theology reflection of higher education should be attentive to John Henry Newman, *The Idea of a University*, edited by Frank M. Turner (New Haven, CT: Yale University Press, 1996).

# R. ART, LITERATURE, AND FILM
## *Beginner Resources*

Benner, Juliet. *Contemplative Vision: A Guide to Christian Art and Prayer.* Downers Grove, IL: InterVarsity, 2010.

Best, Harold M. *Unceasing Worship: Biblical Perspectives on Worship and the Arts.* Downers Grove, IL: InterVarsity, 2003.

Cowan, Louise. *An Invitation to the Classics.* Minneapolis: Bethany, 2006.

Dyrness, William K. *Visual Faith: Art, Theology, and Worship in Dialogue.* Grand Rapids, MI: Baker Academic, 2001.

Godawa, Brian. *Hollywood Worldviews: Watching Films with Wisdom and Discernment.* Downers Grove, IL: InterVarsity, 2002.

McEntyre, Marilyn Chandler. *Caring for Words in a Culture of Lies.* Grand Rapids, MI: Eerdmans, 2009.

Reinke, Tony. *Lit!: A Christian Guide to Reading Books.* Wheaton, IL: Crossway, 2011.

Reynolds, John Mark. *Great Books Reader.* Grand Rapids, MI: Baker, 2011.

Taylor, W. David O. *For the Beauty of the Church: Casting a Vision for the Arts.* Grand Rapids, MI: Baker, 2010.

Veith Jr., Gene Edward. *Reading Between the Lines: A Christian Guide to Literature.* Wheaton, IL: Crossway, 1990.

### Intermediate Resources

Barge, Laura. *Exploring Worldviews in Literature: From William Wordsworth to Edward Albee.* Abilene, TX: Abilene Christian University Press, 2009.

Bradbury, Malcolm, ed. *The Atlas of Literature.* New York: Greenwich Editions, 2001.

Cunningham, David S. *Reading Is Believing: The Christian Faith Through Literature and Film.* Grand Rapids, MI: Brazos, 2002.

Geivett, R. Douglas, and James S. Spiegel, eds. *Faith, Film and Philosophy: Big Ideas on the Big Screen.* Downers Grove, IL: InterVarsity, 2007.

Horner, Grant. *Meaning at the Movies: Becoming a Discerning Viewer.* Wheaton, IL: Crossway, 2010.

Jacobs, Alan. *The Pleasures of Reading in an Age of Distraction.* New York: Oxford University Press, USA, 2011.

Jeffrey, David Lyle, and Gregory Maillet. *Christianity and Literature: Philosophical Foundations and Critical Practice.* Downers Grove, IL: IVP Academic, 2011.

Johnston, Robert K. *Reel Spirituality: Theology and Film in Dialogue.* Grand Rapids, MI: Baker Academic, 2006.

Markos, Louis. *From Achilles to Christ: Why Christians Should Read the Pagan Classics.* Downers Grove, IL: IVP Academic, 2007.

Wolfe, Gregory. *Beauty Will Save the World: Recovering the Human in an Ideological Age.* Wilmington, DE: ISI Books, 2011.

### Advanced Resources

Cahn, Steve. *Aesthetics: A Comprehensive Anthology.* Malden, MA: Wiley-Blackwell, 2007.

Detweiler, Craig. *Into the Dark: Seeing the Sacred in the Top Films of the 21st Century.* Grand Rapids, MI: Baker Academic, 2008.

Johnston, Robert K., ed. *Reframing Theology and Film: New Focus for an Emerging Discipline.* Grand Rapids, MI: Baker Academic, 2007.

Lane, Belden C. *Ravished by Beauty: The Surprising Legacy of Reformed Spirituality.* New York: Oxford University Press, USA, 2011.

McGrath, Alister E., ed. *Christian Literature: An Anthology.* Malden, MA: Wiley-Blackwell, 2001.

Scruton, Roger. *Beauty.* Oxford: Oxford University Press, 2009.

Siedell, Daniel A. *God in the Gallery: A Christian Embrace of Modern Art.* Grand Rapids, MI: Baker Academic, 2008.

Taylor, Barry. *Entertainment Theology: New-Edge Spirituality in a Digital Democracy.* Grand Rapids, MI: Baker Academic, 2008.

Titus, Craig Steven, ed. *Christianity and the West: Interaction and Impact in Art and Culture.* Arlington, VA: Institute for the Psychological Sciences Press, 2009.

Zangwill, Nick. *Aesthetic Creation.* New York: Oxford University Press, USA, 2007.

Zangwill, Nick. *The Metaphysics of Beauty.* Ithaca, NY: Cornell University Press, 2001.

To read further in this area, please consult *British Journal of Aesthetics, Journal of Aesthetics and Art Criticism, Journal of Religion and Film, Mars Hill Audio Journal, Film-Philosophy Journal, Mars Hill Review, New York Review of Books, Times Literary Supplement.* See also the resources mentioned in Philosophy and Ethics.

Please also pay attention to the content and craft of the essays, fiction, and poetry writings by T. S. Elliot, G. K. Chesterton, Joseph Epstein, Michael Dirda, C. S. Lewis, J. R. R. Tolkien, Dorothy L. Sayers, Richard Wilbur, Walker Percy, Annie Dillard, and John Ruskin. See also Phillip Lopate, ed., *The Art of the Personal Essay: An Anthology from the Classical Era to the Present* (New York: Anchor Books, 1997).

## S. PSYCHOLOGY AND SOCIOLOGY
### Beginner Resources

Beck, James R. *The Psychology of Paul: A Fresh Look at His Life and Teaching.* Grand Rapids, MI: Kregel, 2002.

Berger, Peter L. *Adventures of an Accidental Sociologist: How to Explain the World Without Becoming a Bore.* Amherst, NY: Prometheus Books, 2011.

Berger, Peter L. *Invitation to Sociology: A Humanistic Perspective.* Garden City, NY: Doubleday, 1963.

Best, Joel. *Stat-Spotting: A Field Guide to Identifying Dubious Data.* Berkeley, CA: University of California Press, 2008.

Boyd, Jeffrey H. *Reclaiming the Soul: The Search for Meaning in a Self-Centered Culture.* Cleveland, OH: Pilgrim Press, 1996.

Campolo, Anthony, and David A. Fraser. *Sociology Through the Eyes of Faith.* New York: HarperOne, 1992.

Johnson, Eric, and Stanton Jones, eds. *Psychology and Christianity: Five Views.* Downers Grove, IL: IVP Academic, 2010.

Poythress, Vern. *Redeeming Sociology: A God-Centered Approach.* Wheaton, IL: Crossway, 2011.

Wright, Bradley R. E. *Christians Are Hate-Filled Hypocrites . . . and Other Lies You've Been Told: A Sociologist Shatters Myths from the Secular and Christian Media.* Minneapolis: Bethany, 2010.

Wright, Bradley R. E. *Upside: Surprising Good News About the State of Our World.* Minneapolis: Bethany, 2011.

### Intermediate Resources

Berger, Peter, and Thomas Luckmann. *The Social Construction of Reality: A Treatise in the Sociology of Knowledge.* Harmondsworth, Middlesex: Penguin Books, 1991.

Coe, John H., and Todd W. Hall. *Psychology in the Spirit: Contours of a Transformational Psychology.* Downers Grove, IL: IVP Academic, 2010.

Collins, Randall. *Four Sociological Traditions.* Oxford: Oxford University Press, 1994.

Collins, Randall. *Sociological Insight: An Introduction to Non-Obvious Sociology.* 2nd ed. New York: Oxford University Press, USA, 1992.

Evans, C. Stephen. *Wisdom and Humanness in Psychology: Prospects for a Christian Approach.* Vancouver, British Columbia: Regent College Publishing, 1997.

Fowler, James W. *Stages of Faith: The Psychology of Human Development and the Quest for Meaning.* New York: HarperOne, 1995.

Goetz, Stewart, and Charles Taliaferro. *A Brief History of the Soul.* Malden, MA: Wiley-Blackwell, 2011.

Green, Joel B., and Stuart L. Palmer, eds. *In Search of the Soul: Four Views of the Mind-Body Problem.* Downers Grove, IL: InterVarsity, 2005.

Hagberg, Janet O., and Robert A. Guelich. *The Critical Journey: Stages in the Life of Faith.* 2nd ed. Salem, WI: Sheffield Publishing, 2005.

Stevenson, Daryl H., Brian E. Eck, and Peter C. Hill. *Psychology and Christianity Integration: Seminal Works That Shaped the Movement.* Batavia, IL: Christian Association for Psychological Studies, 2007.

**Advanced Resources**

Beck, James R. *Jesus and Personality Theory: Exploring the Five-Factor Model.* Downers Grove, IL: IVP Academic, 1999.

Cooper, John W. *Body, Soul, and Life Everlasting: Biblical Anthropology and the Monism-Dualism Debate.* Grand Rapids, MI: Eerdmans, 2000.

Coplan, Amy, and Peter Goldie. *Empathy: Philosophical and Psychological Perspectives.* New York: Oxford University Press, USA, 2011.

Emmons, Robert A., and Michael E. McCullough, eds. *The Psychology of Gratitude.* New York: Oxford University Press, USA, 2004.

Entwhistle, David. *Integrative Approaches to Psychology and Christianity.* Eugene, OR: Wipf & Stock, 2004.

Johnson, Eric L. *Foundations for Soul Care: A Christian Psychology Proposal.* Downers Grove, IL: IVP Academic, 2007.

McMinn, Mark R. *Sin and Grace in Christian Counseling: An Integrative Paradigm.* Downers Grove, IL: IVP Academic, 2008.

Menuge, Angus. *Agents Under Fire: Materialism and the Rationality of Science.* Lanham, MD: Rowman & Littlefield, 2005.

Moon, Gary W., and David G. Benner, eds. *Spiritual Direction and the Care of Souls: A Guide to Christian Approaches and Practices.* Downers Grove, IL: InterVarsity, 2004.

Smith, Christian. *Moral, Believing Animals: Human Personhood and Culture.* New York: Oxford University Press, USA, 2009.

Smith, Christian. *What Is a Person?: Rethinking Humanity, Social Life, and the Moral Good from the Person Up.* Chicago: University of Chicago Press, 2010.

To read further in this area, please consult *Journal of Biblical Counseling, Journal of Psychology and Christianity, Journal of Psychology and Theology, Journal of Pastoral Counseling, Pastoral Psychology, Studies in Formative Spirituality, Journal of Religion and Society, Sociology of Religion, Review of Religious Research, Society, Social Forces, Journal for the Scientific Study of Religion.* Please also see the recommended resources in the areas of Philosophy, Ethics, and Theological Studies.

# T. SCIENCE AND THEOLOGY
**Beginner Resources**

Berry, Wendell. *Life Is a Miracle: An Essay Against Modern Superstition.* Washington, DC: Counterpoint, 2000.

Gonzalez, Guillermo, and Jay Richards. *The Privileged Planet: How Our Place in the Cosmos Is Designed for Discovery.* Washington, DC: Regnery Publishing, 2004. DVD companion from Illustra Media (IllustraMedia .com).

Herrick, James A. *Scientific Mythologies: How Science and Science Fiction Forge New Religious Beliefs.* Downers Grove, IL: IVP Academic, 2008.

Johnson, Phillip E. *Reason in the Balance: The Case Against Naturalism in Science, Law and Education.* Downers Grove, IL: InterVarsity, 1995.

Lawler, Peter Augustine. *Modern and American Dignity: Who We Are as Persons, and What That Means for Our Future.* Wilmington, DE: ISI Books, 2010.

Midgley, Mary. *Science and Poetry.* London: Routledge, 2001.

Morris, Tim, and Don Petcher. *Science and Grace: God's Reign in the Natural Sciences.* Wheaton, IL: Crossway, 2006.

Nichols, Terence L. *The Sacred Cosmos: Christian Faith and the Challenge of Naturalism.* Grand Rapids, MI: Brazos, 2003.

Stark, Rodney. *For the Glory of God: How Monotheism Led to Reformations, Science, Witch-Hunts, and the End of Slavery.* Princeton, NJ: Princeton University Press, 2003.

Verhey, Allen. *Nature and Altering It.* Grand Rapids, MI: Eerdmans, 2010.

### Intermediate Resources

Bradley, James, and Russell Howell. *Mathematics Through the Eyes of Faith.* New York: HarperOne, 2011.

Collins, C. John. *Did Adam and Eve Really Exist?: Who They Were and Why You Should Care.* Wheaton, IL: Crossway, 2011.

Dembski, William A., ed. *Mere Creation: Science, Faith and Intelligent Design.* Downers Grove, IL: InterVarsity, 1998.

Dubay, Thomas. *The Evidential Power of Beauty: Science and Theology Meet.* San Francisco: Ignatius Press, 1999.

Evans, C. Stephen. *Preserving the Person: A Look at the Human Sciences.* Grand Rapids, MI: Baker, 1977.

Hannam, James. *God's Philosophers: How the Medieval World Laid the Foundations of Modern Science.* London: Icon Books, 2009.

Lennox, John C. *God's Undertaker: Has Science Buried God?* Oxford: Lion, 2009.

Meyer, Stephen C. *Signature in the Cell: DNA and the Evidence for Intelligent Design.* New York: HarperOne, 2010.

Richards, Jay W., ed. *God and Evolution.* Seattle: Discovery Institute Press, 2010.

Thaxton, Charles B., and Nancy R. Pearcey. *The Soul of Science: Christian Faith and Natural Philosophy*. Edited by Marvin Olasky. TURNING POINT CHRISTIAN WORLDVIEW Series. Wheaton, IL: Crossway, 1994.

### Advanced Resources

Baker, Mark C., and Stewart Goetz. *Soul Hypothesis: Investigations into the Existence of the Soul*. New York: Continuum Press, 2010.

Barr, Stephen M. *Modern Physics and Ancient Faith*. Notre Dame, IN: University of Notre Dame Press, 2003.

Gordon, Bruce L., and William A. Dembski, eds. *The Nature of Nature: Examining the Role of Naturalism in Science*. Wilmington, DE: ISI Books, 2011.

Kaiser, Christopher B. *Creational Theology and the History of Physical Science: The Creationist Tradition from Basil to Bohr*. Leiden: Brill, 1999.

Koons, Robert C., and George Bealer, eds. *The Waning of Materialism*. New York: Oxford University Press, USA, 2010.

Lindberg, David. *The Beginnings of Western Science: The European Scientific Tradition in Philosophical, Religious, and Institutional Context, Prehistory to A.D. 1450*. 2nd ed. Chicago: University of Chicago Press, 2007.

McKnight, Stephen A. *The Religious Foundations of Francis Bacon's Thought*. Columbia, MO: University of Missouri Press, 2006.

Moleski, Martin X. *Michael Polanyi: Scientist and Philosopher*. New York: Oxford University Press, USA, 2004.

Rescher, Nicholas. *The Limits of Science*. Revised edition. Pittsburgh, PA: University of Pittsburgh Press, 1999.

Walton, John H. *The Lost World of Genesis One: Ancient Cosmology and the Origins Debate*. Downers Grove, IL: IVP Academic, 2009.

To read further in this area, please consult *British Journal for the Philosophy of Science, Perspectives on Science and Christian Faith, Science as Culture, Techne: Society for Philosophy and Technology, New Atlantis, Syntheses, Theology and Science Journal*. See also the resources mentioned in Philosophy.

# RECOMMENDED ORGANIZATIONS

Further resources, including reading and audio/video materials, are accessible at the websites of the following organizations. Please also visit www .jpmoreland.com for more information.

## A. APOLOGETICS, WORLD RELIGIONS, WORLDVIEWS, AND CAMPUS MINISTRIES

Apologetics.com
ApologeticsEvents.com
Apologetics315.blogspot.com
BeThinking.org
BiblicalWorldview.com
BigQuestionsOnline.org
Biola University Christian Apologetics Program (lectures, degree programs) (biola.edu/academics/sas/apologetics)
Campus Crusade for Christ International (ccci.org)
Centers for Christian Study International (studycenters.org)
Conversantlife.com
CrossExamined.org
Consortium of Christian Study Centers (studycentersonline.org)
EPSapologetics.com
InterVarsity Christian Fellowship (intervarsity.org)
JPMoreland.com
L'Abri Fellowship International (www.labri.org)
LeeStrobel.com
Library of Historical Apologetics (historicalapologetics.org)
The Navigators (navigators.org)
Patheos.com
Ratio Christi Student Apologetics Alliance (ratiochristi.org)
Ravi Zacharias International (rzim.org)
Reasonable Faith with William Lane Craig (reasonablefaith.org)

Reasons To Believe (reasons.org)
SeanMcdowell.org
Stand to Reason with Greg Koukl (str.org); STR Place (strplace.org)
Summit Ministries (summit.org)
ThinkChristianly.org
WebEvangelism.com
Worldview Academy (worldview.org)
The Veritas Forum (veritas.org)

## B. ART, LITERATURE, AND FILM
Affirmation Arts (affirmationarts.com)
Art & Entertainment Ministries (a-e-m.org)
Art House America (arthouseamerica.com)
Church and Art Network (churchandart.org)
Culture-Making.com
*Image Journal* (imagejournal.org)
KickStarter.com
Q: Ideas for the Common Good (qideas.org)
ViaAffirmativa.com

## C. BIBLICAL AND THEOLOGICAL STUDIES
Alpha Course (alphausa.org)
BestCommentaries.com
Biblical-Studies.ca
BiblicalTraining.org
Boston University's Center for Practical Theology (bu.edu/cpt)
Calvin Institute of Christian Worship (worship.calvin.edu)
London Institute for Contemporary Christianity (licc.org.uk)
The Gospel Coalition (thegospelcoalition.org)
NTGateway.com
OTGateway.com
The Theology Program (reclaimingthemind.org)
VineyardBibleInstitute.org

## D. BUSINESS, ECONOMICS, AND WORK-LIFE INTEGRATION
A Call to Business (acalltobusiness.co.uk)
Acton Institute (Acton.org)
Aspen Institute (aspeninstitute.org)
Aspen Institute's Center for Business Education (aspencbe.org)
BusinessAsMission.org
BusinessAsMissionNetwork.com

Call of the Entrepreneur (calloftheentrepreneur.com)
Christian Management Scholars Network (baylor.edu/business)
Center for Faith and Business (centerforfaithandbusiness.net)
Center for Faith and Enterprise (faithandenterprise.org)
Center for Faith and Work (faithandwork.org)
Center for Integrity in Business (spu.edu/depts/sbe/cib)
Center for Leadership and Social Responsibility (tacoma.uw.edu/clsr)
Faith & Work Initiative (princeton.edu/csr)
Faith & Work Life (faithandworklife.us)
TheHighCalling.org
KingdomCompanies.org
Kiros.org
London Institute for Contemporary Christianity (licc.org.uk)
Max De Pree Center for Leadership (depree.org)
Marketplace Institute (marketplace.regent-college.edu)
TheologyofWork.org
Transformational Business Network (tbnetwork.org)
WorldPartners.org

## E. CHRISTIAN ACADEMIC ASSOCIATIONS

Academy of Homiletics (homiletics.org)
American Association of Christian Counselors (aacc.net)
American Catholic Philosophical Association (acpaweb.org)
Association for Practical and Professional Ethics (indiana.edu/~appe)
Association of Christian Economists (gordon.edu/ace/acefande.html)
Association of Christian Schools International (acsi.org)
Association of Practical Theology (practicaltheology.org)
Christian Association for Psychological Studies (caps.net)
Christian Community Development Association (ccda.org)
Christian Educator's Association International (ceai.org)
Christian Medical and Dental Associations (cmda.org)
Christians in the Visual Arts (civa.org)
Conference on Faith and History (huntington.edu/cfh/default.htm)
Council for Christian Colleges and Universities (cccu.org)
Emerging Scholars Network (intervarsity.org/gfm/esn/)
Evangelical Philosophical Society (epsociety.org)
Evangelical Theological Society (etsjets.org)
International Arts Movement (internationalartsmovement.org)
International Society of Christian Apologetics (isca-apologetics.org)
Light University Online (lightuonline.com)
Society for Business Ethics (societyforbusinessethics.org)

Society for the Advancement of Ecclesial Theology (saet-online.org)
Society for the Study of Christian Spirituality (sscs.press.jhu.edu/index.html)
Society of Christian Philosophers (societyofchristianphilosophers.com)
Society of Christian Psychology (christianpsych.org)
Society of Vineyard Scholars (vineyardusa.org/site/content/society-vineyard
    -scholars)
The Religious Communication Association (americanrhetoric.com/rca)

## F. CHRISTIAN SPIRITUAL TRANSFORMATION
ApprenticeOfJesus.org
Biola's Institute of Spiritual Formation (biola.edu/spiritualformation)
EnjoyingGodMinistries.com
Foundations for Laity Renewal (laityrenewal.org)
Metamorpha.com
TheHighCalling.org
Renovare.us (and their Christian Spiritual Formation Institute)

## G. CULTURE AND SOCIAL RESPONSIBILITY
Biola University's Center for Christian Thought (cct.biola.edu)
Culture-Making.com
Center for Leadership and Social Responsibility (tacoma.uw.edu/clsr)
ChristianAllianceForOrphans.org
ChristianVolunteering.org
CityReaching.com
Compassion International (compassion.com)
EuropeanDignityWatch.org
Food for Orphans (foodfororphans.org)
Freedom Summit (freedom-summit.org)
Global Outreach Development (godevelop.org)
HopeChest.org
HopeLineInstitute.org
International Justice Mission (ijm.org)
Institute for Advanced Studies in Culture (iasc-culture.org)
London Institute for Contemporary Christianity (licc.org.uk)
Marketplace Institute (marketplace.regent-college.edu)
Markets, Culture, and Ethics (mceproject.org)
TheMediaProject.org
MissionAmerica.org
Mission America Coalition (mac-global.net)
Mission Resource International (missionresource.org)
NotForSaleCampaign.org

PartnersWorldwide.org
PovertyCure.org
Prison Fellowship (pfm.org)
Q: Ideas for the Common Good (qideas.org)
SevenFund.org
SpringHillUk.com
TechMission.org
Teen Challenge (teenchallengeusa.org)
TheCarpentersFund.org
FishermanFoundation.org
WilberforceAcademy.org
World Relief (worldrelief.org)
World Vision (worldvision.org)
WorldWideVillage.org
Yale Center for Faith & Culture (yale.edu/faith)

## H. ELECTRONIC BOOKS AND DISTANT-LEARNING RESOURCES

BiblicalTraining.org
BigThink.com
Biola's Certificate in Christian Apologetics (biola.edu/academics/sas/
    apologetics/certificate)
Christian Classics Ethereal Library (ccel.org)
ChristianCourses.com
Classical Texts in Ethics (iipe.org/resourcedocs/classics.html)
TheGreatCourses.com
iTunesU
KhanAcademy.org
MIT Open Courseware (ocw.mit.edu)
Online Library of Liberty (oll.libertyfund.org)
OpenCulture.com
TED.com
The Theology Program (reclaimingthemind.org)
Tyndale's Christian Theology Reading Room (tyndale.ca/seminary/
    mtsmodular/reading-rooms/theology)
Vineyard Bible Institute–Bachelors & Certificate (vineyardbibleinstitute.org)
Xenos Christian Fellowship (xenos.org/classes/index.htm)

## I. PHILOSOPHY AND ETHICS

Center for Bioethics and Human Dignity (cbhd.org)
Institute for Advanced Studies in Culture (iasc-culture.org)

International Institute for Public Ethics (iipe.org)
Internet Encyclopedia of Philosophy (iep.utm.edu/)
National Catholic Bioethics Center (ncbcenter.org)
PhilPapers.org
Prosblogion.ektopos.com
Stanford Encyclopedia of Philosophy (plato.stanford.edu/new.html)
Virtual Library of Christian Philosophy (calvin.edu/academic/philosophy/
     virtual_library)

## J. Public Policy
Acton Institute (Acton.org)
Atlas Economic Research Foundation (atlas-fdn.org)
Cardus.ca
Center for Public Justice (cpjustice.org)
Christian Legal Society (clsnet.org)
Emory Center for the Study of Law and Religion (cslr.law.emory.edu/)
Institute for Advanced Studies in Culture (iasc-culture.org)
Institute for Global Engagement (globalengage.org)
LibertyFund.org
Manhattan Institute (manhattan-institute.org)
Witherspoon Institute (winst.org)

## K. Religious Philanthropy
Arthur S. DeMoss Foundation (1747 Pennsylvania Ave. N.W., Ste. 1000,
     Washington, DC 33401-6158)
Douglas & Maria DeVos Foundation (dmdevosfoundation.org)
Duke Endowment (DukeEndowment.org)
Fieldstead & Company (Fieldstead.com)
The Gathering (thegathering.com)
John Templeton Foundation (templeton.org)
Kern Family Foundation (kffdn.org)
Lazarus Foundation (lazarusfoundation.com)
Lilly Endowment (lillyendowment.org)
Maclellan Foundation (maclellan.net)
National Christian Charitable Foundation (nationalchristian.com)
Open Doors International, Inc (opendoors.org)
Richard and Helen DeVos Foundation (P.O. Box 230257, Grand Rapids,
     MI 49523-0257)

## L. LEADERSHIP FORMATION

Alban Institute (alban.org)
Center for Faith and Work (faithandwork.org)
Center for Leadership and Social Responsibility (tacoma.uw.edu/clsr)
Marketplace Institute (marketplace.regent-college.edu)
Max De Pree Center for Leadership (depree.org)
Socrates in the City (socratesinthecity.com)
SoderQuist Center (soderquist.org)
The Trinity Forum (ttf.org)
The Washington Institute (washingtoninst.org)

If you benefitted from the resources in this book, please consider becoming a one-time or recurring donor to the Eidos Christian Center, founded and directed by Dr. J. P. Moreland. To learn more, please go to www.jpmoreland.com.

# NOTES

## Chapter One: How We Lost the Christian Mind and Why We Must Recover It

1. James Davison Hunter, *Culture Wars* (San Francisco: Basic Books, 1991); J. P. Moreland, *Kingdom Triangle* (Grand Rapids, MI: Zondervan, 2007).
2. Neil Postman, *Amusing Ourselves to Death* (New York: Penguin Books, 1985), 31.
3. For more on the Puritans, see Allen Carden, *Puritan Christianity in America* (Grand Rapids, MI: Baker, 1990).
4. Carden, 186.
5. George Marsden, *Fundamentalism and American Culture* (New York: Oxford, 1980), 212.
6. For an accessible statement of Hume's and Kant's arguments, along with a Christian response and a development of theistic arguments, see Norman L. Geisler and Winfried Corduan, *Philosophy of Religion*, 2nd ed. (Grand Rapids, MI: Baker, 1988), chapters 5–9.
7. For a critique of evolution, see Jonathan Wells, *Icons of Evolution* (Washington, DC: Regnery, 2000); Stephen C. Meyer, *Signature in the Cell* (San Francisco: HarperOne, 2010).
8. For a treatment of how these shifts played out in our universities from 1880–1930, see Julie Reuben, *The Making of the Modern University* (Chicago: University of Chicago Press, 1996).
9. Carl Henry, *The Christian Mindset in a Secular Society* (Portland, OR: Multnomah, 1984), 145–146.
10. Charles Malik, "The Other Side of Evangelism," *Christianity Today* (November 7, 1980): 40.
11. See Marsden, 184–188. As Marsden points out, after the Scopes trial, fundamentalism became associated with obscurantism partly because fundamentalists could not "raise the level of discourse to a plane where any of their arguments would be taken seriously" (page 188).
12. R. C. Sproul, John Gerstner, and Arthur Lindsley, *Classical Apologetics* (Grand Rapids, MI: Zondervan, 1984), 4.
13. For more on this, see J. P. Moreland, *Christianity and the Nature of Science* (Grand Rapids, MI: Baker, 1989); J. P. Moreland, ed., *The Creation Hypothesis* (Downers Grove, IL: InterVarsity, 1994); Nancy Pearcey and Charles Thaxton, *The Soul of Science* (Wheaton, IL: Crossway, 1994).

14. For more on this, see Phillip E. Johnson, *Reason in the Balance* (Downers Grove, IL: InterVarsity, 1995).

15. For a brief discussion of the classic understanding of happiness, see J. P. Moreland and Klaus Issler, *The Lost Virtue of Happiness* (Colorado Springs, CO: NavPress, 2006).

16. Ernst Mayr, *Populations, Species, and Evolution* (Cambridge, MA: Harvard University Press, 1970), 4.

17. David Hull, *The Metaphysics of Evolution* (Albany, NY: University of New York Press, 1989), 74–75.

18. Daniel Callahan, "Minimalistic Ethics," *Hastings Center Report*, October 1983, 19–25.

19. Joel Kitkin, "A Nation Divided," *The Seattle Times*, section C (May 9, 2004): C1.

20. For a helpful introduction to postmodernism, see Joseph Natoli, *A Primer to Postmodernity* (Oxford: Wiley-Blackwell, 1997).

21. Michael D. Lemonick, "How the Universe Will End," *Time* (June 25, 2001): 48–56.

22. Mark Hartwig and Paul Nelson, *Invitation to Conflict: A Retrospective Look at the California Science Framework* (Colorado Springs, CO: Access Research Network, 1992), 6. The statement is from page 20 of the Framework.

23. Carolyn Kane, "Thinking: A Neglected Art," *Newsweek* (December 14, 1981): 19.

**Chapter Two: Sketching a Biblical Portrait of the Life of the Mind**

1. These incidents are presented in Augustine's *The Confessions: Faustus* in book 5, chapters 3, 6; *Ambrose* in book 5, chapters 13–14, book 6, chapters 1–4; *Pontitianus*, book 8, chapter 6.

2. Waltke states: "Since it (*galah*) is used of men as well as of God, it must not be thought of as a technical term for God's revelation. . . . Though not a technical term for divine revelation, the verb galah frequently conveys this meaning." See R. L. Harris, Gleason Archer, and Bruce Waltke, *Theological Wordbook of the Old Testament* (Chicago: Moody, 1988), 160.

3. John Wesley, "An Address to the Clergy," in *The Works of John Wesley*, 3rd ed. (Grand Rapids, MI: Baker, 1979; 1st ed., 1972), 481.

4. John Wesley, *A Plain Account of Christian Perfection* (London: Epworth Press, 1952; 1st Epworth ed.), 87.

5. Richard Baxter, *The Reasons of the Christian Religion* (London: printed by R. White for Fran. Titon, 1667).

6. Augustine, *De genesi ad litteram* 1.21.

7. See Alan F. Johnson, "Is There a Biblical Warrant for Natural-Law Theories?" *Journal of the Evangelical Theological Society* 25 (June 1982): 185–199.

8. See Norman L. Geisler, "A Premillennial View of Law and Government," *Bibliotheca Sacra* 142 (July–September 1985): 250–266.

9. For an excellent discussion of the nature of faith, see J. P. Moreland and Klaus Issler, *In Search of a Confident Faith* (Downers Grove, IL: InterVarsity, 2008).

10. Billy Graham, in "Candid Conversation with the Evangelist," *Christianity Today* (July 17, 1981): 24.

11. Billy Graham, "An Interview with the Rev. Billy Graham," *Parade* (October 20, 1996): 6.

12. Roy McCloughry, "Basic Stott," *Christianity Today* (January 8, 1996): 32.

## Chapter Three: The Mind's Role in Spiritual Transformation

1. James L. Crenshaw, *Old Testament Wisdom: An Introduction* (Atlanta: John Knox, 1981), 17–18.

2. Technically, the problem is not that God is too big because God is not in space at all. Rather, God is too great to be the kind of being that could be spatial.

3. I cannot argue for this position here. I have done this elsewhere. See J. P. Moreland, *Scaling the Secular City* (Grand Rapids, MI: Baker, 1986), chapter 3; J. P. Moreland and Scott Rae, *Body and Soul* (Downers Grove, IL: InterVarsity, 2000).

4. For more details on biblical anthropology, see Robert Saucy, "Theology of Human Nature," in *Christian Perspectives on Being Human*, ed. J. P. Moreland and David M. Ciocchi (Grand Rapids, MI: Baker, 1993), 17–52.

5. The connection among anger, anxiety, depression, and brain chemistry is discussed repeatedly in Daniel G. Amen and Lisa C. Routh, *Healing Anxiety and Depression* (New York: Berkley Books, 2003).

6. Biblical terms for different aspects of the human being ("heart," "soul," "spirit," "mind") have a wide range of meanings, and no specific use of a biblical term should be read into any occurrence. The context should be our guide. I am focusing here on a more narrow, specific use of the term "spirit."

7. The connection among anger, anxiety, depression, and brain chemistry is discussed repeatedly by Minirth and Meier.

8. J. Gresham Machen, address delivered on September 20, 1912, at the opening of the 101st session of Princeton Theological Seminary.

9. George Marsden, *Fundamentalism and American Culture* (New York: Oxford University Press, USA, 1980), 188.

10. If someone else told me what a dog was supposed to be (for example, a brown, furry animal that barks), then I could recognize a dog the first time

I saw one, provided I had already experienced the relevant parts of what it is to be a dog (brownness, furriness, the sound of a bark).

11. Richard Foster, *Celebration of Discipline* (New York: Harper & Row, 1978), 55. All of our mental states have intentionality and are about things. I am focusing on the mind because, often, the mind directs the other faculties, as we saw in the case of seeing.

## Chapter Four: Harassing the Hobgoblins of the Christian Mind

1. Stephen L. Darwall, introduction to *Joseph Butler: Five Sermons* (Indianapolis: Hackett Publishing, 1983), 1. Butler's series was titled "Fifteen Sermons Preached at the Rolls Chapel" and was collected in 1726.
2. Though I disagree with much in the article, nevertheless, the following is helpful: Edward E. Sampson, "The Debate on Individualism," *American Psychologist* 43 (January 1988): 15–22.
3. Martin E. P. Seligman, "Boomer Blues," *Psychology Today* (October 1988): 55.
4. See Christopher Lasch, *The Culture of Narcissism* (New York: Warner Books, 1979), especially chapter 2.
5. Lasch, 262.
6. Jane M. Healy, *Endangered Minds: Why Children Don't Think and What We Can Do About It* (New York: Simon & Schuster, 1990), 196.
7. Healy, 114–116, 195–217.
8. Lasch, 97. See also 96–98.
9. Neil Postman, *Amusing Ourselves to Death* (New York: Penguin Books, 1984), 7.
10. Pitirim A. Sorokin, *The Crisis of Our Age* (Oxford: One World, 1941).
11. Roy Baumeister, "How the Self Became a Problem: A Psychological Review of Historical Research," *Journal of Personality and Social Psychology* 52 (1987): 163–176.
12. Philip Cushman, *Constructing the Self, Constructing America* (Cambridge, MA: Da Capo Press, 1996), 600.
13. Robert Banks, *The Tyranny of Time* (Downers Grove, IL: InterVarsity, 1983), 59.
14. Os Guinness, *The Gravedigger File* (Downers Grove, IL: InterVarsity, 1983), 83.
15. For practical advice on several aspects of good health, see Richard Swenson, *Margin: Restoring Emotional, Physical, Financial, and Time Reserves to Overloaded Lives* (Colorado Springs, CO: NavPress, 1992), chapter 8.
16. John G. Gager, *Kingdom and Community: The Social World of Early Christianity* (Englewood Cliffs, NJ: Prentice-Hall, 1975), 86–87.
17. Doubt is one form of the fear of losing control. For more on doubt itself, see William Lane Craig, *No Easy Answers* (Chicago: Moody, 1990); Os

Guinness, *In Two Minds* (Downers Grove, IL: InterVarsity, 1976); Gary Habermas, *Dealing with Doubt* (Chicago: Moody, 1990).

18. Roger Trigg, *Reason and Commitment* (Cambridge: Cambridge University Press, 1973), 44.

## Chapter Five: Clearing the Cobwebs from Our Mental Attics

1. For a more detailed treatment of these issues, see A. G. Sertillanges, *The Intellectual Life: Its Spirit, Conditions, and Methods* (Washington, DC: Catholic University Press, 1987), especially chapter 2. For an overview of different views about virtue in general, see John W. Crossin, *What Are They Saying About Virtue?* (New York: Paulist, 1985).

2. Joseph Pieper, *The Four Cardinal Virtues* (Notre Dame, IN: University of Notre Dame Press, 1954), 117–133.

3. Dallas Willard, *The Spirit of the Disciplines* (San Francisco: Harper & Row, 1988), 156.

4. Jane M. Healy, *Endangered Minds: Why Children Don't Think and What We Can Do About It* (New York: Simon & Schuster, 1990), 105.

5. See Dallas Willard, "The Absurdity of Thinking in Language," *Southwestern Journal of Philosophy* 47 (1973): 125–132.

6. There are numerous good ones, but two books with which to start are Patrick J. Hurley, *A Concise Introduction to Logic* (Belmont, CA: Wadsworth, 1982), and Norman L. Geisler and Ronald M. Brooks, *Come Let Us Reason* (Grand Rapids, MI: Baker, 1990).

7. Pair 1: P is sufficient, Q is necessary. Pair 2: P is necessary, Q is sufficient. Pair 3: P is sufficient, Q is necessary. Regarding pair 3, if something is a human, that is sufficient to guarantee that it is a person (there are no human nonpersons), but something could be a person and not a human (God and angels are persons, if God had created Martian or Vulcan persons, they would be persons but not humans).

8. Though false, the statement is not self-refuting because it is a philosophical statement about morality, not an absolute ethical rule of morality. Since the statement refers only to all moral rules (and claims that none of them is an absolute), and since the statement is not itself a moral rule, the statement does not refer to itself and, therefore, cannot be self-refuting. What makes the statement false is the existence of different sets of moral absolutes, not the self-refuting character of the statement itself.

9. These fallacies are called "informal" because they make it possible to reason from true premises to a false conclusion, but they can only be detected by examining the content of the argument and not simply by looking for defects in the argument's logical structure.

292 \ LOVE YOUR GOD WITH ALL YOUR MIND

10. I have adopted this argument (and some others in this section) from Francis Beckwith, *Politically Correct Death* (Grand Rapids, MI: Baker, 1993), part 2. Beckwith does a masterful job of cataloging the various informal fallacies used by pro-choice advocates. This book is must reading for anyone who desires to reason carefully about the abortion debate.

11. One can start by taking the Bible as merely a set of historical documents and not an inspired book, argue for its general historical trustworthiness, use its general trustworthiness to argue for both Christ's divinity (which would imply that as God, Christ would speak the truth since, for most forms of monotheistic belief, the Deity speaks all and only truths) and the fact that the New Testament contains enough history to know Christ's view of Scripture, and then show that Christ held to the full inerrancy of Holy Writ. Therefore, the Bible is inerrant.

### Chapter Six: Evangelism and the Christian Mind

1. Thomas Sowell, "Playing with Fire on Church Burnings," *Orange County Register*, Metro section (June 21, 1996): 7.
2. Os Guinness, *The Gravedigger File* (Downers Grove, IL: InterVarsity, 1983).
3. William Wilberforce, *Real Christianity* (Portland, OR: Multnomah, 1982; based on the American edition of 1829), 1–2.

### Chapter Seven: The Question of God (Part I)

1. For more detailed overviews of this argument, see J. P. Moreland, *Scaling the Secular City* (Grand Rapids, MI: Baker, 1987), chapter 1; J. P. Moreland and Kai Nielsen, *Does God Exist? The Debate Between Atheists and Theists* (Buffalo, NY: Prometheus, 1993).
2. See the objections by Anthony Flew and Keith Parsons in Moreland and Nielsen, *Does God Exist?*, 163–164; 185–188. See also J. L. Mackie, *The Miracle of Theism* (Oxford: Clarendon Press, 1982), 93.
3. Michael D. Lemonick, "How the Universe Will End," *Time* (June 25, 2001): 48–56.
4. Robert Jastrow, *God and the Astronomers* (New York: Norton, 1978), 116. Additional sources for this chapter, ranging from more basic to more difficult are: Paul Copan, *Loving Wisdom* (St. Louis: Chalice Press, 2007); Chad Meister, *Building Belief* (Grand Rapids, MI: Baker, 2006); Lee Strobel, *The Case for a Creator* (Grand Rapids, MI: Zondervan, 2003); Norman L. Geisler and Chad V. Meister, eds., *Reasons for Faith* (Wheaton, IL: Crossway, 2007); William Lane Craig, *Reasonable Faith* (Wheaton, IL: Crossway, 1994); Paul Copan and Paul Moser, eds., *The Rationality of Theism* (London: Routledge, 2003); William Lane Craig, ed., *Philosophy of*

*Religion: A Contemporary Reader* (Edinburgh: Edinburgh University Press; New York: Rutgers University Press, 2002); William Lane Craig and J. P. Moreland, eds., *A Companion to Natural Theology* (Oxford and Malden, MA: Wiley-Blackwell, 2008).

## Chapter Eight: The Question of God (Part II)

1. See Antony Flew, *There Is a God* (New York: HarperCollins, 2007).
2. Michael J. Behe, "Evidence for Design at the Foundation of Life," in *Science and Evidence for Design in the Universe*, ed. Michael J. Behe, William Dembski, and Stephen Meyer (San Francisco: Ignatius Press, 2000), 119.
3. See Michael J. Behe, *Darwin's Black Box* (New York: The Free Press, 1996), 69–73.
4. William Dembski, *Intelligent Design* (Downers Grove, IL: InterVarsity, 1999).
5. Robin Collins, "The Evidence of Physics: The Cosmos on a Razor's Edge," in Lee Strobel, *The Case for a Creator: A Journalist Investigates Scientific Evidence That Points to God* (Grand Rapids, MI: Zondervan, 2004), 130.
6. Paul Davies, *God and the New Physics* (New York: Simon & Schuster, 1983), 189.
7. John Warwick Montgomery, *Law Above the Law* (Minneapolis: Dimension, 1975), 24.
8. J. L. Mackie, *The Miracle of Theism* (Oxford: Clarendon Press, 1982), 115. Compare J. P. Moreland and Kai Nielsen, *Does God Exist?* (Buffalo, NY: Prometheus, 1993), chapters 8–10.
9. Michael Ruse, "Evolutionary Theory and Christian Ethics," in *The Darwinian Paradigm* (London: Routledge, 1989), 262–269.

## Chapter Nine: The Evidence for Jesus

1. See Edwin Yamauchi, "Jesus Outside the New Testament: What Is the Evidence?" in *Jesus Under Fire*, ed. Michael Wilkins and J. P. Moreland (Grand Rapids, MI: Zondervan, 1995), 208–229.
2. A. N. Sherwin-White, *Roman Society and Roman Law in the New Testament* (Oxford: Clarendon Press, 1963), 188–191.
3. See Collin Hemer, *The Book of Acts in the Setting of Hellenistic History* (Winona Lake, IN: Eisenbrauns, 1990).
4. In my view, one of the most sophisticated treatments of the dating question is John Wenham's *Redating Matthew, Mark, and Luke* (Downers Grove, IL: InterVarsity, 1992). Wenham argues that the synoptics should be dated between the early forties to the late fifties.
5. Martin Hengel, *Between Jesus and Paul* (Minneapolis: Fortress, 1983), 93.

6. Larry Hurtado, *How on Earth Did Jesus Become a God?* (Grand Rapids, MI: Eerdmans, 2005), 25–29, 202–204.

7. See Paul Barnett, *The Birth of Christianity: The First Twenty Years* (Grand Rapids, MI: Eerdmans, 2005).

8. G. N. Stanton, *Jesus of Nazareth in New Testament Preaching* (Cambridge: Cambridge University Press, 1974).

9. Royce Gruenler, *New Approaches to Jesus and the Gospels* (Grand Rapids, MI: Baker, 1982).

10. J. Ed Komoszewski, M. James Sawyer and Daniel Wallace, *Reinventing Jesus* (Grand Rapids, MI: Kregel, 2006), 33–34.

11. James D. G. Dunn, *A New Perspective on Jesus* (Grand Rapids, MI: Baker, 2005), 44.

12. Dunn, 49–50.

13. Barnett, 113.

14. In what follows, I am deeply indebted to Paul Rhodes Eddy and Gregory A. Boyd, *The Jesus Legend* (Grand Rapids, MI: Baker, 2007), 447–454.

15. Richard Bauckham, *Jesus and the Eyewitnesses* (Grand Rapids, MI: Eerdmans, 2006), 67–84.

16. See the painstaking treatment of these historical accuracies in Colin J. Hemer, *The Book of Acts in the Setting of Hellenistic History* (Winona Lake, IN: Eisenbrauns, 1990).

17. N. T. Wright, *The Resurrection of the Son of God* (Minneapolis: Fortress, 2003).

18. For more in evidence for the resurrection of Jesus, see Gary Habermas, *The Risen Jesus and Future Hope* (Lanham, MD: Rowman & Littlefield, 2003); Paul Copan, ed., *Will the Real Jesus Please Stand Up?* (Grand Rapids, MI: Baker, 1999).

19. There are two books I'd like to recommend. First, for a helpful discussion of stories and illustrations for sharing your faith with others, see J. P. Moreland and Timothy Muehlhoff, *The God Conversation* (Downers Grove, IL: InterVarsity, 2007). For an incredibly interesting, fast-paced novel that covers some of the issues of the last three chapters in an easy-to-read story form, see Craig J. Hazen, *Five Sacred Crossings* (Eugene, OR: Harvest House, 2008).

## Chapter Ten: Recapturing the Intellectual Life in the Church

1. Roger Trigg, *Reason and Commitment* (Cambridge: Cambridge University Press, 1973), 44.

2. Brad Stetson, "The Promise of a Mature Masculinity," *Orange County Register*, Metro section (July 3, 1996): 8.

# ABOUT THE AUTHOR

J. P. Moreland is Distinguished Professor of Philosophy at Biola University in La Mirada, California, and Director of The Eidos Christian Center. Dr. Moreland has four earned degrees: a BS in chemistry from the University of Missouri, a ThM in theology from Dallas Seminary, an MA in philosophy from the University of California-Riverside, and a PhD in philosophy from the University of Southern California.

Dr. Moreland has authored, edited, or contributed papers to thirty-five books with publishers ranging from Oxford University Press, Blackwell, Routledge, Wadsworth, and Prometheus to InterVarsity and Zondervan. Among his books are *Christianity and the Nature of Science, Does God Exist?* (with Kai Nielsen), *The Creation Hypothesis, Philosophical Naturalism: A Critical Analysis, Kingdom Triangle, The Lost Virtue of Happiness,* and *Body and Soul.* He has also published more than 120 magazine articles in such publications as *Christianity Today* and *Christian Research Journal,* and more than 80 journal articles in venues such as *Philosophy and Phenomenological Research, American Philosophical Quarterly, Australasian Journal of Philosophy, MetaPhilosophy, Pacific Philosophical Quarterly, Southern Journal of Philosophy, Religious Studies,* and *Faith and Philosophy.*

Dr. Moreland served for eight years as a bioethicist for PersonaCare Nursing Homes, Inc. headquartered in Baltimore, Maryland. His research interests lie in analytic ontology, philosophy of science, and philosophy of mind, and in the interface between Christian thought and spiritual formation. He has also planted two churches, served with Campus Crusade for Christ for ten years, spoken and debated on two hundred college campuses and in hundreds of churches, and appeared numerous times on radio and television as a spokesperson for a Christian worldview.

# *The Message* Means Understanding

*Bringing the Bible to all ages*

*The Message* is written in contemporary language that is much like talking with a good friend. When paired with your favorite Bible study, *The Message* will deliver a reading experience that is reliable, energetic, and amazingly fresh.

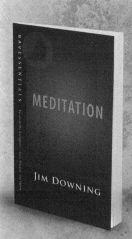